Moving Nearer to Heaven

The Illusions and Disillusions of Migrants to Scenic Rural Places

Patrick C. Jobes

PRAEGER

Westport, Connecticut
London

Library of Congress Cataloging-in-Publication Data

Jobes, Patrick C.
    Moving nearer to heaven : the illusions and disillusions of migrants to scenic rural
places / by Patrick C. Jobes.
        p.   cm.
    Includes bibliographical references and index.
    ISBN 0–275–96689–5 (alk. paper)
    1. Urban-rural migration—Montana—Bozeman Region.   2. Moving,
Household—Montana—Bozeman Region—Psychological aspects.   3. Environmental
psychology—Montana—Bozeman Region.   4. Community—Montana—Bozeman Region.
5. Rural-urban migration—Montana—Bozeman Region.   I. Title.
HT381.J62   2000
307.72′09786′662—dc21   99–055875

British Library Cataloguing in Publication Data is available.

Library of Congress Catalog Card Number: 99–055875
ISBN: 0–275–96689–5

First published in 2000

Praeger Publishers, 88 Post Road West, Westport, CT 06881
An imprint of Greenwood Publishing Group, Inc.
www.praeger.com

Printed in the United States of America

The paper used in this book complies with the
Permanent Paper Standard issued by the National
Information Standards Organization (Z39.48–1984).

10 9 8 7 6 5 4 3 2 1

Contents

Tables

Preface

This book is based on information that was initiated as quasiexperimental field research. In the end, it more resembles a naturalist observation of an ecosystem. We enjoyed good fortune from many people and institutions who contributed to the effort in various ways. Fortunately, I do remember the names of some of the people involved. The following acknowledgments are organized from the beginning of the project and data collection, through the analyses and to manuscript preparation.

The data were collected in phases. Students in two of my classes in Human Ecology at Montana State University acted as interviewers during the initial stages. A few dedicated professional interviewers collected information in the later stages. My colleague, Anne Williams, worked alongside us during the early 1980s. The data were analyzed throughout the entire project by a friend and colleague, Lee Faulkner, sometimes with the advice of Jack Gilchrist. Data analysis was complex and tedious, especially during the final analyses that required the careful merging of different data sets. Lee remained cheerful and helpful as she flawlessly kneaded the data sets for over 20 years. Equally important and dedicated has been Diane Fuhrman, who has typed the manuscripts related to this project since the 1970s. Even as I have learned to word process and have traveled to far corners of the Earth, I have always turned to Diane to prepare the next serious draft.

Several colleagues have also provided academic insight, advice, and camaraderie. Leslie B. Davis edited an early manuscript and final version. Ed Marston, editor of the *High Country News*, offered encouragement and suggestions. Fellow members of research committees investigating rural migration were especially supportive and encouraging. Bill Stinner, Mike Toney, Jack Gilchrist, Ed Knop, Annabel Kirschner-Cook and Audie Blevins could all be depended upon to positively criticize the research. The most important colleague, the man who encouraged us to work together, was John Wardwell, who unfailingly supported all of us until his death in 1998.

The manuscript has been written and rewritten at five universities on four continents. The outline was developed at Montana State University. The first draft was written while on a Fulbright at the University of Bucharest 1994-95. It was revised the next year in Pakistan, while I was at the University of Agriculture at Faisalabad. The third draft was edited at the University of New England at Armidale, New South Wales. The final draft was prepared at the University of New Mexico, which provided an adjunct professorship and a quiet office. Special thanks are due to Professor Philip May, director of the Center on Alcoholism, Substance Abuse, and Addictions (CASAA), and to Professor Richard Coughlin, chairman of the Department of Sociology. Following that, the copy editorial assistance of Deborah Whitford and Nancy Lucas was superb.

The research was initiated without funding. Fortunately, the U. S. Department of Agriculture (USDA) sporadically supported the research from the mid-1970s until the late 1980s. The final stage of the project was made possible through a grant from the Liz Claiborne-Art Ortenberg Foundation. Art Ortenberg and Jim Murtaugh were incredibly supportive and patient through the final analyses and manuscript preparation.

Finally, I am grateful for the people I have known in beautiful rural (and formerly rural) areas scattered throughout the Rockies. My ideas were stimulated through conversations with friends, colleagues, and fellow residents in northern New Mexico; Boulder and Lyons, Colorado; and throughout Montana. Sandy and Adele Pittendrigh, Don McLaughlin, Hugo Tureck and Bob Swinth have been as supportive as friends can be. Finally, I am grateful to the residents of the Gallatin Valley and other rural areas where I have conducted research. Without their cooperation, conversation and coffee, the research could never have been conducted.

I am grateful to my parents, who made this book possible through two gifts. First, they allowed me to assume that a university education was part of my life. That assumption established me in the profession to which I have remained dedicated ever since. Second, they took me to a lovely and fascinating variety of beautiful places.

Chapter 1

Introduction

"GIVE ME LAND LOTS OF LAND UNDER SUNNY SKIES ABOVE"

This book is about how and why people move to beautiful, safe and somewhat remote places. Although the underlying factors and explanations are similar wherever the setting, this book is based on observations in the rural American West, particularly the Gallatin Valley of southwestern Montana. A special concern is the profound differences between what many people say they want to do and what they actually do. It is about how they change, how they say they want to stay forever and move tomorrow. Such confusion, ambiguity and change can be understood through contrasting their wishes and their beliefs with their behavior. Even so, such understanding is eternally incomplete. Their illusions about deciding where to live and why they want to live there are central to understanding what, for some, is a hope to find paradise.

The search among many migrants to the beautiful areas of the West is a sensitive exploration for the highest ideals in a period of disillusionment. Theirs is a hunger for community in a world in which precious little exists and in which symbols are unwittingly regarded as realities. Theirs is one image of high hopes and frequent disillusionment with contemporary society. The values placed on a good life in a decent place and the opportunities and limitations for satisfying those values are implicit throughout this book.

The story of newcomers inevitably is the story of old-timers, who also cherish a hope for a good life in a decent place. Their accommodations to newcomers, a status once occupied by most old-timers, is bittersweet. The strain between the old and the new is exercised around struggles over the physical and planned environments, participation in local organizations and in style of life, literally how they dress, talk, drive and conduct themselves with others.

These observations are of a dynamic setting. They focus on how migration is related to life in a small town in a beautiful setting. Migration is an eternal human process which is particularly definitive of the American psyche. Migration is neither an independent variable nor dependent. It is caused by social events while causing still more. It is part of the experience of a never ending transformation of people and the places where they reside. The diverse considerations that people make before, during and after they decide to move are described. Their considerations are affected by their particular and idiosyncratic qualities. Their decisions are made with imperfect and often inaccurate knowledge. Their decisions evoke continual and long-term consequences on the local community, since there is a never ending stream of newcomers and out-migrants.

No general or systematic theoretical observation is presented here. Unless it be this: Humans are simultaneously rational and irrational, some seemingly more one than the other. There is a certain fuzzy logic in what they say and do. Contemporary theory about migration contributes enormously to understanding and explaining how people move, but no single theory systematically explains most of what they say and how they behave. More broadly, social theory has much to offer to this understanding. Perhaps what is most valuable, social theory expresses eternal paradoxes about behavior. Is it rational or irrational? Is there reality to life or is life, that is, social behavior in its environment, a matter of construction and interpretation? Can a community be planned effectively or does planning create more problems than solutions? Should sociologists give advice about applying ideas to society or should they remain locked away, academic monks in cells lined with books?

The answers to these and other fundamental questions have no singularly correct answers. They place an intellectual framework around these observations regarding how people in a small town in the Rocky Mountains act and think about their lives. Migration is an inflow and outflow process that links social values expressed through individual decision making to physically relocate. Migration creates effects by the arrival and departure of these people, taken as individuals and as a collective, a cohort coming and going. It is one tiny flow in the river of life that shares many common qualities with the ebbs and flows of the broader stream.

The fuzzy and poetic foundations of social life acknowledged, this also is a study of very practical and tangible elements of personal and town life in a modern industrial urban nation. Subdivisions with toxic weeds and stray dogs are real and annoying impacts on the physical environment from population growth and expansion. Increased and aggressive traffic, and the loss of semipublic lands, affect the constructed environment. Higher prices and an expanding concentration of cosmopolitan elite are other residues of change in the social system.

My observations are heavily influenced by my training and experiences as a sociologist. I often think of the impacts of social development more than merely the process of change. My personal values and beliefs also have influenced what is written here. I have been passionate about understanding the reasons why people move from city to country, and then back again. Communities, meaning deeply entrenched small populations with common values sustaining themselves in the same place for multiple generations, are precious social systems to me. They also frequently are prejudiced, bigoted, ignorant and destructive. I have spent much of my time in small towns and rural areas since I was a boy, living with my grandparents on farms in Oklahoma. Finally, I measure my joy more by how few people I encounter on a trout stream or along a ski trail than by the number of fish I catch or the number of runs I make. And I love to catch dozens of fish and ski many runs. Not coincidentally, skiing and fishing in solitude is possible only in low population rural places.

The observations presented here are largely drawn from two longitudinal research projects that stretched across 20 years. The data and examples were drawn from interviews collected during these projects centered in the Bozeman, Gallatin Valley, area of southwestern Montana. Those data are complemented by data drawn from other studies I conducted in the region. Perhaps the most important influence on what is written here is my own participation as a resident of this area during these years. No scientist could possibly have enjoyed his or her laboratory more than I enjoyed mine. I lived in it, deeply loved its environment and its people and know it very well.

"O give me land, lots of land . . . don't fence me in."

THE ROMANCE OF MONTANA

The romance of moving to a small town in the open spaces of Montana (or some other idyllic place) seems to be ubiquitous. Wherever I am, when it becomes known that I come from Montana, people begin to appear who want to move there. I began writing this book in Bucharest, Romania, an unlikely spot to find such people. Within three weeks of my arrival in Bucharest, two men, and later their wives, told me of their dreams and plans to retire to Montana. Les, a robust red-haired school teacher in his early forties, called himself a "wannabe Montanan." His mother had been born in Livingston. A Californian, he had been a base brat, following his father from military post to military post, a semitransient life he had cultivated into adulthood. The life he and his wife envisioned was very clear. They wanted five to 10 acres with a house costing less than $100,000. They wanted to create mobile home spaces with water and sewer connections so that visiting friends and relatives could have privacy and the spirit of community. They wanted to be within two hours of a city in order to shop, find medical care and use an airport. They wanted to spend springs and summers in Montana, and to head for California at the start of the football season. From there, they would drive to Mexico or Arizona for the winter. When I told them that spring in Montana was like winter in most places, they blithely switched their imaginary travel calendar to arrive in May or June. Les had been in Montana once, two years earlier, while visiting his father in Rexburg, Idaho. He spoke of his hope to fish for trout, although he had not fished for sport in the other places he had lived.

Later, as I edited the earlier draft in the undulating tablelands of eastern Australia, the same attraction to Montana became apparent. Several people I met soon after arriving in Australia wanted to talk about Montana and the Rocky

Mountains. Within three days, a range scientist and I met coincidentally. He was considering accepting a post-doc at Montana State University in Bozeman, where he would start a new life in Montana. Later, I asked a woman where she had found the Boulder (Montana) Hot Springs T-shirt she was wearing. She said she had bought it in Boulder, and then commented, "I reckon Montana must be the best place to live in the whole world."

Not many people have the Montana fantasy, certainly not as hopefully envisioned as Les and Michelle. People who have it are sufficiently uncommon where they live so that, from their perspective and the perspectives of those around them, they seem unique individualists. Collectively, though, a few from Bucharest, hundreds from New York, thousands from Los Angeles, and millions from the places in between, they are a mass of humanity. Like Les and his wife, their thoughts run rampant in the romanticized vacuum of their imagination.

The general outline of their dream is common, shared by many exurbanites who move to the Northern Rockies. They seem to have a dreamscape geographic image which they think can be objectively played out like chess or Monopoly®. They only want a few affordable acres, which they intend to develop only a little bit. They want urban amenities and a flexible, mobile lifestyle. They want community to almost magically, though sensibly in their minds, to converge around them. Yet, they want to be somewhere else several months each year. Multiply this lovely individualistic vision by tens of thousands and there is a traffic jam in Yellowstone National Park, a subdivision crisis in hundreds of small towns in the vast terrain of the Rockies which stretches from the Mexican border well into Canada. Also, such objectified treatment of the place creates a social system that is increasingly devoid of sustained engagement with local affairs and superficially active with other concerns.

Neither the dreamers nor their dreams are evil. By some reckoning, the dreams express commendable thought: caretaking of the environment, a return to a simpler life in nature, the hope for community. The people are commendable, too, courageous and independent, competent and industrious. Yet, however laudatory the dreams and the dreamers, collectively they manifest into a bad (one hopes temporarily bad) dream for individuals and communities. Migration to the relatively small towns and open spaces is considered throughout this book as a social problem. As will become apparent, migration also creates an opportunity for some triumphs and successes in spite of the frequent failures and disappointments. As a sociologist, I see effects of migration as social change. Most people, though, described the changes as problematic, often forgetting or taking for granted those aspects of change that bring personal joy and community well-being.

Since its inception, sociology has been concerned with big questions that incorporate moral philosophy and social problems. Sociologists have passionately argued these questions, sometimes practically and often esoterically. After all, sociology is an academic discipline, which means that most of its work is scholarly. In the Middle Ages, scholars are reputed to have debated how many angels could dance on the head of a pin. As absurd as that question may seem to hard-headed empiricists, who know the answer cannot be measured by any available instruments, the question has deeply important philosophical implications. A new scholasticism is embroiled in an argument about what is a social problem. One aspect of modern scholasticism is the assertion that problems are entirely subjective, reflecting how people feel and act rather than having any real objective substance. Called by different names, such as social constructionism and deconstructionism, the advocates maintain that a problem is only a culturally created orientation by an influential segment of society about something they don't like and believe should be changed. As in historical scholasticism, the modern form may seem to be asserting ridiculous claims like, the criminals are the real victims or clearcutting is important only because of how people respond to it. The true causes of crime, according to many such theorists, are the powerful and wealthy who close opportunities to others and create laws to protect their own advantage. Similarly, when the nature of problems related to clearcutting are reduced to the social struggle between proponents and opponents, the real and objective consequences of what happens to the land, wildlife and ultimately the people — or mining or subdividing — are neglected or ignored. Another aspect of the new scholasticism is an obsession for measurement. This obsession leads to relying on simple, rarified data.

At one extreme, modern scholastics requires huge data sets that permit the cranking out of statistically significant analyses. At the other extreme are social scientists who are convinced that only particular cases, examined in painstaking detail, are the foundations for scientific truth. Contributions are made at both esoteric extremes, although their insights are likely to be limited to the time and place under which the data were collected. The extremes rarely are engaged accurately with the broader world, which is extensive, general and complex. The approach used throughout this book is multifaceted. It is more philosophical and descriptive, although the research began as empirical and quantitative. In character with sociology, it is based on the conviction that the underlying moral philosophical issues are fundamental for examining the nature of how people interact in the context of their personal communities and in conjunction with the broader society.

Given the illustrious and serious contributions from sociology, how is it possible to justify thinking about a phenomenon as benign as the migration of relatively privileged white people into mountain Shangri-las? No claim is made that the movement of people to the Northern Rockies is more or, for that matter less, important than the contemporary ravages of the Four Horsemen of the Apocalypse. Massive poverty, epidemics and wars surround us, demanding attention. Unfortunately, as aspects of the human condition, these will be present whether they are studied or not. One of the discouraging realizations of the 20th century is that attempted solutions sometimes exacerbate problems. Life goes on around them, in spite of them, as unreconcilable as that is with the perfect wish to make them go away. There is an important link between these problems and the migration to safe, beautiful and peaceful places. People want to remove themselves from those problems, geographically, socially and psychologically. The problems won't disappear, although migrants can personally escape being so close to where they concentrate. Classic social problems undeniably influence the migration; the problems are not forgotten as people move a bit farther out of harm's way.

Justifying the study of rural migration to scenic recreational areas, as a happenstance of more serious social crises, is warranted, although neither necessary nor sufficient. Rural migration to scenic enjoyable locations has its own set of problems for people, the community and the environment. These are important independent of any other justifications. It is a mass phenomenon, affecting millions of people who move, who are left behind and who are residents into which the new people move. The magnitude of people affected by migration alone makes it an important subject for study. This is not an esoteric phenomenon, although it lacks the immediacy of the human suffering evident in the classic studies of social problems.

Although migration, primarily by middle- and upper middle-class people, to scenic rural areas may seem mundane in comparison to homelessness or AIDS, the subjects are all fundamentally human. It is fashionable among social activists to claim primacy for the problems with which they identify, particularly those of an underclass. The problems, whatever they are, are genuine and human. So, too, are the aspirations, joys and sufferings of middle-class migrants, many of whom experience abuses of social class, race, gender and age in their newfound homes, just as they did in the settings they left behind. Their families suffer from the spectrum of disease, insanity, poverty and alcoholism, a full complement of human misery. The deserved attention given to identified groups who suffer often forgets or neglects others who are or who seem to be more fortunate. While suffering occurs in small rural Rocky Mountain towns, that itself is not a primary justification for studying them. It would be ludicrous to claim that the problems faced by either residents or communities in the scenic developing areas are as intense or as difficult to resolve as those in urban ghettos and in the rural Black Belt. On the other hand, the levels of poverty and human tragedy on nearby Indian reservations equal those of any place in the nation (Ward, 1995).

Individually, most in-migrants suffer from their moves in some manner. Their moves were more than changes in residence, typical of most urban moves. Most migrants in this study were moving to change their lives rather than their houses. Even newcomers who honestly settled down into happiness everafter felt sad to leave friends, family and the familiarity of their previous homes. That level of suffering is difficult to avoid for people who feel love and attachment. Many, particularly those who did not find what they expected, have suffered considerably. The loss of their dream, whatever wisdom the loss conveyed, was hurtful. Sometimes disillusionment is tragic and devastating. Many lost their financial reserve, a place on a career track or a supportive community they appreciated too late. Some lost their hopes of a stable family and community. In their suffering, some grew wiser, others bitter. In time, their accommodations to the difficulties may change. Their suffering, of course, was not necessarily due to residing in the Northern Rockies or to becoming migrants. Many would have faced similar and perhaps worse difficulties wherever they lived. That they happened to experience their difficulties in the Rockies is an important fact, for the story is about the place as well as the people.

The community suffered problems, too. Many of the problems, experienced by residents who live there, seem ordinary, benign, hardly worth mentioning. They are not considered seriously by radical students of social problems. The region in general continues to be beautiful and clean. Even those towns most severely impacted by the siting of major developments, except for reservations, bear little resemblance to devastated slums in cities.

The region is a natural respirator, a living zoo and museum. It is the largest relatively intact natural area in the middle latitudes in the northern hemisphere. Any environmental loss diminishes that important fact. The Louvre or the National Gallery of Art would become gradually diminished if people were allowed, for the highest purposes of profit and personal satisfaction, to gradually remove pieces of art. The loss of a few haystacks by Monet, a few nudes by Rubens a few Ming vases . . . after a while the loss of the *Gioconda* smile. In retrospect, people would talk about how lovely their marvelous museum had been, and how they wished one could have seen it then.

Analogies are deceiving. The Northern Rockies, particularly the Greater Yellowstone Ecosystem, is not a museum, although increasingly it is a zoo. Museums are collections of objects preserved away from where they were created. The Northern Rockies are the objects in their place of creation and in their somewhat original relationship with each other. The objects in museums have been identified as special by authorities. A natural ecosystem is precious in its entirety. The objects identified as particularly noteworthy, the geothermal features, mountains, streams and wild animals, are especially precious because they are in a natural setting. Seeing a bison or bear in a zoo brings joy to visitors. In this era of species extinction, zoos are necessary, protective habitats in spite of the tragedy of captivity they impose. Seeing a free-ranging herd of antelope and elk or a solitary grizzly in its naturally evolved home is majesty that cannot be constructed. The immensity of the Northern Rockies as a natural setting is beyond the imagination of most people, including those who have been there. I have taken well over a thousand trips into the Northern Rockies. Sighting a herd of antelope north of Harlowton still stops the conversation with my companion or causes joy to leap in my chest when I am alone. Wandering along a stream, any of hundreds of streams, watching fish rise still brings me peace in solitude. Being under the stars away from any human sound or sign still humbles me. I suspect there is a similar primal joy and peace within every woman and every man.

I was born in Compton, at that time a working-class suburb of Los Angeles. Southern California was probably one of the most comfortable natural ecosystems on Earth. The absolute development of the southern California coastline is a terribly fragmented and selfish dissolution of natural beauty for the profit and participation of a very few. By the early 1950s, my parents had moved to the mountains of northern New Mexico. I began to go to Aspen in the mid-1950s. It was still a friendly little town with one tiny old market. I haven't been back since 1970, when it already had begun to resemble the poshest suburbs of Los Angeles.

Aspen and the entire Roaring Fork Valley and the surrounding region have continued to explode with population and development since then. The development of Aspen has been replicated dozens of times, although less ostentatiously, in hundreds of rural towns in the West.

There is a story of a farmer who had a marvelous three-legged pig who accompanied him wherever he went. The pig could sing and once had been able to dance. It had saved his daughter's life. A curious acquaintance asked the farmer what happened to the pig's leg, as well as its ears and cheeks. The farmer said he had cut them off to eat. "Isn't that an awful way to treat such a wonderful animal?" the acquaintance asked. "Oh, no, you wouldn't want to kill a good pig like this," replied the farmer.

The problems suffered by the environment are perhaps the most obvious and easily talked about consequences of growth. They are objective and relatively impersonal and safe to discuss. Only the crass and insensitive can feel unmoved by the plight of an endangered species or the pollution of a pristine stream. The social system of the community also experiences problems as a result of migration, growth and development. Changes to the social system are less often taken with sufficiently seriousness to prevent them than are the changes to the natural environment. Social changes seem more subjective since they affect people rather than objective places and things. Besides, people, being responsible for their own conditions, are expected to adapt to changes imposed upon them. People are indeed flexible and adaptive. And certainly there is no single form of community or social life which is superior to all others. It would be an error, however, to confuse adaptability and relativity with an absence of individual suffering or the capacity of the community to function as people say they want it to function. Studying and telling about the special and unexpected difficulties people experience with the neighbors, friends, work and organizations is as central as considering impacts on the environment. It also is objective. People hurting and organizations failing are as factual as a bulldozed stream bed or an overgrazed pasture.

THE POSITIVE SIDE

There is a temptation in social science and, more broadly, in the serious side of the Judeo-Christian ethic to focus on the problems, the dark side. While enormous and discouraging changes and trends are manifested in the Northern Rockies, discussing only the problems would leave out much of the beauty of the place, the joy of its people and the creative joining of the two for the benefit of both.

Most people who moved to the Gallatin Valley were very happy, at least during the earliest stage of their residence there. Recent in-migrants who were being interviewed for the first time were ebullient, overflowing with happiness and hope. They brought with them what often is referred to as human capital, their own education, energy, insight and enthusiasm (Becker, 1962). Although the hopes of most were dashed within a few years and they moved away, they spoke fondly of some of their friends, experiences and the area in general. Fewer than a quarter of those who moved away left with essentially nothing good to say about the place and their experience there. Among those who left, their years in Montana were at least a reality check, a lesson about what they wanted and what they could have. Even for the vast majority of residents who left, living there had had many gratifying aspects. A few, very few, said they hoped to move back. Leaving the area was usually the closing of a chapter in their lives.

People who moved away often contributed to community. At the very least, most had made a few friends and performed some useful work. Some left lasting legacies that made the place more beautiful or safe or interesting. A designer, who left angry and bitter about having had to struggle just to earn enough for food, clothing and a house for his family, initiated the hanging of colorful pennants along Main Street during the summer festival. The former wife of a faculty member left the area following a wrenching divorce. She had been the impetus behind the first public meetings to plan bicycle paths. A renowned musician joined the faculty merely because the university was located near where he wanted to live, fish and be with his wife, who raised beautiful horses and exotic animals. He moved away following his divorce, but returns each year to teach a class for young master musicians. The performances literally have added music to the community for many years.

The people who do not move away, particularly those who remain for more than a generation, contribute a deeper structure to the community. Their stabilizing contributions to neighborhoods, friendships and voluntary organizations are the dependable and familiar foundation of life. These are the people who own the businesses and manage the organizations on which residents depend. Collectively, they are cautious, even conservative, about moving too quickly. Theirs is perhaps a wisdom that comes from enduring hard times when others failed. It is thrifty, perhaps myopically thrifty, to plan for the future in a dynamic area that needs so much protection from the adverse effects of inevitable growth.

The people who reside in the area and its towns have many accomplishments about which to feel proud as they accommodate growth. A few have effectively implemented local planning ordinances to complement protective state and federal legislation. Some have developed public facilities such as museums and athletic facilities. There are so many beautiful and aesthetic characteristics that are easily neglected. Yet, each historic building or artifact is a remnant of the past to be nurtured for the future. And each sparkling stream, lush hill and grove of trees in which the towns are located is a gem which, if protected for the public, will make these places more attractive and viable communities for centuries to come.

Most of the long-term residents hardly live in unremitting ecstasy and fulfillment much more than residents in other rural places. Rather, they seem to find the measure of happiness and joy they want and believe that it is commensurate with what they deserve. Their dreams are reasonably tangible and can be satisfied. Theirs is the joy of shivering and watching their children play Little League, soccer and ski. Theirs is the comfort of being one of the familiar faces on the street, at a school performance or in church. Theirs is the happiness of trekking the same streams and hillsides year after year, chasing elk, catching fish and finding mushrooms. Theirs is the completeness of modestly having work, friends, family, organizations and place, all together; frustrations and sadness intermixed with successes and happiness. The story of the people and the place is much more than failure and disintegration. It also is a story of triumph and integration, of community.

ECONOMIC TRADEOFFS

There is no economic bottom line in life. There are, of course, simple limitations if the financial goal is to purchase a Rolls Royce, a mansion in Palm Beach or an ocean cruise. The more complex reality is that there are other forms of transportation, lodging and recreation. Viewing life in specific tangible terms limits alternatives and forces the criteria for success into the single dimension of economic feasibility. Bottom-line thinking has ensnared most of this generation. They are convinced they must take a second job or employment out of the home because they have to have X, where X is a larger house, new athletic gear, dancing lessons or savings for education. The questions are more than how much things cost and whether one has that much. They also include issues about what the alternatives are and what has been lost by being locked into a single choice. The tradeoffs often are unrecognized or dismissed as consequences that can be avoided, odds that can be beaten. For example, analyses of delinquency indicate that a middle-class mother's choice to get a divorce for self-fulfillment is likely to be at the expense of her childrens' delinquency and subsequent adjustment (Gottfredson and Hirschi, 1990). Her determination to experience a socially contrived level of well-being may contribute to anxiety, alienation and to delinquency among her children.

Immigration to beautiful small towns is generally a phenomenon that involves the middle- and upper middle-classes (Fuguitt, Brown, and Beale, 1989). Ironically, the immigration often increases the proportion of poor people in many communities. Some are poor more by technical definitions than by more valid meanings. Some people who moved to be near outdoor recreation, such as fishing, skiing and mountain biking, regard work as an imposition to or as a mechanism for being able to play. An optimal strategy among a small visible minority of young adults in recreation regions is to work part-time or seasonally, just enough to spend as much time pursuing their favorite forms of recreation as possible, usually in the company of like-minded spirits. Such people often proudly describe what an enjoyable life they experience on so little income. Their poverty is largely a matter of choice, often a proud choice. They often have education and skills that permit eking out just as much of an income as they need to engage in as much recreation as they want; most could easily earn much more if they were willing to forego the environment and their beloved lifestyle.

Many others are far less fortunate. These are the poor people who were never interviewed in this research. They are a deep and transient poor who wander throughout the land. I have witnessed an occasional ramshackle family bus, camped for weeks in a nearby national forest. Ministries and welfare workers frequently see them, talk to them and about them. Lucky ones occasionally stay, become established and self-supporting, but most move on in their own stream of homelessness and disassociation.

Most of the poor in recreational scenic areas fall between these extremes. They are the poor generated within the middle-class, migrants and established residents alike. The bases for their poverty are complex and the tenure of their poverty usually temporary. The loss of income and the difficulty in finding work can lead to a rapid plunge into poverty among migrants. The eagerness and competitiveness of migrants also make earning a decent living difficult for established residents. Recently arrived tradesmen and women, eager to establish a reputation for future work, often take on work at very low wages. Meanwhile, they gradually spend a nest egg brought with them until it is gone. This, in turn, can bankrupt established business with higher fixed costs that must compete with these newcomers who are undercutting the local labor market. The result, especially when the local economy is contracting, is that both newcomers and some established residents lose their jobs and their businesses. Of course, this process creates bargains for consumers, but most consumers are part of the low-paying competitive spiral. And, once again, since there is an endless stream of newcomers entering and competing in the local labor market, it creates eternally depressed incomes and tenuous job security for wage earners throughout the spectrum of occupations.

Other reasons for poverty among people who by other standards and in other times and places would be middle-class resemble those endemic to the fragility of the middle-class anywhere. Illness, death and divorce occurred among many households in the study. The financial implications of these personal tragedies are multiplied in scenic recreation locations because their economic marginality affects so many residents. The loss of employment because of illness for a dual-income, let alone a single-income, family can be devastating, particularly since expenses soar while income declines. Many respondents recounted the personal tragedy and financial consequences of illness, death and divorce.

A GOOD PLACE TO LIVE

The story of America is intricately founded upon the search for a good place to live. How that search unfolds differs enormously from person to person. The differences are partially determined by their sociodemographic characteristics (age, sex, race, occupation), an extensive list of qualities people were given at birth or achieved through opportunity which affected their life chances, perspectives and behavior. People have changed their minds about what a "good place" means as times and cultures have changed. During the founding phase of America, a good place was likely to offer the prospect of owning a farm or practicing religious freedom. In this late stage of industrialization, a good place is more likely to offer stable and fair employment, a safe comfortable environment and dependable services. Differences also occur over the life course. Retirees, couples with children and young single adults now frequently live in settings that reflect their phase in life. Crucial passages to other phases often are accompanied by moving to new places.

The demographic differences among people, and the phases in their lives, establish infinite variations about what is regarded as a good place to live. For example, the retired and elderly typically consider health facilities, the presence of family and weather more than do young people (Barsby and Cox, 1975). Older migrants also are more circumspect and cautious about financial implications of their moves (Flynn, 1982). Sociologists have provided explanations to help make sense of why people move (Howell and Frese, 1983). Scientific explanations inevitably are imperfect simplifications. Sociological explanations about how and why types of people move to new places are simplifications, no matter how detailed their attention to personal predispositions and societal conditions. Classic and modern sociological explanations richly contribute to understanding why people move by describing ageless themes about human behavior. Rather than arriving at a single statement of universally accepted fact, sociological explanations offer competing explanations. Sociological truth lies in the rich theoretical mosaic composed of evolving knowledge generated as social issues, disagreements among competing theories, are creatively expressed in the craft (Argyris, Putnam, and McLain, 1985).

WHAT THIS BOOK IS ABOUT

Social Theory

Most chapters begin with a discussion of a timeless issue that has been explored by sociologists. These issues pertain to practical and intellectually stimulating ideas which have occupied generations of migrants. Some of these issues involve paradoxes since they are not resolvable by either logic or data. Such issues deserve attention because they express enduring and important positions that continue to plague people as they adapt to their environments. The presentation of sociological theory is an efficient way of summarizing a wide spectrum of knowledge that has occupied minds dedicated to understanding migration. Each theory, however different from the others, is relevant to currently accepted beliefs, and contributes to understanding some aspects of migration. Kant (1934) described the always imperfect, yet always more accurate evolution of knowledge. The discussion of issues in terms of competing explanations of why people move and the effects of their movements also provides unifying themes for organizing the chapters. The disagreements about why and how people move are a demographic analogue to what is true.

Those disagreements about migration are more than intellectual exercises dispassionately based on the rational interpretation of facts. Sociologists are passionately convinced that theirs is the valid and reliable way of looking at the world. Since all are in disagreement with other sociologists, not to mention geographers, psychologists and economists, somebody must not be providing the right answer some of the time. The author passionately believes that each theorist has identified a crucial dimension for understanding migration. Equally passionately, he believes that none, either independently or in toto, comprehensively explains the causes or effects of migration. Their explanations are conscientious, thoughtful attempts, which is as much as can be expected of anyone. The reality of migration is, and probably always has been, more complex than any or all theories can explain. The theories and issues presented are not exhaustive. They are only a small selection from the broad repertoire of sociology. Theories are developed from insights based on limited observations. Sociologists, being human, are neither clairvoyant nor privileged to see the entire picture of all migrants at all times (Ritchey, 1976). Some of the theories have considerable predictive value, but only for specific times, places and conditions. They seem to accurately account for why particular types of people move under particular situations, such as being transferred as a corporate decision (Rosenbaum, 1983). Other theories are much broader, applying across different historical periods and diverse conditions to a broad spectrum of migrants (Roseman, 1983). No theory accounts accurately for all types of people in all kinds of situations. Effective theories increase the ability to understand and predict migration beyond what would be possible without them, that is, beyond trying to understand and predict the behavior as if it were a randomly occurring phenomenon. The more a theory establishes an accurate understanding and prediction of a phenomenon over long periods of time, whether migration or the relationships among celestial bodies, the more effective that theory is considered to be.

Distinguishing between understanding and prediction is a tricky yet extremely important matter. Understanding, fundamentally, is believing that an explanation makes sense. Its literal meaning is to "stand under," to provide a foundation, a cornerstone, for explaining what is being made apparent. Until satellites containing telescopes were launched into space, stargazers had always stood under what they sought to understand. By implication, that was a heliocentric perspective since standing under implies that the base platform is Earth. "Prediction," in contrast, means to say what is going to happen before it happens. Ideally, prediction is built upon understanding although they frequently diverge.

Gothic cathedrals are built upon enormous stone foundations that support the more visible naves, arches and buttresses. The architectural theory, of course, involves many cornerstones; a thorough understanding of stress loads, qualities of materials and much more in addition to an aesthetic design. Credible social theories also are built upon a thorough understanding of social foundations and social structures and processes. To the extent that social theories explain the successes and failures of communities and societies in order to provide people with what they want and need to live satisfying and fulfilling lives, the more morally valid the theory. Relatively few gothic cathedrals remain standing, as is evidenced by the hundreds that have collapsed because of inadequate understanding of fundamental concepts (Vale, 1992). So, too, social theories that lack solid foundations, if taken seriously, can lead to a mass of unforeseen environmental and social rubble. For example, Wallerstein (1989) warns of the dangers of continuing to justify consumption as a foundation for modern society. Imminent catastrophe follows building upon such theories or building upon the wrong theory for the matter at hand. Some of the theories presented here seem to provide a greater understanding, a more sensible explanation, of broad social phenomena than in fact they do. Theories, like apparel and humor, are attractive as temporary fads and fashions. Some seem to work, but eventually are deemed inappropriate, unworkable, even distasteful, at least until they pass through another cycle of popularity a few years later.

Theories are intellectually stimulating in and of themselves. They are interesting stories that are usually more fact than fantasy. They may be sufficiently powerful that people are convinced to act upon them. Attempting to implement theory is still another and independent dimension from either understanding or predicting. Implementation of social theory (or policy and planning, as it is more popularly known) tries to incorporate the pure and simplified conceptual systems of theory into the infinitely varied and complex real world. The intent is to protect or improve the real world, the community and society. Through such application, theory also is refined, improved and occasionally rejected. Even with perfect knowledge, which never exists, there are realistic limitations (geographic, economic, social and cultural) that prevent the complete implementation of theory. Such stumbling blocks indicate the limitations of theories themselves since each is created under an assumption that it would work if only the rest of the world would behave the way it is supposed to behave.

Most of the theories discussed throughout this book are only complementary parts of a larger theory. While entities on their own, they actually explain, predict and advocate only one aspect of a broad and complex continuum. The tendency is to embrace one theory and, in doing so, to exclude the valid aspects of the theories rejected. The author advocates the consideration of multiple, frequently conflicting theories. He theorizes that the deepest understanding and the most successful planning will result from considering conflicting theories, because each contains some lasting and inescapable truths, ignored or forgotten by their antagonists.

Planning: Past, Present and Future

This notion of competing theories being part of a single broader understanding, may, at first, seem foreign and inconsistent. An example may help to clarify what is meant. During the early years of this century, Lester Frank Ward (1906) advocated what he called *social telesis*, the application of sociological knowledge to help guide future development. Ward distinguished such applied knowledge from pure abstract theory. His nemesis, William Graham Sumner, was an adamant spokesman for the free market (1940). Sumner opposed any notion of social planning, instead placing his faith in the "invisible hand" that guides society. The enmity between Ward and Sumner expressed a classic dilemma that serious scholars had addressed for centuries. Machiavelli advised his Prince in the ways of planning and control (1944). Adam Smith (1992) radically advocated letting market forces alone determine the course of progress. Karl Marx (1970) was equally adamant that the natural course of progress was through communist planning which would inevitably supplant the capitalist marketplace. Following Ward and Spencer, the argument of whether to apply social knowledge or keep sociology pure was repeated in bitter dialogues between George Lundberg (1961) and Robert Lynd (1939). The arguments historically have been based on numerous moral suppositions and have involved subtle nuances to justify making points. Social scientist advocates for social justice, who wish to resolve differences in possessions and opportunities that exist across geographic boundaries, are among the latest to articulate this age-old issue (Smith, 1994). The issue is no more resolved theoretically now than when it first was recognized, nor is it likely to be in the foreseeable future.

The favoring and opposing of planning are more than responses to a reactive pendulum that swings in response to the gravity of the other (Rapaport, 1990). The extremes are based around one fragmented and singular truth separated from its equally fragmented and singular opposite. At one extreme is the sanctity of individual freedom and independence leading to the greatest, although unpredictable, good for the social whole. At the other extreme is the faith that the greatest good can be achieved around collective goals obtained by the surrender, forced if necessary, of selfish individuals. Each is a precious half truth so long as it remains in the context of pure theory. In real life, both do, indeed must, simultaneously exist. Any system that excludes one or the other because it is regarded as an inherent evil eventually becomes an ineffective caricature of what it was intended to do. An accurate system of theory must incorporate the extremes, protagonist and antagonist, thesis and antithesis.

In real life, the extremes do exist. The consequences of emphasizing either individual freedom or collective obligations at the expense of the other becomes apparent, yet the attraction of doing so is inescapable and is indeed part of the synthesis. The totalitarian governments of Eastern Europe and the former Soviet Union eventually imploded within paranoid systemic planning. They expended their limited financial capabilities on competing with the capitalistic West as though they were at war. They became incapable of producing, distributing and selling goods and services taken for granted in the West. Their obsession wrought economic, social and environmental catastrophes when their plans failed. Similarly, an absence of planning has left many catastrophic legacies in the free market West, from Bhopal, India, to real estate devastation in the Sun Belt of the United States. Inner cities and large blocks of rural areas in both capitalist and communist countries are social catastrophes filled with residents who are marginally productive, whether in a command or free market.

Planning also occurs at the less lofty level of community. The question is not whether planning occurs so much as who does it and how it is done. Planning at the community level is a crude and personal exercise of the philosophical spectra across a free (or a command) market. The typical real estate proposal proceeds like this. Investors and developers cautiously consider and decide on optimal strategies for converting resources to profit, that is, they plan. Simultaneously, they shrewdly help create or convert legislation and statutes to their purposes while wooing decision makers at every political level. Irving Goffman (1959) distinguished between front stage and backstage. Most community planning, whether in America or elsewhere, is largely conducted backstage, presenting neither sight nor sound of how decisions are being constructed. The public has the right and opportunity to respond after the plan has been drawn up following tacit private acceptance by the political leaders and planning bureaucracy. Except in highly publicized and outrageously objectionable cases, the plan is rarely rejected. The competence and foresight of the planning becomes evident only after a community matures or a project unfolds and becomes operational (Russell, 1992). Some planned unit developments are functional and aesthetic masterpieces; some are visual and environmental junk.

Planning applies to the lives of individuals as well as to global political and economic systems and to community development. A common and recurrent theme of contemporary popular psychological and self-help literature is "living in the now." The implication of this contemporary wisdom is that inordinate dwelling upon the past or anticipation of the future removes one from sanely enjoying life and contributing to the well-being of others. Living in the now implies being attentive and responsive to the people and conditions in one's life. As with any theory, it contains powerful and obvious elements of truth. Certainly, living with obsessions about the past and the future means that a person is not effectively coping with the present, is probably miserable and quite likely making others miserable. Besides, the past is certainly and the future is eternally out of one's control, hence something of a waste of time and energy to worry about. Yet, sane and rational people plan their lives on the basis of what they think can be expected based on prior experiences and knowledge. Taken to an extreme, "living in the now" implies being sociopathic or psychopathic. These are people who don't learn from the past in order to prepare for the future.

One of the seminal thinkers in sociology posed a different ideal about individuals living in the present. The adjusted mature person, according to George Herbert Mead, learns from past experience. Such knowledge becomes part of the self, the individual psyche, to be drawn upon when anticipating and planning for the future (Mead, 1934). The wise and adjusted person, in effect, lines up past, present and future to increase the predictability and satisfaction of their lives. It is a never ending and always imperfect process, although predictability and satisfaction increase as people gain wisdom by learning from the past and being able to apply those lessons to the future. However, taken to an extreme, people can become trapped by the past, drawing upon knowledge and experience which no longer is appropriate for new conditions posed by the future.

In-migrants to Montana traverse the broad continuum ranging from living in the present to immersion in the future or the past. Those who lived primarily in a single dimension of time generally did not stay very long. What do people attach to when they have dissociated from the personal connections with people in a previous community? How do they develop commitment when they leave a place behind? Newcomers who lived only in the now, who left where they came from without commitments in friends, family, work and community, were not likely to stay. Newcomers who had reasonable experience and expectations to plan for a future were much more likely to stay, especially if they enjoyed the activities of building a consistent connection in their daily lives. Not all of those who had such reasonable experience and information planned accurately. Many changed their plans. For example, some discovered that they wanted more financial rewards or occupational opportunities, or more diverse educational and cultural experiences for their families. Having learned that, they moved on with clearer knowledge toward a revised plan.

Lining up the past, present and future is a life-long process. It does not preclude occasionally making fast and spontaneous decisions, although, typically, considerable time is required to learn and reflect about what has been important, why it is important and how it has operated so that the knowledge can be thoughtfully applied to the future. A few of the more permanent and satisfied residents made almost split-second decisions to move to Bozeman. They intuitively recognized that what they had anticipated from the past had not and was not likely to occur. The young woman, the daughter of parents from Central Europe, who left the New Jersey suburb driving her VW Beatle filled with her possessions within 48 hours after learning that her fiancé was going to marry her best friend, was such a case. She stayed for 12 years, married and, by all indications, was happy. During our last interview, she said she was satisfied and would be willing to remain in the Gallatin Valley for many years to come, had her husband not accepted a job that was forcing them to move. However, she and the very few other in-migrants who decided to move at a moment's notice and who stayed for more than a decade had backgrounds upon which to build and hopes for commitment into the future. They had not been living for the moment nor were they cognitively dedicated to doing so. They had educational and occupational competencies and histories of responsibility. They moved with the hope of extending those assets into the future.

As more is known about what approaches and designs work for particular needs and environments, a growing faith in planning is increasingly moving it to front stage. Development is becoming more visible to the audience of community members, creating a middle ground where the shibboleth distinction between planning and the free market becomes transparent. In the community, the quality of clothes of both the emperor of social engineering and the emperor of the invisible hand are becoming apparent and are being challenged. Many investors trying to make a buck object to such visibility and challenge. But, then, local citizens rightly object to destructive impacts on their lives and property. Simultaneously, the naive and unworkable assumptions of some planning advocates are open to challenge and ridicule (Seamon, 1983).

The presentation of theories and the intensive discussion of individuals and communities, in most instances, will make the success and failures, the applicability and inapplicability, apparent. Not all theories are created equal, nor are the strategies built on those theories (Gottlieb, 1993). That theories persist is testimony to their reflecting an important, perhaps timeless and inescapable aspect of social life. That element of truth, though, is unlikely to be applied as a singular and rarified theoretical idea, such as to plan or not to plan, whatever the substance of any particular plan.

The stars of this particular story are people who live in small towns in beautiful places. Most are migrants to Bozeman and the Gallatin Valley, and more generally to the Rocky Mountains. As with any tale, there are heroes and villains, geniuses and fools, although those labels in themselves denote ordinary people. Their common wish was to live in a beautiful place — or to be dragged along by someone who had that desire. Their stories illustrate the spectrum of backgrounds and aspirations, and the consequences and relative success of their moves.

ILLUSIONS AND MIGRATION TO BEAUTIFUL LOCATIONS

Most migrants to beautiful places have relatively inaccurate illusions about what the new community and their life within it will be. For most people, the distance between that illusion and reality determines how long they stay. About half of the newcomers to rural, scenic, recreational locations in the Northern Rockies were gone within five years. Most of those who moved away had intended to stay longer, even for life or at least a major portion of it. For some, their illusion may have been a matter of incomplete or inaccurate information. Their decision to move was based on bad facts. For most, including many of those whose knowledge was insufficient or inaccurate, another more universal flaw affected their judgment. Their illusion led them to filter and color the image of what they expected to find and to experience. Their image was so simplified and pleasing that the more complex and difficult reality was not anticipated. Most didn't like the unexpected types of people they encountered and ways in which they treated each other and the environment. The perspective of their new experience admitted a darker view than the rosy tint they had wanted to see.

From one lofty philosophical perspective, the migration may be interpreted simply as an experience, albeit to reflect upon and learn from (Nietzche, 1955). Such an existential perspective simplifies what happened to the people who moved or remained. We are more sympathetic to the ideas of Karl Mannheim (1936) who analyzed the relationship between ideology and utopia. We consider how crude utopian ideas, illusions, affect a search for a place to live, utopia. Unlike Mannheim, our focus is more on practical day-by-day experience and thought than upon pivotal political philosophies. Before arriving, most in-migrants had aspirations of what they wanted. They provided their own definitions of acceptance and rejection, and ultimately of their own success and failure. While many of those who later moved away became more circumspect, most also judged the place as unacceptable or themselves as inadequate for failing to be able to stay there. Most were disappointed and wiser although a few were rabid and devastated.

It is tempting to adopt a dispassionate view of people coming and going. An honest narrative requires reporting what happened and how newcomers reported their successes and failures. Most people made some big mistakes. A few made some whoppers. A fortunate few seemed to pursue a clear, even and accurate course; settling, staying and finding what they had wanted all along. The success or failure of remaining is partially a consequence of the magnitude of their illusion about what they wanted, partially a result of the quality of actual information they considered before moving and partially a result of the rigidity of their illusions. In-migrants fall into several categories with regard to their illusions and the information they consider. These categories strongly determine their likelihood of staying in their newfound home.

People who arrived with strongly developed illusions were very likely to leave. Nearly all those with strongly held illusions based on inaccurate information, whether derived from facts or fantasy, left within two or three years. Even when their information was accurate, most migrants who arrived with illusions left within a few years. Newcomers who arrived with fewer illusions were much more likely to stay. If they premised their move on inaccurate information, such as an apparently open and well-paying job market, most had to move relatively soon. Most newcomers who eventually become old-timers were people who arrived with few illusions and with fairly accurate information about becoming a functioning member of the community. They also were looser, more capable of adjusting and being satisfied with what their new world had to offer to them.

The conceptualization of migrants holding illusions about their new home is an ideal type (Weber, 1946). In fact, all newcomers have some illusions, some suppositions about what the place will be like based on imagination (McHugh, 1984). People who imagine that the attributes of their new location are wonderful (or awful), and that their happiness and satisfaction will derive from those attributes, are arriving with illusions. As the research unfolded, it became apparent that those recent arrivals who intensely listed the beautiful environment, the friendly community, and the developed cultural resources as the sources of their future happiness were unintentionally waving a red flag that they were likely to be moving away soon. Surprisingly, newcomers with self-assured enthusiasm were emitting a signal almost as strong as people who despised their new home. Both were looking to an imaginary environment, whether social or natural, to be the necessary and sufficient conditions for their life. The social and natural environments of the Rockies, magnificent as they are, are realities that transcend imagination.

Most people who remained for a decade or longer arrived with few such illusions. Instead, they spoke more modestly of what they were doing to fit into the community. Certainly, not all of these people were oblivious to the surrounding mountains, the clean air, or the postfrontier Victorian Main Street facade. However, they were not likely to say that those qualities were the primary factors that brought them to the area or that they intended to organize their lives around them. They were much lower keyed, more likely to say the size of town, the presence of mountains, the friendliness of people were okay, acceptable, even nice; but not that they were the best, the greatest, the most. Those with few illusions more quickly settled into a job they had secured before arriving, doing things together if in a family, taking care of the house, being involved with institutions in which they were practically interested and not rushing into close friendships and neighbors. They liked their lives in the place rather than expecting the place to provide what they liked.

EFFECTS OF MIGRATION ON THE COMMUNITY

Rapid in- and out-migration have profound consequences for the community and the surrounding region. From a purely scientific perspective, migration is essentially a mechanical process that leads to similarly mechanical local effects (Price and Sikes, 1975). The cause and its effects are also much more than mechanical process and structure. Analyzing them merely as science fails to acknowledge them as the more complete phenomena they are: a rich mixture of people and their values in the social structure. People define what they think they want in moral terms. Those dimensions carry into the community and society so that the fit between what the community residents say they want and what they actually do can be observed. The differences between what residents say they want and then actually do creates confusion and conflict among residents and even within the individuals themselves. Because people and their beliefs differ, clashes of values are inevitable. Individuals are sometimes ignorant and logically inconsistent, so there is confusion. Some differences are unresolvable qualities of life, paradoxes. The community is the testing site where those clashes, confusion and paradoxes become apparent. It is the place where people must live with their differences, disagreements and inevitable difficulties.

Migration is an energetic force that imposes itself on communities and society (Goldscheider, 1971). It is a classic manifestation of the philosophical glass, half full and half empty, constructed and satisfying from one perspective, destructive and insufficient from the other. To those who believe the glass is full, it may sometimes even seem to runneth over. New people are often full of vitality and energy. Research has continually demonstrated that migrants are among the better and the brighter. Categorically, they are more ambitious and better educated. The popular scientific phrase is that they are human capital, carrying an investment of ability within them. Migrants also carry real capital. Newcomers to Bozeman brought money and investments from where they had lived. They bought homes and the materials for living and started businesses. They brought new skills and innovative ideas. Many gave their time, abilities and economic support to local organizations. Newcomers also added new color to the community, a different appearance and ways of doing things. The more famous and accomplished contributed an aura of recognition. The glamour locations throughout the West have all attracted a smattering of media stars and performers, accomplished scholars and artists and successful, wealthy professionals and executives.

Not all new migrants fill the glass, that is, contribute to the community. Even more importantly, those who bring vitality, fortune and recognition also contribute to negative consequences which even they oppose. While migrants, especially the relatively educated, energetic and capable migrants common to the Northern Rockies, are typically a wealth of human capital, many are not. Migrants to scenic recreational places are not drawn from a normal distribution of residents. They are bimodal. Most are above average in education and status. At the same time, some, a disproportionate number, are more likely to be sources of serious social problems. Migrants, mostly from this small but disruptive disadvantaged minority, contribute much more than their share of local social problems. They are more likely to be mentally ill (Sanua, 1970), to become criminals (Crutchfield, Geerken, and Gove, 1982) and to be incapable of supporting themselves (Fichten, 1991). Consequently, they are more likely to impose their needs on local social service institutions.

The police and welfare agencies spend much of their time responding to problems associated with recent arrivals (Jobes, 1997). The impacts created by problem migrants are endured by more established residents, even in institutions devoted to stability and preparation, especially churches and schools. The heavy demands by newcomers take away from the time and quality of service to the more permanent congregations and students. Ministers are exhausted by pastoral counseling demands of these lost sheep, leaving little time and energy for their resident flocks. Teachers complain of overflowing classrooms in which a third or more of the students had been enrolled in a different school system the previous year. Migration is terribly trying on children under most circumstances. They lose classmates, friends, family and other familiar sources of support. School systems operate with different curricular texts, materials and philosophies. Establishing a stable routine in the classroom is difficult when so many students are suffering from social upheaval, geographic displacement and a disjuncture in their education. The process is relentless. The same disequiliberating difficulties are repeated year after year, wearing down teachers, ministers and welfare workers who are forced to struggle continually with those changes that their colleagues in more stable communities do not have to face.

Continual, inexorable, problematic effects of migration also accompany even those changes in the community that generally are considered to be beneficial. Flying in and out of Bozeman during the early 1990s made visible the effects of rapid development after nearly a decade of much slower growth. Roads were being constructed for subdivisions to the tops of what seemed to be every hillside or the edge of every stream front within a 20-mile radius. Newcomers have immediate and direct needs for space and services. They often want the most precious spaces and the most extensive services available. Population growth consumes the scenic, recreational and aesthetic places as roads are constructed, lands are subdivided and access to beautiful places is closed off.

A complex of overt effects from such development is required or demanded. Infrastructures such as schools, sewage systems, parking, recreational development and other construction follow. Environmental effects are perhaps inevitable as the population grows and the sensitive habitats are invaded. Rural subdivisions and nature create the nexus where fire dangers and noxious weeds are most likely to occur. Together, the direct effects of development and their consequences on the social and physical environments pique local attention to protect and preserve what is left. Burning ordinances to keep air pollution from getting worse, riparian ordinances to protect streambeds and other precious wetlands and land use designations to establish some order become public issues that enter the arena of community planning. They also impose a new layer of controls and enforcement, another effect of invasion by new people.

The physical consequences of growth command most of the attention to working toward practical solutions. The effects of growth in farming areas can raise farm prices and drive away agriculture (Buttel, Larson, and Gillespie, 1990). Purely social effects, which frequently are just as obvious, are talked about, but are scarcely more amendable to solutions than are the environmental effects. Newcomers bring their new and different ways of doing things, of behaving with others. For example, as the most recent wave of exurbanites poured into the northern Rocky Mountains during the late 1980s, they brought their styles of competent, but aggressive driving with them. Often purchasing what they seemed to believe were obligatory four-wheel drive symbols of recreational rural life, they drove faster, cut corners, ignored pedestrians and were discourteous to other drivers, just like back home in the city. This caused considerable consternation to the slower, more courteous, although admittedly less competent small-town drivers. Newcomers increasingly treated themselves and others as they did in the city. Salespeople and public officials gave similar reports to shifts in how they were being treated. Prior to the mid-1960s, customers and clients were patient and considerate, generally grateful for the personal service they received and to the person providing it. Besides, slow service provided an opportunity to catch up on local activities and gossip. Customers and clients knew the people who waited on them. By the early 1990s, the typical treatment of clerks combined the personal and the haughty. Customers critically expected, and generally received, efficient service. They treated clerks more as personally familiar objects rather than as neighbors or as feeling human beings.

How to cope with or resolve such obvious changes in the way people behave with each other, what sociologists call the interaction system, is neither as clear nor prescribed as are the impacts on the physical environment. The interaction system is a definitive aspect of community and residential satisfaction. Less apparent and obvious social characteristics also have profound impacts on how the community functions. Kemmis (1990) has sensitively rued the passage of community in small-town Montana. Perhaps the definitive special feature of small-town life is how people treat each other on the street, in the office, at church, in the neighborhood and in other situations that involve them personally. They most likely know each other, which encourages them to be acknowledged. A handshake, a wave and a smile are expected and given to an individual. Those patterns become so ingrained that they are extended even to strangers. Such patterns persist even in rapidly growing towns until the informal interaction system finally disintegrates. The gestures sometimes remain for many years after they have lost their personal implications, symbols without their deeper, earlier meaning. The Italian sociologist, Vilfredo Pareto (1976), referred to these and other vestiges of past social life as residues. Newcomers from cities are extremely adept at symbolically learning the gestures, without truly experiencing them in the context of their original meaning. The gestures are exhibited with the same authenticity as the new pair of cowboy boots worn to the annual rodeo or barbeque. The importance of trustworthy, dependable, personal interaction is the foundation of stable small-town life. It offers recognition, compassion and support to a real and whole person.

It is all too easy to give a rosier description of small town informal interaction than it deserves. Blatant discrimination is widely practiced. Minorities rarely, and usually uncomfortably, mix with the majority. The elite doesn't cross to the wrong side of the tracks, at least not officially. People are two-faced. Everyone knows about the skeletons in each other's closets while acting as though there are no bones in their own. The deceits and dishonesties of small-town life are built into and understood in the informal interaction. Despite their prejudices and inequities, the predictability and trust in the way people treat each other remains personal and is cherished and protected. These same biases and prejudicial advantages exist in the city, though they are masked behind the impersonal and superficial interaction of urban life (Riesman, 1953).

Small towns have their own ways of coping with change brought from the outside. The most effective defense is that generally they haven't had to cope with much. In fables, Shangri-la is protected by distant remoteness, hidden by the deserts and the surrounding mountains. Small towns with low migration and growth have their unique and difficult problems, but they don't include the intensive changes and problems brought by a mass of outsiders. The unfortunate aspect of the defense of being off the beaten path is that such places usually do not have the organization or expertise to react when their sleepy hollow is awakened by the sound of backhoes and cement trucks. Their lack of knowledge and preparedness makes them naive, hopeful and vulnerable to incursions by greedy developers and environmental advocates seeking seclusion.

The familiar, personal interaction of rural life is itself a mechanism for informally adapting to the kinds of changes that occur year in and year out. Rural people talk, gossip, complain and sometimes, though rarely, confront each other to work through what they want. Their agreements are made verbally around the amalgamation of personal interests. They rely on formal institutional, particularly legal, solutions as a last resort, because "you don't treat people that way." Urban society looks to externally imposed rules to solve problems, reversing the foundations of rural social life. A naive arrogance comes from living in rural areas over many years. Residents, especially the leaders, come to think that they are on top of the local problems since they have managed to survive the past. However, their established methods of coping with economic contraction and population decline are usually inadequate and inappropriate for responding to the demands imposed by high migration and population growth. They also lack the economic or political resources for developing or implementing a plan. Their towns and the surrounding areas will be permanently altered. One hope of planning is that the alterations will incorporate the personal face of rural life.

THE BEAUTIES OF SMALL TOWNS IN THE ROCKIES

The desirability of small towns and rural areas seems intrinsic to many people. Their attractiveness in these last years of the millennium are particularly apparent in contrast to the enormous environmental decay and the insecurity and hostility of urban life. Scenic and recreational areas are especially attractive, the last extensive vestiges of natural beauty and solitude. The proximity of water clean enough for trout and wilderness vast enough for bison and elk, wolves and grizzlies is purifying and humbling. The Northern Rockies, from south of the great ecosystem surrounding Yellowstone and Teton National Parks to the equally wild and rugged vastness of the International Peace Parks (Glacier and Waterton National Parks), may be the largest relatively undeveloped region in the temperate portions of the Northern Hemisphere (Jobes, 1991). This is ironic since the Northern Rockies are not in a Third World country that has been passed over by exploration and growth: they are in the wealthiest nation on Earth. The Northern Rockies and other natural areas in the West are huge gems beyond value that are rarely calculated into national wealth. They deserve protection if for no other reasons than those entitled to any precious environment. There are so many recreational, economic and scientific reasons for protecting them that space is insufficient here to describe them (Calvert and Jobes, 1990).

There also are purely social and aesthetic dimensions for preserving both the areas and their towns. They afford spaces to find peace and solitude simply beyond the imagination or capacities of more urbanized nations. In industrialized Europe, for example, there are no comparable habitable regions of low-population density and relatively undeveloped environments. The scenic recreational areas of Germany and Japan are largely symbols in which development is extensive. Ironically, the Germans and Japanese particularly recognize, even make sacred, those symbols. In America, there still is the opportunity for conserving much of the reality of nature rather than symbols of what once was.

The preservation of the Rocky Mountains can no longer depend upon their harsh weather, geographic remoteness, and rugged landscape. Modern wealth has created large numbers of people who can afford to live where they want, even if only for a few months each year. Modern transportation, communication and other technologies have made the bitter Montana winter comfortably habitable, at least for the hardy. Simultaneously, the comparative attractiveness of the Rockies to the deteriorating urban world has increased the motivation to reside in Montana and the surrounding states. This is the crucial phase for preservation planning for this natural region, lest it be the final phase for the lack of a natural region to preserve. It will require enormous courage and strength of leadership based on faith and foresight. It must strive to protect the informal and personal qualities of a rural life. At the same time, it must incorporate some of the practical experience and wisdom of urban society to make the decisions and solutions solid enough to withstand the endless challenges of exploitation that ultimately would destroy it as an extensive natural environment.

I have been part of the phenomena discussed here since the early 1950s. My parents moved from Los Angeles to Los Alamos in the Jemez Mountains of northern New Mexico when I was 13 years old. My choices of universities to attend and of job opportunities have been based largely on close access to nature. Within that parameter, I have been fortunate to find university positions in which to do work I love in equal measure to the natural environment in which I have lived.

Chapter 2

People Who Migrate, People Who Stay: An Overview of Data and Theories about Migration

Economic explanations of migration are among the oldest and most established theories in the social sciences. The classic notion that people move as a consequence of weighing the economic alternatives between places and selecting a site that optimizes their material well-being has been the predominant model of migration in the social sciences. The pervasive and long-established use of this explanation gives it considerable legitimacy. Rational Man (Person) Theory, of which this model is a part, has no serious contenders as an explanation of social behavior caused by forces external to the individual (Cebula, 1979). Any alternative seems to imply that behavior occurs in a cipher unrelated to awareness and adaptation among people. The assumptions and propositions seem so self-evident that they are taken for granted and are passed with minimal review.

The durability of economic theories of migration has more support than historical priority and logical attractiveness. They have proven to be both empirically valid and reliable for migrations ranging from primitive hunting and gathering bands through mature industrial societies. These theories are versatile, applicable to individuals and to mass streams of migrants (Speare, Kobrin, and Kingkade, 1982). However, the fact that economic theories have seemed to make sense for centuries and that they have been used to explain considerable amounts of migration under incredibly varied conditions, does not mean that they are appropriate or even the most efficient explanations for particular types of migration which seem to be motivated on bases other than economic factors.

Classic economic theorists would maintain that the criticisms made in this section are ill-founded because we construe the meaning of economic factors too narrowly, that is, classic economic theory considers any variable that is brought to consciousness and weighed in order to make a choice to be an economic variable. This classic position is rejected here because it effectively defines any motive as essentially economic, merely because it can be compared to all others. Such logic usurps all other explanations. If taken seriously, it becomes untestable, a monolithic theory elevated to the status of religion.

Classic economic theory is treated here as if it excludes other social factors. A more pointed criticism is aimed at the tendency among demographers who have largely restricted their research to the use of economic variables when examining migration. Demographers have primarily selected changes in potential jobs, income and investments as the predisposing facts for migration. The use of these and other economic variables is partially an artifact of the available actuarial data on national populations. Governments have been concerned with and consequently collected systematic economic information in censuses and national surveys. Little systematically collected national data exist for social interaction systems, like familiar recreational or religious groups. Demographers, then, have been relegated to using what has been available, rather than what might complement and expand upon existing findings. The relatively recent use of specialized demographic surveys is a departure from the limitations of existing data. Surveys collected for special purposes, such as the ones upon which our observations are based, are being collected for a variety of specific research purposes.

Another problem related to the almost exclusive reliance upon economic data and theory to explain migration is that the perspective becomes reified to the exclusion of other explanations. Given the widespread acceptance of the metaphor of rational economic decision making as the salient explanation of human behavior, such analyses express how migration occurs in a familiar conceptualization assumed to be correct in everyday life as well as by demographers and governments. However, the use and acceptance of the economic metaphor does not make it universally correct. The analysis of migration through the metaphor provides a forum for demonstrating its limitations. Scientists and policymakers may create, measure and use alternative, important noneconomic variables to interpret and plan for migration into communities.

Having criticized the nearly unilateral use of economic data and theory in-migration, their merits deserve iteration. They may empirically account for more migration than any other variable for most people most of the time (Goldscheider, 1971). Even when persons are primarily motivated for noneconomic reasons, economic factors are almost a universally necessary, if not sufficient, condition for moving or staying — or living. The mere fact that so many people believe in the efficacy of earnings and material possessions as the reason for explaining their own behavior, or the behaviors of others, makes economic analyses essential and powerful (DeJong and Fawcett, 1981). The attendant fact that so many people establish a minimally acceptable income and standard of living for themselves means that most at least consider economic factors, however much their actual incomes and living standards differ from those minima. Finally, the data of economics are attractive. Economics is the social science with the most clearly defined and universally accepted measures that are external to the person: currency, jobs and possessions (Friedman, 1962). These are tangible elements. They can be seen, felt, flaunted and measured with considerable agreement. This strength is also their weakness. They appear to be so clear and universal that values people hold regarding family, friends, nature, community and religion are likely to be ignored or forgotten in their presence.

Research that has considered economic factors as the primary determinants of migration falls into two general types of explanation (Brown and Wardwell, 1980). The most traditional approach has looked to relative increases in job opportunities in rural areas to account for in-migration or, conversely, to job losses as the cause of out-migration. The other interpretation has emphasized the increase in technological amenities made possible by economic development. As rural areas have become almost as "up-to-date as Kansas City," and more easily accessible through advanced industrial, transportation and communication technologies, they have become more attractive to urbanites.

Both explanations account for large populations of migrants. Direct evidence for economically stimulated growth comes from research on energy development boomtowns. In many locations, including some in the Northern Rockies, towns with thousands of residents have sprung up where only a few hundred people lived before resources began to be tapped and facilities associated with those resources were constructed. Coal Strip, Montana, ballooned from 150 residents in 1970 to nearly 5,000 by 1980 as coal mines and power plants were developed. Boomtown migration can be considered a direct function of job opportunities. Where few people and fewer jobs existed, many people suddenly flow to gain employment. Conversely, when development slows or ceases, the population moves away.

The nearly singular importance of these frequently temporary jobs is especially evident, considering how undesirable such locations usually are at least during the early phases of development. Quite frequently, the locations were so geographically undesirable that people did not want to live there. Icy cold winters, hot dry summers and bug- and reptile-infested swamplands are not intrinsically attractive to most people. During the development phases, living quarters are generally cramped, uncomfortable and expensive. Most public services taken for granted in stable communities don't even exist locally or are woefully inadequate. Perhaps the most undesirable quality of boomtowns, though, is how people treat each other. Blatant abuses occur in public, especially at bars, which are the scenes of fighting and hustling (Jobes, 1986). Less visible are the increased spouse and child abuse. Self-abuse in the forms of increased alcohol and drug dependence, suicide and automobile accidents also multiplies. Old-timers from the predevelopment era of agriculture and small business ignore or are critical of newcomers, excluding them from community activities. The problems signify an overload of the capacity of the local community to accommodate the needs of too many unfamiliar people in too short a time, resulting in nearly everyone feeling angry and deprived of what they believe should be theirs.

During the late 1960s, Calvin Beale (1975), a demographer with the U.S. Department of Agriculture, reported that, for the first time (except for the bleak depression year of 1932) in the history of the United States, rural areas were growing faster from in-migration than were urban areas. He called this reversal of population growth the urban-rural turnaround. The turnaround excited demographers and students of rural society because it signaled a reversal in a routine process. It also raised the morale of administrators and business people in the rural hinterlands as they optimistically hoped for economic growth and population stability. Most of the rural turnaround was discovered to have been concentrated in retirement and recreation areas, and in university towns and boomtowns. Much of the growth was spillover of population from cities that were expanding into their nonmetropolitan periphery. By the later 1970s, the initial turnaround was over (Gorham, 1993). Beale and his long-time and frequent collaborator at the University of Wisconsin, Glenn Fuguitt (1996), now are documenting that the phenomenon has begun anew, perhaps becoming cyclical, waxing and waning according to complex social and economic factors.

Most of the nonmetropolitan growth has been expansion into areas adjacent to cities. It is essentially an urban process. The expansion of mining, agriculture, industrialization and university growth have significantly contributed to population expansion in many rural towns. Tourist recreational and retirement growth has been the most widely spread foundation for the true turnaround (Glasgow, 1980). The growth of tourist recreation towns in the Rockies is only one form of the reversal of urban-rural population growth (Johnson, 1989). However, it persisted when other types of urban-rural turnaround almost ceased. Growth in rural Rocky Mountain scenic and recreational areas promises to be persistent for at least a few decades (Knop and Jobes, 1997).

Boomtowns are peopled by economic migrants. Although some may also be attracted by a wish to live in the area of development, money and jobs are the primary drawing factors. Some become part of a new migrant labor force, moving from boomtown to boomtown, as jobs are completed and new ones started. Boomtowns are the local equivalence of a gold rush, whatever the resources precipitating the rush may be. Whether for pipeline development, coal-powered electrical generation or offshore oil drilling, the effects are much the same. The people who are drawn to them are especially economic in orientation, although they, too, have other motives for their moves (Freudenburg and Jones, 1991).

In 1885, E. G. Ravenstein (1885, 1889) published a paper to which serious scholars of migration have been indebted ever since. Ravenstein introduced the notion that population sizes and distances within a geographic area influence migration. People, he maintained, move according to the opportunities they are hoping to find. Most will move only as far as is necessary to reach those opportunities. They are least attracted to low-density remote areas, other factors considered. They are most likely to gravitate to population centers. Perhaps more importantly, Ravenstein then systematically described how patterns of migration are determined by demographic characteristics of the population: age and gender. Young adults move most. Those with young children make migrants of them, too. People in the more settled middle years move less. During the past 30 years, retired people have been moving more (Biggar, 1982). The migration reflects economic incentives to find work and economic abilities, such as decent retirement incomes and affordable places to retire. In their study of retirees at Sun City, Gober and Zonn (1983) documented how economic factors were integrated with considerations of family and friends. The migration also implies powerful social change such as a reduction in commitment to the family, when people who could afford to stay choose to move. Women moved more often, but shorter distances, usually within the region to a nearby city. Most people moved short distances. Places with large populations send and receive more migrants than smaller places.

Ravenstein's laws of migration have proven remarkably accurate and resilient for generalizing about the characteristics of who moves and where they move. They are important to keep in mind when there is a temptation to try to explain migration in purely personal or psychological terms. Humans are social beings which routinely behave in much the same way as entire groups or categories of which they are parts. However personal and individual one's motives are, they are systematically similar to others. The commonality of the experiences of types of people moving into and out of scenic and recreational places is emphasized throughout this book, despite their individual idiosyncracies and the substantive differences in their lives. Ravenstein's laws, while implying an economic efficiency, need only be interpreted in purely demographic and geographic terms. His theory is not specifically an economic explanation.

Other demographers also have developed theories that require no universal assumptions about rational economic choices motivating people to move. William Peterson (1961) created a general typology of migration which specifies that some migration is not based on open and free choices. Petersen specified impelled and forced migration. Such migrations can be massive, as in the transportation of criminals to prison or to a new continent. They also are broadly and historically recognized, as in the Babylonian captivity of the Israelites. More recently, Jobes, Stinner, and Wardwell (1991) have compiled case studies of migrations which are largely noneconomic in origin.

Some similarities among the people moving into the Northern Rockies are most clearly evidenced by who they are not. Larry Blackwood and Ed Carpenter (1978) were among the first scholars to acknowledge an anti-urban and ethnically homogeneous bias among many turnaround migrants. They are not racial minorities. The faces in Sun Valley, Jackson, Bozeman, and the hundreds of other small towns in Idaho, Wyoming, and Montana are almost entirely white. The primary exceptions are on or near Indian reservations or Hispanic settlements created during the days when migrant agricultural workers dug sugar beets and sheared sheep. Despite the rapid national increase in minority populations, the percentages of nonwhite residents in these areas has remained constantly below 3 percent for decades.

Newcomers are likely to be well-educated, with professional, managerial or trade skills. Their incomes are lower than could be expected given their education. Many are technically poor: they have low incomes. They are likely to have moved more than a thousand miles from where they had been living, which was quite likely a long distance from where they were born. One reason for the long distance from where they had moved is that the population density in the region is low. There are so few people in the region that most newcomers, by necessity, have to move a long way to get there. A more intriguing factor, though, is that migrants into the Northern Rockies are anomalies within Ravenstein's Laws. They are people who have moved a long distance to a place with few people. The reason they have moved such a long way is that there are no places, at least to the east, that offer the qualities they are looking for that are to be found in the Northern Rockies. There are few intervening opportunities for mountains and the beauty and recreation in small-town settings to be found between the East Coast and the Rockies. In addition, women move about as frequently as men, although they often move to accompany their families rather than having initiated the move.

SOCIETAL CHANGES AND COMMUNITY CHANGE

The rapidly growing towns in the Rocky Mountains mirror their in-migrants. The population growth, the cosmopolitan character of residents and the anticipations of tourists increase expectations and eventual development of diverse attractive businesses and semipublic services, such as preschools and recreational organizations. The differences along Main Street between these towns and nontourist towns in agricultural areas are immediately visible. The Main Street tourist town has a cultivated ambience combining cosmopolitan retail goods and services with small-town appearance. Arts and crafts, stockbrokers, galleries, book and antique stores and restaurants make up a disproportionate number of store fronts. The businesses on Main Street in small recreational tourist towns more resemble gentrified urban shopping areas than small towns in agricultural areas. Their businesses, or at least the business owners, turn over rapidly. In Bozeman, the long-standing joke when a new restaurant opens is "We better hurry to find out how it is before it closes." A scale of cosmopolitanism for rural towns probably could be constructed by examining the per capita presence of espresso shops, microbreweries, antique shops and ethnic restaurants across towns in the region.

Changes in actual local goods and services in a small town are largely determined by how much it has grown. Population loss generally is accompanied by fewer and less diverse goods and services. Population growth generally leads to concomitant expansion. Changes in perceptions of goods and services are more complex and related to factors that are beyond the locality. Unlike actual increases or decreases in facilities or businesses, perceptions differ according to who beholds them. That who is determined by their reference points. Some reference points are exogenous, beyond the locale. Recent newcomers from still smaller and less-developed towns have comparatively more favorable perceptions about the services of these tourist towns than newcomers from cities. Those from cities take the local market as given, inferior to the city, but think the ambience makes up for the inferior local goods and services.

Another exogenous reference point is that of a common standard. Such a standard, while constantly shifting, creates general expectations beyond any particular experience or locale. Suppositions about the worst and best possible provisions for goods and services occur along with notions of an average. The new locale is evaluated in relation to such extralocal experiences and suppositions. Perceptions about local goods and services derive in part from exposure to alternatives. The longer people reside in a town and the less they visit other places, the more their perceptions become based on what is available locally. After a couple of decades, newcomers become downright local. When residents comment that a local steakhouse is better than one to which they were taken in Chicago or New York, it may be both a cosmopolitan and a local statement of pride. However, when someone says the same thing about local ethnic restaurants, it is a pretty clear indication that that person has gone native, that they have forgotten just how many and how superior the ethnic restaurants are in San Francisco or Boston.

An irony exists around the bases for evaluating local goods and services because of the mixture of exogenous and endogenous factors that affect perceptions. Evaluations of local goods and services may decline, even as their numbers increase and their diversity expands. There are several reasons for lowered perceptions of a growing goods and services sector. One reason is that past experience, particularly among newcomers, leads them to have especially high expectations. They actually have had experiences with great bookstores, medical centers and universities.

Another reason is that the standard expectation, however realistic it may be, may lead residents to evaluate their locality relatively low. Local high school students, for example, frequently consider their hometowns to have little compared to what they imagine other places offer. It really does not much matter if there are more high-quality athletic clubs, music societies, book guilds and church groups in a town than anyone can join. The evaluation by small-town youth is that there is nothing to do. That becomes the standard perception, with an attendant belief that some place, like Seattle, has lots to do. More endogenously, locals may not like the loss of some community qualities, even as the cosmopolitan scene is expanding. The loss of a favorite greasy spoon or local market may be considered greater than the simultaneous establishment of gourmet restaurants and larger supermarkets. True locals may rank their goods and services especially high when most outsiders would consider them mediocre or worse. Old-timers brag that a local ethnic restaurant is as good as the best in San Francisco when, by any standard of comparison, the statement is a matter of poor judgment or poor taste.

On the other hand, local establishments can be excellent. In Bozeman, a landmark diner, the Burger Inn, popularly known as Manny's, was a historical reference point among pre-1980 and post-1980 residents. The tiny counter-only diner was renowned for its gigantic helpings of grilled food for bargain prices, which was perhaps a deciding factor in its ultimate closure. It was even more renowned for its curmudgeon owner, cook and raconteur, Manny Voulkos, brother to influential artist, Peter. Manny seemed to enjoy shocking or insulting patrons, to the great delight of nearly everyone. To those who understood the scene, it was an honor to be insulted. Manny regularly created a menu with items that were never available. He was said to have served pancakes that had dropped on the floor, after carefully dusting them off. (They probably had been deliberately dropped and then were replaced by a larger stack that seemed to have been set aside for that purpose.) Hundreds of Manny stories still circulate years after the doors closed for good.

A PERSONAL NOTE ABOUT THE AUTHOR AND THIS RESEARCH

The information in this book comes from many sources. The author conducted two extensive research projects which together spanned 23 years. In both of these projects, residents and newcomers into the Gallatin Valley repeatedly were interviewed and observed in considerable depth. He also conducted several research projects of shorter duration throughout the region during that period (1968-1995). Existing data, especially from the U.S. Census, provided solid foundations for measuring many changes and comparing localities. The research of other authors, especially demographers in the region with whom the author has worked throughout this period, has also provided data and insights.

I am a long-time witness to what is being described here. I have lived in beautiful rural areas in the West most of my life. The truth of science is limited to the observable data which are extremely limited. My personal experiences and observations go beyond those that could be precisely replicated by me, let alone another scientist. The facts, then, are partially enthographic, the study of the intricacies of individual communities through close observation. Ethnography makes it essentially impossible to separate the data drawn from personal interviews and secondary sources, such as the census and surveys administrated by social scientists.

Some scholars advise students to study subjects with which they are not personally involved in order to avoid prejudice and increase objectivity. This is sound advice so long as the subject conceptually captures their passion. I have not followed that wise advice. I have been more than interested in and fascinated with small towns and rural areas in beautiful areas since I was a little boy. I love them, care about them and feel badly about their demise. I spent many holidays with my grandparents on a wheat farm near a tiny prairie town in Oklahoma. I began to think about change in scenic recreational places that I most loved during the late 1950s: Santa Fe and the surrounding towns in northern New Mexico and Aspen and other emerging ski towns in Colorado. By the early 1970s, I didn't want to visit these places anymore because of their conversion to the modern, with only symbolic preservation of the original town and environment. They had surrendered most of their idiosyncratic or regional character. Friends, including long-term residents, harped endlessly and fatally about the new people and the undesirable changes they were bringing. They also felt excited by the presence of movie stars and begrudgingly enjoyed the prosperity as their little towns became cosmopolitan. A young architect and former skiing buddy from Steamboat Springs visited me in Bozeman in 1972. Already discouraged by the growth of Steamboat, he was even then looking to Bozeman and Bend as places to resettle. Ultimately and ambivalently, he decided to stay in Steamboat, accommodating new people, growth and financial success with deteriorating fishing, loss of fresh powder snow and natural beauty.

I have experienced camaraderie with other newcomers as we rejoiced in finding the promised land. I have endured sadness as that temporary community unraveled through job losses and transfers, divorce, ambition and death. On a mountain pass outside of Bozeman, in an old farmstead, we raised black sheep for hand spinning. Our 47 acres included the farms and sheds for a century-old sheep ranch that had been subdivided. The first year on the top of that snow-covered hill, there were only three other families in a one-mile radius. The next year, there were three more, and there were two or three each year after that for a decade. We watched eagles learn to fly and coyotes kill the sheep. We heated with firewood, raised a large garden and had a menagerie of chickens, geese, rabbits, as well as the sheep, one steer each year and an occasional goat. I hunted and fished more than most sportsmen can even dream about. My daughter and son rode horses to a one-room schoolhouse where I was a board member. Neighbors initially shared every conceivable task, fencing, haying, working with animals, building houses, cutting firewood, repairing vehicles and, for six months each year, pulling each other out of snowdrifts. We talked, ate, sang and drank with each other. We cared for each other's children. All this sharing, self-sufficient life cost most of my salary and half of my time. And, it was worth every dollar and every hour.

Darker sides of the experience eventually appeared. Several residents worked for the Burlington Northern Railway, which closed a large repair shop in Livingston. This forced most of them to accept transfers or lose their jobs. In either case, most left. Alcoholism, drug abuse, infidelity and spouse abuse took their tolls in divorce. The interminable snows and mud of serious mountain living led some to move, again, to a warmer climate with a growing season longer than 85 days. At least one, usually a few, frosts would hit the gardens between Memorial Day and Labor Day. A perfunctory snow fell every few years in July or August. There were almost always big snowfalls in September and May. The personal, social and environmental hardships did more than eventuate in moving away. They strained and eventually destroyed much of the hope, faith and trust that many neighbors had for each other as an enduring community.

I mention my personal story for three reasons. First, it is an example of the process of hope and disillusionment that is integral to migration. It has some of the most romantic and enjoyable aspects of the idyll of country life. Those qualities were and are genuine. They really can and do exist, even — perhaps most vividly — in communities of newcomers bursting with energy and illusions. It also depicts the disintegration of intense families, friendships and neighboring which were initially anticipated to last forever. It is an extreme example that is not representative of the places where most newcomers live or of how they work and play. The second reason is to clearly identify the difference between the physical geography and the community. Social life occurs in the context of the physical environment. Both must be minimally tolerable. I loved the physical characteristics of Montana and most of my community life.

The third reason for telling my story is to remind readers about where the words are coming from. My experiences undoubtedly have influenced how I have perceived and interpreted the experiences of others. Ski touring, canoeing and sailing have occupied many of my more fulfilled moments. They share a common quality in that in each of these activities, perspective constantly changes. Landmarks become obfuscated by other features. What lies around the next bend is never entirely visible or certain. I hope that my perspective permits me to have an accurate perception of the experiences of the people who move into and out of the scenic rural West. I hope it helps make a true reading of the voyages of others. I hope it will help other people and communities to plan their destinies along the way. I had left Colorado partly because of the development that was sweeping the state. There was a new light on the horizon every evening when I drove home west of Lyons from the University of Colorado where I taught. I chose Bozeman because it was a beautiful small town located in the middle of probably the best trout fishing in the lower 48 states, and it had a ski area nearby. Not incidentally, it had a university where I could teach and conduct research in sociology, work I preciously honored.

A research problem had begun to gel in my mind by the time I moved to Montana. I hypothesized that, as growth and development occurred, long-term residents would dislike the changes. They would become dissatisfied and many would move on. The hypothesis had practical implications. If it were possible to demonstrate that the satisfaction of residents was declining in spite — even as a consequence — of growth, then residents and leaders would eagerly begin planning and organizing to protect this place they loved, their home. The simplicity of the hypothesis and the naivete of the assumption that the community would seriously act upon the findings are humorous in retrospect. I was 30 years old, bright, informed, and "I came from Boulder to help them," restating the cynical phrase often voiced in Washington, D.C. Reality turned out to be far more complex and interesting than the hypothesis. Planning has slowly lurched along, never really hampering growth.

Bozeman and south-western Montana turned out to be the perfect place to study this phenomenon. There were no metropolitan areas to inundate surrounding rural areas and towns, as had happened around Denver and Salt Lake City. There were huge undeveloped tracts of land with varied and precious natural resources. The growth, while sustained, was never catastrophic, as had occurred in energy boomtowns I studied at the same time. The changes could be studied as a gradual and continuing process that was occurring throughout the recreational areas of the rural West, growth that promised to continue into the foreseeable future.

It would be scientifically deceptive to claim absolute objectivity about what is described here, although it is all honest and, I hope, true to Bozeman and other small towns in the Northern Rockies. I am a human with preferences and dislikes for places and their qualities. I believe that some are better places for very human reasons: supporting places to raise children; slower places to talk with family, stable friends and neighbors; safer and far healthier places for ordinary residents. These are biases. Sociology does not have a conscience about such matters. The disappearance or formation of a town is merely a fascinating phenomenon from a scientific perspective. Scientists do frequently pursue a research problem because of a hope that their findings will improve the lot of humankind. I cross the threshold beyond mere intellectual fascination in the study of community. I hope that it is apparent to readers when that personal mixing of science, opinion and advocacy occurs.

Separating fact from interpretation is sometimes difficult, even impossible. I experienced so many facts and so many changes that my thoughts and interpretations have evolved. I have been affected and changed as a scientist, as a resident and as a maturing human being. Each aspect of my life has affected the others. While I try to be objective, three decades is a long time to invest in a project. The perspectives that have emerged undoubtedly have foreclosed the use of other reasonable and applicable ways of looking at residential satisfaction, rural growth and planning.

Table 2.1 summarizes my own expectations and my perceived expectations of how other residents, especially newcomers, would feel and act with regard to protecting the natural and social environments in the study area. Before initiating the research, I had deduced that most local residents would both stay and fight to protect the existing locale. By the 1980s, I had reversed those expectations, as facts led me to alter what I thought had been a logical expectation. However, newcomers retained considerable hope that residents, especially themselves, would stay and only minimally disturb the community and surrounding countryside.

Table 2.1
Changing Expectations That Residents Will Stay and Want to Protect the Natural and Social Environments: The Author and Newcomers, 1970s-1990s

1. My expectations (logic) before collecting data in 1973 that residents would want to stay and to protect the natural resources and quality of social life that is, "Others Behaviors."

My Expectations: 1973

Stay and protect	Most residents
Develop and/or leave	Few residents

2. My expectations following initial analyses and the actual likelihood of residents staying and protecting natural resources and quality of life 1980s and 1990s.

	My Expectations: 1980s	My Expectations: 1990s
Stay and protect	Few residents	Some residents
Develop and/or leave	Most residents	Most residents

3. The expectations of a broader audience (e.g., Newcomers and Old-timers during the 1970s-1990s) that residents will stay and protect natural resources and quality of social life.

	Audience Expectations	
	Newcomers	Old-Timers
Stay and protect	Most residents	Some residents
Develop and/or leave	Few residents	Many residents

The reader is cautioned, then, about the limitations of what is written here. These words may help people appreciate and understand the great hunger for community that motivates people to move to rural areas, the successes and failures of such migration and the impacts of the migration on communities and the surrounding areas.

The question of whether a scientist should discuss a subject in any manner other than as direct objective facts is a classic issue of contention. Max Weber, one of the giants of social science, believed that a scientist should be only an objective reporter of facts and their interrelationships. He believed that, if scientists allowed their personal beliefs to influence their analysis, the analyses would be biased by those beliefs. He advocated an absolute separation of personal references in research. He insisted that no allusions to any characteristics, position or beliefs by the scientist should be made in the analyses. *Value free sociology*, as Weber (1946) termed this approach, strives for purely objective analyses, letting the facts speak for themselves within a theoretical perspective through the rigorous rules of scientific method.

Weber (1885, 1889) had a liberal political justification for value free analysis. He believed that scientists using their prestige to influence others (students, politicians, the public) took unfair advantage of impressionable, less-informed people. This violation of trust did more than manipulate others: it made scientists into lackeys for nonscientific causes. Ultimately, it would undermine science, as public trust for facts was lost. This position typified American sociology prior to World War II and continues to be the prevailing ideal for research among serious scientists. It is worth noting that Weber, who probably foresaw the depersonalizing nature of emerging industrial-urban society more clearly than any scholar of his era, suffered from intense and debilitating depression.

The extreme opposite of value free analysis is the notion that scientists should work directly for a cause. This position, common among activists and in totalitarian societies, regards science as a tool for facilitating a designated political philosophy. At its extreme, it has justified medical torture in Nazi concentration camps and mass-forced transfers of Balkan peoples to Siberia. This extreme subservience of science to political beliefs can lead to the exact manipulation and loss of trust that Weber warned against. Writing this as I reside in Bucharest, I am personally familiar with the social and scientific catastrophes which have resulted from an extreme mixing of science with advocacy.

A more recent challenge to value free analysis incorporates some inescapable realities, while seeking objective analysis. This position, most often identified with Alvin Gouldner (1970) and Irving Horowitz (1975), says that, as humans, scientists inescapably believe and act in certain ways that preclude pure objectivity. In social science, which is so intimately enmeshed with social life, it is especially important for scientists to express their biases and other factors about themselves which might affect the objectivity of their analyses. To fail to do so is dishonest and nonobjective. Then, given their biases, scientists have the obligation to be as scientifically rigorous as possible. This realistic middle ground between value free analysis and the subservience of science to political positions admonishes scientists to become political critics when the political system ignores facts or acts immorally.

There is no clear point at which personal beliefs destroy objectivity. What is now called the postmodern perspective says that there can be no true objectivity. This perspective creates a cynical paradox that ultimately denies both science and morality. As an extreme esoteric way of looking at the world, this perspective cannot be logically disproved because the subjective interpretation by people is never totally apparent to observers. That makes objectivity always questionable. Postmodernists explain the world in terms of power, the power to persuade or impose a world as it is defined, rather than a world as it exists. However, most of us live in a world that is fairly real, with facts and rules that most of us believe and follow.

This book is written in the middle ground, where real people are making decisions and acting upon them, and where real communities with recognizable structures are affected by those people. Most of the time, they behave fairly predictably and sort of honorably. Trying to make sense of this reality is, to me, attempting to be totally objective while appreciating that there are inevitable limitations of knowledge and personal preferences. These shortfalls influence what I see as facts and how I explain them. Even postmodernists, despite their denial of the real and objective, talk about some chardonnay as better than others, expect their stockbrokers to make profitable investments, and wear comfortable shoes. These are matters of fact for them, not merely matters of definition and persuasion.

The notion of "free will," freely by choosing a course of action, is a fundamental and universal concept that has plagued thinkers for millennia (Finkelman, 1986). The position taken in this research is that, while considerable decision making occurs among individuals, many of the factors that determine who moves are beyond the awareness or control of individuals, hence not really a matter of choice. For example, almost no inner city black and non-European minority people have moved to scenic recreational areas in the Northern Rockies. Since they have not been interviewed about why they have not chosen to make such moves, the reasons for their choice are not known. However, the influence of being born into an inner city racial or non-European minority is sufficient to predict and, by inference, to explain why so few have moved. Now, given these factors, where does free choice occur? It is not likely that they chose their genetic and geographic characteristics: they were born with them. And, because of these statuses, the choice to move to rural Montana is not likely to occur to them. Because of their experiences, they are unlikely to have feasible connections and pathways to generate either the thought about moving to such destinations or the methods for doing so.

This example distinguishes between two different levels of factors that "cause" people to behave as they do. *Macrolevel factors* are broad influences that often are beyond much control by individuals. They rarely can be modified by the choice of a single person. When many people sharing common hopes and aspirations band together, of course, they can become a social force, even a revolution. Migration to scenic recreational places does not seem to be part of the worldview or the social movement among many inner city minority people.

Microlevel factors are influences that more personally affect individuals. Individual migrants may be consciously aware of many of these factors. At this level of analysis, there clearly is considerable choice making, which might be called free will from an ethical perspective. They are free to make choices within their parameters of life. But few are free to set most of those parameters. In time, a few make the choice to move. If they become established, those they left behind may gradually recognize the opportunity to move, thus increasing the likelihood of their choice to move. The choice is present as an abstraction. Realistically, it affects very few, though it is part of a slow process.

THE UTOPIAN VISION AND CHOOSING A PLACE TO LIVE

Choosing a community is fundamentally an exercise in architectural choice. One is looking for a home, an environment in which to reside. While some few dreamers have the strength and fortitude — or naivete and arrogance — to imagine that they can create their environment, most restrict their choices to what is available. The special qualities of visionary designers, like L'Enfant or dreamer architects, like Solari, are manifested with less systematic vision in places to which people are attracted (Rapaport, 1990).

The utopian dream of designing and creating a place integrated into nature and providing the essentials for a happy life is perhaps now more consciously developed than it has been throughout most periods in human history. The past has periodically flowered under such conscious attempts to create the ideal environment in which to live. The Old Testament is testimony of the attempt by the Hebrew nation to flourish under God's laws in the Holy Land. The Garden of Eden personified the perfect and unsustainable balance of humans in nature. The monastic period saw similar attempts to reach an inner City of God (Augustine, 1972) through an ideal composite of work on the land and life in cloisters in the human community. Brigham Young led his brethren on a more tangible quest toward Zion, which is now less than a day's drive from Bozeman (Arrington, 1966). Scott and Helen Nearing (1970) advocated a return to the simple life close to the land, a theme common among earlier American communards. The hippie communes of the 1960s sought, albeit with brief success, to accomplish their dream without doctrinaire religion or politics. Currently, there are dozens of ambitious attempts to unite the environment of God and the works of humans into a harmonious home. The followers of the Rajneesh (Carter, 1990), the Church Universal and Triumphant led by Elizabeth Clare Prophet, and the entourage of Shirley MacClaine are three examples.

Less spiritually guided, yet still oriented toward the ideal of constructing a community in a desirable physical environment, has been the proliferation of planned unit developments during the past two decades. Their object is to create community acceptable to worthy residents, excluding the unacceptable. Exclusionary elitist communities, like the Meadowlands outside Houston and Ponte

Vedra in Florida, are large and profitable examples of a commercial process repeated thousands of times in the United States during the past three decades.

Intentional communities are filled with hope and excitement, especially during the planning and early development phase when newcomers and dreamers simultaneously experience and share the exhilaration of creating community (Coser, 1974). Residents must then face the day-to-day realities of making their lives work in conjunction with neighbors and community residents who, like themselves, have idiosyncratic personalities and characters, not to mention diverse beliefs and behaviors. This realization often leads to the abandonment, destruction and disintegration of the community or a standardized approach to life within it. The excitement and promise of the utopian phase is not unique to choosing a community. Similar processes occur in the course of many valued changes in life: choosing a new house, a marriage partner or a new vehicle. The effects of tolerating imperfections can become too much, particularly in the fast, demanding and transient life in contemporary America. The dreamed promise often ends up on the trash heap of the local community. And new dreams and promises grow out of it.

Once established and functioning, intentional and planned communities offer themselves on a take-it-or-leave-it basis. Some, like the Shakers and the Moravians, gradually disappear as members leave and possible recruits fail to join. The hippie communes of the 1960s rarely lasted long enough to leave such a legacy (Kanter, 1972). Others, such as the more conventional planned communities in American suburbs, provide a ready-made environment that appeals to a target market. Potential buyers personally decide whether and eventually to move into a place conceived, designed and marketed by designers and planners as part of a collective dream shared by future residents. During the 1950s, these might have been the vision of Levit Town or Del Webb. Now, there are dozens of themes catering to particular market niches, ranging from young adults to retirees across a wide spectrum of wealth. Meanwhile, the entire mass of people moving to scenic recreation places are part of a common flow to architecturally distinct ponds. A recent trend is for small acreage to be sold while keeping the original theme of the total property intact. A farm continues to operate around elegant houses. Cattle and sheep graze just outside the fenced yard. Housing sites are discretely hidden from neighbors' views. Meanwhile, there have been and will continue to be a few hardy and dedicated souls who want to be primitively self-sufficient (Jacobs and Brinkerhoff, 1986).

Selecting a community, then, involves shopping for a home, where home means more than a house. This selection clearly involves many choices about which people may or may not be aware. Most people in cities probably never seriously consider moving to small rural western towns. Among those who do consider it, some seem to make their choices without much reliable substantive experience or information. Are either of these genuine choices? Does a choice occur if a person never considers it? Is it a real choice if it is based on inaccurate or superficial information? The information implied by answers to these questions provides a matrix for considering migration. The migrants are in effect trying to plan their lives to become more fulfilling and satisfying. Their presence then stimulates the community to respond to them across the varying dimensions of satisfaction that community members believe are important (Michelson, 1977).

What is implied is a diffuse mass phenomenon that operates among a public the members of which are exposed to some general set of values and information. Most act upon these while remaining largely unfamiliar with the fact that there is a stream of people like themselves. Most are generally ignorant about many crucial aspects of their reasons for moving that may be related to a successful permanent move. For some, the absence of awareness is part of the "hang loose" philosophy of the fragmented urban society. For others, it is a combination of late 20th-century practical, uptight economic considerations and rejection of the urban world of which that system is a part. There are hundreds of factors that people who are thinking about moving might consider. Certainly, people who have carefully investigated and thought about the move in order to become thoroughly informed is one style of choice making. But, is it more of a choice than one made with less information or information that is flat wrong? What about the extreme cases of newcomers who say that they really had not thought much about it; it just felt right, so they moved? Is their cavalier approach less of a choice or merely a less-informed choice?

Residents interviewed were asked about the choices they had made and continued to make as they lived in the Gallatin Valley. We were interested in knowing generally if they had thought about and obtained any information about matters related to employment and finances, commitments with families and friends, as well as the natural and the constructed environment. We also were interested in specific idiosyncrasies among residents and in social and demographic characteristics that might have influenced their choices.

This book describes changes in a specific type of turnaround area. A broad, lush valley surrounded by mountains and rolling hills, it is a center for fishing, hunting, skiing, horseback riding, canoeing and hiking. Bozeman, its urban center, is the site of a state university and is among the most educated and cosmopolitan towns in the region. Industrial development and pollution are minimal. The Marlboro® image among residents is common in Bozeman and prevalent elsewhere in the region. The son of Wally McCrae, one of the first Marlboro® men, attended Montana State University while I taught there. Wally is a rancher, author and renowned cowboy poet, a genuine old-time Montanan.

People who move to the Gallatin Valley are attracted to its safety and beauty. People choose these qualities without the urban compromise that would be implied had they been sought in a nonmetropolitan county adjacent to a city. Bozeman has a population of about 30,000, and is the service and commercial center for a radius of roughly 100 miles. As people move to the area, their attraction to this rural setting is clearly not agrarian. These people were moving for a quality of life, not to live off the land.

There are prices to pay for living in this Shangri-la. The climate is harsh. A 90-day growing season is an abbreviated way of summarizing a long, cold season with frosts from Labor Day until Memorial Day. Snow usually covers the ground from early November until early April. Bozeman is geographically and culturally isolated. Its population is 98 percent Caucasian, severely ethnically homogeneous. By the standards of towns with 30,000 residents, the area is a cultural oasis. It has a symphony and hosts an annual opera. Major performers occasionally stop by enroute to or from the West Coast. It has been the site of national athletic finals for skiing, gymnastics and rodeo. It has wonderful country and western music and dance. Still, its entertainment and social activities, by metropolitan standards, are limited, change slowly and are easy to become familiar and bored with, at least, among people who expect more. The community is composed largely of newcomers, strangers lacking rooted personal attachments with family, friends and organizations. The town and area also are rapidly taking on the appearance and characteristics of Everytown, USA, with suburban sprawl, fast-food strips, malls, minimum wage service employment and pollution.

Previous research regarding community satisfaction has provided a profile of major dimensions of satisfaction as well as significant differences between rural and urban places. Campbell, Converse, and Rogers (1976) have demonstrated how satisfaction is a function of expectations. People are relatively satisfied if they achieve roughly what they expect. Rural people generally are more satisfied with life than are people living in cities, despite lower incomes and poorer job opportunities (Goudy, 1990). People who live in the country are more critical of a few local services, such as medical care and local shopping, but are more satisfied across a wide spectrum of quality-of-life considerations. They like their neighbors, friendships, interactions and organizations in their communities. They also are more satisfied with the quality of their surrounding physical environment than are city dwellers.

Community is a holistic concept (Hawley, 1986). The differences between community and society, while quantitatively measurable, are fundamentally qualitative. Take, for example, the meaning of "neighbor." There always are neighbors. By definition, neighbors are close proximate residents. In a community, neighbors reside near each other for long periods, sometimes even generations. They are familiar and known, and, for better or for worse, they are dependable. In a society, neighbors constantly change. They are interchangeable people who fill the same space, much as modules fit into a machine. The loss of neighbors in a community is emotionally wrenching, usually a cause of great sorrow, occasionally a reason for joy. The loss of neighbors in society is relatively unimportant, frequently hardly noticed. It is normal. The entire social fabric of community is based on quasipersonal, emotionally attached social relationships. In Romania, there is a word for a deep, heartfelt malaise that never stops aching when someone leaves their village. The relationships are qualitatively intense, personal and permanent. Maria Povika, the famous potter of San Ildephonso (Marriott, 1948), wrote of a similar ache when she traveled from her beloved pueblo to the Chicago World's Fair. "All of my grandparents remained in their villages until they died. My father and his brothers returned to theirs to die." The bond to the social system of community is qualitatively different from society.

A weakness in most contemporary survey research on resident satisfaction is that it fails to consider the changes in satisfaction among individuals and within communities as a whole. These changes are a dynamic and crucial aspect of satisfaction that are essential for understanding the meaning of rapidly changing community. Cross-sectional or actuarial data are unable to accurately and fully address how people change in conjunction with their particular locales. Such data lack continuity for measuring changes between and among individuals; that is, how their beliefs and feelings have changed. Detailed information from individuals is not only essential to measure changes they feel or experience, it also is necessary to understand the composition and changes between and among the components of the community as a unit. Only longitudinal case studies or surveys permit investigating how the resident composition of a community changes and how perceptions of its residents change. One drawback to case studies and surveys like this one for the Gallatin Valley is that inferences beyond the case or the sample are limited. If Bozeman is a representative location of migration to romantic rural areas, then rapid turnover of population elsewhere must be similar although certainly not identical.

REASONS FOR THE MIGRATION TURNAROUND

Migration to high natural-amenity areas, particularly during the 1970s, was motivated by a variety of factors. Rural areas were becoming more attractive (Blackwood and Carpenter, 1978). The high proportion of young adults and a simultaneous interest in the natural environment and outdoor recreation combined to attract unprecedented numbers to rural areas (Beale, 1975). Improved transportation and communications in rural areas facilitated this move (Wardwell, 1977). Simultaneously, the cities were becoming more chaotic places for living and working. And a reawakened desire for rural community was appearing (Nearing and Nearing, 1970).

The notion of community is crucial for understanding urban-rural migration. People who are attracted to high natural-amenity areas are frequently an unusual type of migrant. They are likely to decide to live in such places because they are attracted to the natural settings and the ambience of the community as much or more than for better jobs and income. The prosperity of the 1960s and improvements in transportation and communications made it easier for many of these people to relocate. The towns were aesthetically pleasing and recreationally attractive. They also seemed to be secure havens for raising children and for allowing adults to become part of a stable community.

In spite of those attractions, most people who move to them quickly move away. There is a continuing paradox of people who say they want natural environment and community, only to reject them after obtaining them. This paradox is more than an interesting phenomenon for researchers. It has policy implications for both the natural areas and adjacent communities which the migrants say are attractive at one time, only to be rejected later.

Table 2.2 summarizes how residents typically describe various aspects of the community, depending on whether they have recently arrived, are old-timers or are about ready to move away. Newcomers generally describe the area in very positive terms. They believe the people are helpful and friendly, opportunities are promising, the natural environment is lovely and the life almost idyllic. It is such a wonderful place that many believe that planning is not necessary, although a few want plans to preserve it. The people who are about to move away describe a very different place with unfriendly people and few opportunities. They believe the natural and social environment are in decline, and most believe that planning is essential to preserve what is left. A few believe that the planning controls are preventing the place from developing opportunities. The irony, of course, is that most respondents are the same people; the leavers are interviewed a bit later when the luster of being newcomers has become thoroughly tarnished.

Jim (age 58) and Ruth Cardoza (age 56) moved to Bozeman when their son Jimmy was accepted to Montana State University. Jimmy lived at home. The first interview took over two hours. Ruth brought out plates of fabulous hot chocolate chip cookies and coffee. All of the Cardozas were very heavyset and enjoyed food and conversation. They spoke of their interest in learning to fish and of driving to the nearby national parks and natural areas. "We fell in love with this area the first time we saw it. We drove out when Jimmy was a baby in 1961 and came back twice. Jimmy decided to go to college here at the same time that Jim had his 30 years in with the railroad. It just worked out perfectly." During the next four years, they became increasingly critical of Bozeman and the area. They criticized what it

Table 2.2
Feelings that Respective Categories of Residents Report about Bozeman: How Recent Arrivals, Persons about to Leave and Longtime Residents Feel about Bozeman

How do you feel about:	Type of Resident		
	Newcomers	Leavers	Old-Timers
Residents	Helpful and friendly	Unfriendly, closed	Cliquish but active
Community ambience	Idyllic life	Artificial and declining	A nice place to live
Natural environment	Wonderful	Overrated, declining	Changing but good
Services: medical, roads, education	Fair	Poor	Good
Environmental planning	Polarized necessary or unnecessary	Essential	Moderately helpful
Opportunities for success	Fair and optimistic	Awful and fatalistic	Poor but acceptable

lacked and how it differed in comparison to Cleveland. They never bought a fishing license nor did they even go traveling around the area. The house was sold and they moved back to Cleveland. Jimmy moved into an apartment and graduated a year later.

Old-timers, those who stay for a decade or more, are much more circumspect. They believe the area is changing, not necessarily for better or worse. They recognize the cliquishness of the residents, the diversity of the social groups and the frequent exclusion of recent arrivals. They believe that services are good, better than do the newcomers or leavers. They know good jobs are hard to find. For most of them, it is a good place to live.

TYPES OF TURNAROUND MIGRATION

Rural Agrarian (Back to the Land) Migration

Back to the Land is a misnomer for most migrants' who move to rural agricultural settings. Most of the people we interviewed and observed had never lived in such places and consequently were not, themselves, moving back to a lifestyle in which they had been raised. Moreover, many who had hoped to operate their own agricultural enterprise never did so, whether they originated in the city or from a farm. Back to the Land migrants are attracted to rural areas to live on enough land to farm or raise animals or to participate in other renewable extractive production, like forestry or fishing (McPheat, 1996). Attraction to the work generally is associated with their appreciation for the surrounding environment and the informal and personal way people live in such places.

Back to the Land migration ties people to Earth's cycle of life in the natural environment in a personally fulfilling and physically active way (Jacobs and Brinkerhoff, 1986). It also carries some hope of self-sufficiency and freedom from outside interference in their lives. The economics that affect independent small farming, logging and fishing operations are so tenuous that earning a decent living is impossible for most, difficult for many others. The labor also is so physically demanding that few care to endure the rigors once the excitement of the new experience or the vigor of youth has passed. Only one in 20 residents mentioned coming back to the land. Back to the Land migrants, unless sufficiently financially independent to pay for the luxury of their hardworking lifestyles, must rely on outside support. Many rely on public assistance, occasionally supplementing their lifestyle with hallucinogenic agriculture. Most rural properties were purchased for aesthetics and privacy, not self-sufficiency.

Some locations, particularly coasts and mountains, are so attractive that people want to live in them solely for aesthetic reasons, without any intention of participating in local extractive industries. Residents are likely to romanticize what they imagine to be the small intimate social system which they would like to share as friends and neighbors. Nonetheless, they must depend on some other form of economic support, which is frequently at odds with the local extractive economy. Professionals may establish new and superior services for the community. Tourism and real estate have expanded rapidly in most of these communities, creating a new economic base around playing and living in the environment in addition to primary extraction from it. They engage primarily in occupations dependent on patronage by other residents and tourists. After moving, most discover how economically marginal their occupation is for the local area. Naturally beautiful places away from population areas are likely to attract far more people than can be locally supported even with an expanding economy.

Rural Boomtowns

Boomtown developments attract residents who are primarily interested in capitalizing on temporary financial development in an area. Many boomtown migrants see an opportunity to pay off debts and to build a nest egg during the short period they live there. The work is largely semiskilled and skilled labor performed under demanding physical conditions. The more bitter the cold or blistering the heat, the more isolated the location; the less available a semblance of normal community, the higher the pay. Few boomtown workers remain to become part of an established community. The physical environment to which they are constantly exposed through work is generally seen as isolated and uncomfortable. Some exploit it through trespass and poaching. Many escape it as frequently as they can, often through drugs and alcohol if not by actual distance (Jobes, 1986).

The foregoing scenario is the ideal type of boom cycle. Exact scenarios differ, of course. In some remote places, essentially no municipality existed so new infrastructure had be constructed. In most cases in the West, a small town becomes the center for development (Jobes, 1987). Boomtowns may even be removed from the site of primary employment, as is common during offshore oil drilling. Despite their differences, they exert common impacts because similar underlying processes affect the locality and its residents. A few fortunate locations eventually become permanent and relatively stable towns. Some become almost model towns, at least temporarily, while the newly developed resources are mined and processed. They enjoy the wealth of new schools, public buildings, streets and utilities. Unfortunately, a bust almost inevitably follows. Businesses close, property values decline and infrastructure gradually decays as competition intensifies, resources play out and employment declines.

Metropolitan Expansion

The largest number of persons moving to nonmetropolitan areas during the 1960s and 1970s moved to counties adjacent to cities. This type of migration constituted a recent phase of continuing metropolitan expansion which accelerated with public transportation and the automobile. The motives of any individual moving to one type of nonmetropolitan location may be the same as for any other individual moving to a different type of rural area. Generally, however, there are categoric differences. Boomtown migrants go for the short-term, but high-dollar paycheck. Romantics hope for an ideal community in a natural setting. Metropolitan expansion migrants are extensions of the city, generally hoping to get more and better of what they already have. Some few may harbor illusions about small-town life and agrarian self-sufficiency, largely due to their relative inexperience with or naivete about rural areas. Most expansion migrants enjoy having the city nearby and living around like-minded urbanites. Even so, a successful truck farmer near a large city might well be more self-sufficient and successfully tied to the land than agrarian idealists who fail economically or become disillusioned with their small-town environments.

Table 2.3 illustrates the extent of growth in Bozeman between 1950 and 1990. It, like Gallatin County, has approximately doubled since 1950. Growth has been continuous, with spurts of over 30 percent per decade in the 1940s and the 1960s. The rural county population has more than doubled in comparison to relatively slow statewide growth. The rural county population has grown by over 40 percent every decade since 1940. Rural growth implies recreation, leisure, construction and mobile home development. Growth is increasingly in rural areas. Agricultural employment rose very slightly throughout the period compared to rapid growth in other sectors. Although the economic contribution of agriculture to the area is large, agricultural employment is small in comparison to other sectors. Educational services multiplied over seven times, indicating the relative importance of Montana State University to the local population and economy. The decline in employment in the educational sector signifies the broad economic malaise that occurred in the area during the 1980s. Residents born out of Montana gradually formed a majority during the period, and less than one-fourth of the residents resided in the same house in 1990 as they had in 1985.

These changes illustrate how different Bozeman has been from the State as a whole. The changes in Bozeman typify a high natural-amenity recreation and education center. In sharp contrast to national demographic trends, its growth has been primarily due to white persons. Only three percent of the population was nonwhite by 1990. Changes in the characteristics of residential units also were in clear contrast to the single family dwelling units, typical of more stable, family-oriented social systems. The proportion of single units declined throughout the period, while multiple units and trailers, particularly in unincorporated areas, increased several times. These changes in residential construction correspond to an increase in single persons and poorer small families in a growing population.

Rapid physical changes also occurred during this period, particularly after 1970 when rapid population growth outstripped the capacities of many public facilities. Schools nearly doubled their capacities. A new swimming center, two athletic complexes, a law and justice center and one-way streets were added between 1975 and 1980. Downtown, which retained much of its appearance as a small town Main Street, lost many of its practical retailers following the construction of a mall. By 1980, downtown was rapidly becoming gentrified, retaining much of the facade of a diverse shopping and service center while losing much of the core retail trade establishments. By 1990, gentrification was nearly complete. Only one hardware store and one hometown cafe were left. Condominiums, restaurants and specialty shops replaced hardware, department and drug stores; furniture shops; and family-oriented clothing and shoe shops. Strip development lined the intersecting streets downtown with fast-food restaurants, chain stores and minimalls instead of the elm trees that had been there through the

Table 2.3
Selected Demographic Characteristics for Bozeman, Gallatin County and Montana, 1950-1990

	1950	1960	1970	1980	1990
Population					
State	591,024	675,767	694,409	786,690	799,065
Gallatin County	21,902	26,045	32,505	42,865	50,463
Bozeman	11,325	13,361	18,670	21,645	22,660
Change % in decade	30.7	18.0	39.7	15.9	9.6
Per mile	8.7	9.5	12.9	17.1	20.9
Rural Population					
State	332,990	336,310	323,733	370,431	379.076
(%)	36.3	49.8	46.6	47.1	47.4
County	10,577	12,684	13,835	21,220	24,392
(%)	48.3	48.7	42.5	49.4	43.3
Change % in decade	10.1	19.9	9.1	53.4	13.0
Bozeman Residents					
Same house 5 yrs earlier (%)	NA	32.2	29.5	24.4	21.3
Born in State (%)	NA	59.9	57.2	48.6	40.8
Married couple family	2,540	2,728	3,439	3,533	3,612
Female household, no husband	NA	NA	303	484	725
Persons per household	2.98	2.89	2.80	2.61	2.27
Employment	4,403	4,968	6,985	9,391	12,100
Agriculture	136	152	200	218	344
Educational services	387	1,098	2,433	2,700	2,620
Nonwhite (%)	23 (.01)	498(3.72)	243(1.25)	562(2.59)	665(2.55)
Below poverty level (%)	NA	NA	6.3	9.5	11.8

Source: *Census of the Population: Montana 1950, 1960, 1970, 1980, 1990.* U.S. Bureau of Census, Department of Commerce, U.S. Government Printing Office, Washington, D.C.

mid-1960s. McDonalds opened in 1978 and K-Mart in 1977, making the town visually and culturally more similar to suburban cities in Everywhere, U.S.A.

Michael Sobel (1981) has defined lifestyle as "a recognizable mode of living" that is conceptually independent, although which is actually interrelated to attitudes, values and behavioral orientations (p. 28). Following the early ideas of Thorstein Veblin (1899), lifestyles especially express the consumption preferences that individuals make in accordance with their historical and economic positions. Consumption, demonstrated as leisure, is emphasized even more than work, although all activities and possessions reflect the more general concept, lifestyle.

"Social order arises, in a sense, from a permanent running compromise between constraint and freedom, between the interests of the individual and the goals of the society" (Cumming, 1968, p. 4). In the United States, the right of individuals to migrate with few limitations is taken for granted. Most migration has been regulated informally, except for a few legal constraints, such as not fleeing to avoid prosecution. Migrants seek to achieve a location that will optimally provide what they think they are looking for. Their preferences are based upon how they feel the needs associated with the positions they occupy may be met. People who occupy few roles of responsibility, such as those who are childless, single and unemployed, have fewer responsibilities and are relatively free to move. Others must take their greater responsibilities into consideration in order to meet social standards for family care, employment and consumption patterns. Migration expresses the constraints of social order. Economic opportunity and its linkage to fulfilling roles in socially responsible ways is a major determinant in selecting a location or remaining there. However, it is not the most important consideration for many persons who regard economic factors as insufficient reasons for making a major life choice, such as migrating.

Norms guide behavior toward conventional definitions of social responsibility. Behaviors that potentially create demands on the society in the form of unemployment, child care and low community participation require a collective response to ensure that essential needs are met. Migration is potentially such a behavior. It can provide solutions to some social problems, such as getting work done in places where few people live. And it can create problems when more people move into a place than can be accommodated by local services, jobs and social structure.

Norms evolve around migration in the same way as they do around other potentially beneficial or disruptive social processes. In the United States, people are held personally responsible for finding work, housing and entertainment through their own devices. This is the same underlying strategy as the traditional norm of families providing for their children without collective assistance. Socialist societies accept much of the responsibility for accomplishing such tasks. Individuals in socialist societies are expected to forego individual choices that would interfere with collective solutions for employment and services.

The traditional tendency, then, has been to socialize citizens to internalize norms for taking on social roles with their attendant responsibilities as defined by the society. The conventional roles, at least for the past few centuries in Europe, involved relatively stable residence. People typically would relocate only once, if at all. Some trades involved traveling journeymen. And a few groups have been peddlers or done other work in areas where the norm called for moving.

In addition to people who assume migratory roles, large numbers of persons are imperfectly socialized. They fail to adopt conventional roles and, hence, are freer to follow alternative paths. Some are free by default. Serfs during the Late Middle Ages became free by default. When owners enclosed their properties, serfs had to move. More recently, many people have been freed to move due to the emergence of an ethic that has favored loosely restricted individual experience over conventional collective responsibility. An emerging premise that favors individual satisfaction has evolved in the United States. The extreme of this ethic involves periodically rejecting conventional roles. Decisions to remain or become single, childless, hold marginal employment and to move frequently are manifestations of this ethic. More persons are exercising individual preferences and satisfaction around traditional social obligations.

A BRIEF DESCRIPTION OF BOZEMAN AND THE GALLATIN VALLEY

Bozeman has been a rapidly growing town since 1940. High growth has occurred in spurts. The population increased 30.7 percent during the 1940s and 39.7 percent during the 1960s. It roughly doubled between 1950 and 1980, increasing from 11,325 to 21,645 (Table 2.2). This increase was the same as that experienced throughout Gallatin County, which was approximately three times the Statewide growth. Even the slow growth of the 1980s added another thousand, nearly 5 percent, to the population. The 1990 population density was 20.9 per square mile. While low by the standard for more populated states, density had more than doubled from what it had been in 1950. The population was also becoming poorer. By 1990, more than 10 percent fell below the poverty line.

Population growth in Gallatin County has been equally divided between Bozeman and other locations. Bozeman was the magnet for most of the growth within 30 miles of town. The redistribution of population doubled the rural population. This apparent ruralization of the population is actually an artifact of census definition. Most growth occurred in unincorporated subdivisions and trailer parks within a nine-mile radius of Bozeman. While the number of mobile homes more than quadrupled in town between 1950 and 1990, the increase of mobile homes in rural areas was over fourteenfold.

The rapid growth in Bozeman has been associated with changes in composition of residents. The census asks residents if they are living in the house where they were residing five years earlier. The percentage of residents residing in the same house had gradually declined since 1950, as had the percentage of natives in the State. Recent unemployment characteristics changed markedly, reflecting the influence of the university. Agricultural employment less than tripled to 234 during the same period when educational services grew seven times to 2,700, only to decline. The nonwhite population, although still less than 3 percent, has shown a gradual increase.

Bozeman has many qualities that are reportedly highly desirable in the in-migration literature on the urban-rural turnaround (Brown and Wardwell, 1980). By urban standards, it has a clean physical environment and a safe social environment. It has a land-grant university. Its services are excellent for a city of its size. Medical and health, transportation and shopping services are well developed, again, for a city of its size. The area is relatively remote and pristine and has excellent hunting, fishing, skiing and other mountain environment activities. Tourism is the third largest generator of revenue in the county. Only the university employs more persons. Except for a few summer weeks with 80°-90°F temperatures, the rest of the year is cool or cold and frequently snowy.

The issue of population growth and urban values versus environmental and small-town preservation is the key source of contention in towns like Bozeman. There are numerous, more specific issues that must be negotiated between preserving the natural environment, town life and population growth. The material environment is a finite though elastic resource. Population increase leads to direct competition by converting the natural environment into a constructed environment with uses designed for people (DeVall, 1984). Housing encroaches on natural space. Commercial and residential uses of water replace stream flow, and air and water pollution degrade existing systems. Such direct competition exchanges a previous system for one in which humans become primary components, affecting the space, animals and associated aesthetics in the area. Population increase also leads to indirect competition as more people use the remaining space. More recreationists seek the remaining trees, animals, fish and unmarked paths and slopes. Whatever their expectations, people will be dissatisfied as the criteria they use for evaluating a worthwhile experience fall below a level acceptable to them. The competition involves differences in expectations between people with developmentalist and those with naturalist sentiments. The competition involves differences that are modified over time as the area and its population change. Conflicts concerning development emerge, particularly in rapidly growing, previously undeveloped areas. Planning has become a primary mechanism through which to optimize the relationship between the impacts of development and the environment. It is the legally mandated rational model for resolving conflicts regarding development (Humphrey and Buttel, 1982).

Throughout this century, Bozeman has retained a dominant position in Gallatin and the adjacent counties. Bozeman comprised 45 percent of the county population in 1990, despite the disproportionate rural growth in the county. It had the highest percentage of college graduates in the county. Except for the small tourist town of West Yellowstone, it had the highest income. West Yellowstone, though heavily dependent upon Bozeman for most professional services, was supported by Yellowstone National Park and tourism in the adjacent area. Except for West Yellowstone, the educational levels of towns were inversely related to the distance from Bozeman. However, there were costs to living in Bozeman. Except for the artificially inflated property costs in West Yellowstone, mortgage costs in Bozeman were over $90.00 per month more than in other towns in the area. West Yellowstone is located on a tiny private property grant surrounded by United States

National Park and Forest Service properties. Bozeman also had a higher percentage of poor children than any other town in the county.

The economic domination of Bozeman over the rest of Gallatin County is documented in Table 2.4. Over two-thirds (69%) of the 539 private enterprises in the county were located in Bozeman in 1994. The private retail sector in Bozeman commanded 80 percent of retail sales. Specific technical services were even more centralized. Nearly all (97%) of the health services sector was located in Bozeman. The domination also involved larger enterprises. The only two private organizations in the county that employed more than 250 workers were both located in Bozeman. Although these figures demonstrate only the dominance of Bozeman in the county, that domination also spread to adjacent counties.

Planning is a mechanism through which supporters and opponents engage in a political exchange that establishes rules that govern development. It is a process of negotiated development. Naive supporters may see planning as a method for preserving everything in the environment while permitting appropriate growth. They tend to have a limited and superficial understanding of the varieties and intensities of impacts. As a general rule, some natural qualities are inevitably lost when development occurs, though others may be preserved or even improved. Opponents, on the other hand, tend to see planning as a mechanism that interferes with their particular preference, often their vested interest, for development. Some would prefer no conversion of natural environment through development. Others believe that the natural environment gains its value primarily through development. Still others oppose planning because it interferes with the "natural" process of population growth and community development, which is to say, development without overt guidelines.

Table 2.4
Economic Domination of Gallatin County by Bozeman: Selected Measures of Economic Enterprise and Employment in 1994

	Gallatin County N	Bozeman N	(%)
Retail enterprises	539	367	(69%)
Retail sales ($1000)	519,872	414,146	(80%)
Health services ($1000)	38,778	37,599	(97%)
Businesses employing more than 250 Employees	2	2	(100%)

Source: 1994 Census of Retail Trade, U.S. Bureau of Census, U.S. Department of Commerce, U.S. Government Printing Office, Washington, DC.

Our samples included people with an enormous range of attitudes and activities regarding environmental preservation. While most respondents were neither zealously opposed to unrestricted development nor supportive of it, several respondents were. Bozeman is the national or regional headquarters for several environmental preservation organizations, such as the Greater Yellowstone Coalition and the Wilderness Society. It also is a center for free-market economics as well as being on the regional fringe of radical survivalism; both orientations are opposed to planning. Representatives from these extreme contingents spoke openly and passionately. People from both extremes were convinced that, if their belief about planning did not prevail, something terrible would happen. The prodevelopment advocates focused on the physical environment. Rex Nash, a local environmental leader, was convinced that, if the Northern Rockies were not protected as a natural region, dramatic environmental losses were certain. First, the large carnivores, the wolf and the Great Bear, would become extinct. Gradually, other precious habitat and species would suffer the same fate. Jerry Nelson, an outspoken libertarian representative, was concerned that such planning would further undermine the already eroding freedoms of individual landowners. Jerry considered himself a free-market environmentalist. He was sure that landowners would protect what was valuable because it could be marketed for profit.

The struggle between environmentalists, planners and the free market is endless. The advocates disagree on what is most valuable, the natural environment or individual freedoms. They also disagree on the mechanisms for protecting what is valuable, protecting the abstract environmental user into the distant future or protecting the individual property owner now. The resolution, of course, comes through the struggle between the opposing orientations.

THE ECOLOGICAL FALLACY: WHEN IS COMMUNITY A UNIT GREATER THAN THE SUM OF ITS PARTS?

News of population growth and an expanding economy reaches an increasing number of prospective residents who expect to be able to capitalize on what they interpret as the success of the local economy. What they fail to realize is that very few people, usually the established financiers, realtors and professionals, reap much of the continuing harvest from the growth.

There is temptation among both social scientists and ordinary citizens to draw conclusions about individuals based on general observations. Carried to an extreme, such conclusions may be stereotypes and prejudices. One underlying basis for the error in the logic of extending generalizations to individual behaviors was first referred to as the ecological fallacy by W. S. Robinson (1950). The fallacy occurs in situations where facts have been collected, that is, where the information leads to inductive knowledge. For example, when the boom of the late 1980s was underway, it was generally believed that the prosperity was extending to most individual residents. In fact, the real-estate boom in Bozeman helped those homeowners who already had paid off their mortgages and would be selling and moving away, but excluded the large number of lower income residents who had not been able to buy when prices were low. Even property owners who had no intention of moving were hurt by high taxes. The higher costs led to the expansion of lower priced housing outside of Bozeman, especially in Belgrade, which is about 10 miles away. Many new residents were attracted to the area after hearing that the Gallatin Valley was expanding financially. The reality was that the general trend might not be reflected in their personal lives. Robinson warned against academicians extending general observations to specific individuals, especially when the comparatively interpreting trends between different geographic areas can lead to erroneous conclusions and painful consequences for both residents and decision makers. Growth shouldn't be equated with prosperity. The financial success of a few can mask the failure for many.

The Rogers, who had looked at several towns in the region before settling in Bozeman, put it this way, the first year they were interviewed: "We moved to Bozeman instead of the other towns we considered, particularly Cody and Jackson [Wyoming], because it is more economically diverse." The physical environments of all three places are equivalent, but Bozeman is less dependent on tourism and has steady growth. A year later, Mrs. Rogers was working as a secretary while her husband, an artist, ran their struggling new art gallery. She attributed their economic failure to their gallery's location in a small mall outside the downtown area. She had planned on running the gallery while her husband painted. Both were essentially working two jobs within a few weeks after arriving. "We haven't had time to fish and canoe, which we love. That is why we moved here. But, as soon as we get established, we'll be able to do those things again."

A year later, they were gone. During our final interview, she remarked that, in the three years they had lived in Bozeman, it seemed that most of the people they had met had been locked in the same failing struggle to become established. Both of the Rogers said, "Besides, we really don't like the growth we have seen here in just the time we have lived here. Something really should be done to preserve the farmland, as well as the streams and wilderness. You know there is subirrigated land all around Bozeman that should never be taken out of farming, and it is already being subdivided." The spiral of growth which initially promises success not only often fails in its promise, but it also creates disillusionment because of its exploitation of the natural environment which drew people there in the first place.

Changing Faces in an Evolving Facade

Sometimes, I feel like Bozeman is a movie set for many newcomers. Newcomers imagine what it is like, what its residents are like and then they become actors, acting out what they think is authentic. They actually are acting out a fantasy along with a number of other actors doing the same thing. They think the others are authentic, when in fact most are imitating what they imagine to be reality. Most tire of the acting at some point. Some go broke and can't afford to stay on the set. Others see through the facade, much as most singles eventually stop deluding themselves that bars are a locus of friendship and support. They learn that others are transient, feel transient themselves and move on to another temporary fantasy or to more permanent attachments.

This research was initiated to study satisfaction and life quality. In the end, it has focused more on dissatisfaction although they are, in fact, the same concerns. One asks why people like a location and stay, which the other asks why they don't and leave. The variables that were initially hypothesized to attract and retain residents were the natural and constructed environments and the institutional and personal aspects of social life. Adopting the perspective of newcomers, they might be offended by characteristics of natural physical location. It might be colder, less beautiful than they expected. They might be offended by the constructed environment. It might be less diverse and attractive than they expected. Or they might be offended by the social system. They might dislike local schools or politics. Or they might find neighbors, friends and family displeasing.

Old-timers, on the other hand, can be dissatisfied by changes they perceive or expect they will encounter because of changes. Old-timers might be offended by change in physical location, such as loss of recreational access and privacy. Old-timers might not like new developments such as paved roads or a better airport. Realistically, most old-timers appreciate these and other improvements of services. They also may object to changes in their local institutions or in the way close personal aspects of their lives are working.

There is a profound difference between the permanent physical structure of a community and a community composed of permanent residents. The physical character, the streets, schools and services, are relatively permanent in most established towns, whether the people are transitory or permanent. Transitory towns have few permanent people, but nevertheless have established manners of behavior, a social structure. The permanent structure in a transitory town differs from what newcomers imagine it to be. There are "local ways" just as there are in cities. These are in part rules for transitory people who don't know they are transitory. For people who want to believe they are part of the town, there is an emerging pattern of being a "good citizen" and participating even if one's stay is limited. The gradual process of being accepted as a person applies only to those who stay long enough to become givers rather than merely receivers. Even so, most givers usually are not there very long. Few remain long enough to enjoy or face the consequences of their contributions.

The world of idealism does not necessarily confront the multiple worlds of reality. Even espousing no plan nevertheless implies wanting to live in a particular type of community, whether it has been deliberately planned or not. The homebodies, jingoists and disenfranchised in Table 2.5 oppose planning. The nonplanner conservatives want to live in a community that magically emerges through the invisible hand. Many then engage in as much Machiavellian activity as they can to plan their place around each other while claiming not to plan (Machiavelli, 1944). They end up with a soiled nest. The utopian planners, on the other hand, pretend they can create the good community through foresight regardless of market forces and human frailty. They are characterized as zealots, rational developmentalists and the disillusioned in Table 2.5. At the extreme, they dictate ridiculous or temporary visionary edifices — Brasilia, intentional new towns, the Third Reich, and Soviet Union.

The extremes of planning ideologies reside in an ideological world of self-prophesied failure. Both ignore the structural realities of population, actual desirable land uses — fishing, pollution, open space — that provide real jobs for real people. People have time-bound abilities and ideals. They forget that most people, including themselves, lack commitment and will not remain in a place to conform in the way their idealism presupposes. Whether homebodies or zealots, jingoists or rational developmentalists or disenfranchised or disillusioned, they are intellectually invested in what they believe is right and wrong about the community, and whether planning is the appropriate solution for preserving the good and eliminating the bad. However, their intellectual investments are likely to change. Planning is only one dimension of responding to change. Another crucial dimension involves how people feel about the community in which they live. In spite of their mutual antagonisms regarding planning, the homebodies and the zealots fundamentally appreciate the place. The disenfranchised and disillusioned detest it. What distinguishes them is how they believe the community should respond to protect the place, if they like it, and change it, if they do not.

While advocates and opponents of planning take their battle to the public, most people sit on fences. They fail to take a position because they are disinterested or want to avoid the strain of confrontation. Since there are always a few antagonists in modern society who articulate the issue of development (or any other issue), the strain never completely disappears. To reduce the strain, the activity of planning is turned over to experts. Then it is discovered that the experts are drawn from the same pool of persons with the same variations in knowledge and ideology. Turning planning over to experts makes it easier for residents to avoid making mistakes and the strain of criticism. Professional planners are uniquely trained to circumnavigate complex rules governing land-use development. Ultimately, though, when the decision makers establish policy, residents are once again faced with the final truth that, in modern society, the only solution is eternal evolution and negotiation. The changing circumstances of the people who are affected, along with changing resources of the area and the changing ideologies of the era, make reevaluation a never ending process.

Modern societies encourage individual development, expression and achievement. Planning or opposition to planning acts to block some individuals from achieving what they want. Choosing where to live on the basis of quality of life is similar to choosing what to do on the basis of financial ability. Poor persons may choose to do arts and crafts as an occupation because those activities carry their own rewards. Rich people, because of wealth, can choose much of what they want to do or where they want to live because they perceive that time is so precious that they wish to use it in the most satisfying way. Both perspectives imply choice. In fact, many people have very few choices such as are taken for granted in the West. They may do what they do and live where they live simply because of their inherited place in the world.

Utopia and reality conflict with each other because the vagaries of living influence how people feel about planning in the following ways. First, if circumstances seem good without planning, then planning is not perceived as

Table 2.5
Differing Orientations about the Quality of the Area and Whether or Not Residents Perceive Change: The Present and Future Implications

	Perceivers of No Change	Witnesses of Change
This is a great place to live.	**Homebodies**	**Zealots**
For the present	Stress nothing except "as is." Want no planning. Adapt rather than think.	Stress physical and social environment. Want planning to maintain "as is," even given future growth.
Future consequences	Possible Regret	Feel good because place is optimal and they participate, bad because it changed.
Bozeman can be improved.	**Jingoists**	**Rational Developmentalists**
For the present	Stress jobs and development. Believe nature takes care of itself. Oppose planning. Want place "as is" with more locals.	Stress both place and people. Emphasize planning to optimize built environment and protection of nature.
Future consequences	Survive with some regret about the alterations and some pride about the development.	Appreciate some aspects of constructed environment. Bothered by loss of nature and qualities of the small town
Bozeman is a Terrible Place	**Disenfranchised**	**Disillusioned**
For the present	Obsessed with employment and income. Believe that change could improve job prospects and other characteristics of the area.	Everything is wrong. Want assistance unless it changes. Social environment quickly deteriorating, critical of natural environment.
Future consequences	Probably bad, but better.	No longer relevant — long gone.

necessary because the current good life makes thinking of utopia seem irrelevant. Second, if planning is already successfully in operation, life would not be so good without it. These competing situations particularly apply to people who have very limited comparative perspectives on their communities. People who have comparative perspectives, for example, migrants and educated people or people who have witnessed a variety of changes, may see their lives as more or less ideal than those in other communities. Everybody wants some kind of planning, whether codified or not. The issue is what kind of planning. Nonplanners want a guarantee of noninterference with market forces even if the logical outcome may be the destruction of all of the community qualities they like. Planners favor the protection of those qualities, either natural or manufactured, with some restriction of the market.

The Context of Assuredness and Ambivalence: Liking a Place and Knowing about Alternatives

Services and the natural environment always are in competition. For a few people, services are relatively unimportant compared to nature. For others, nature is relatively unimportant conceptually or as a place for activities. Disagreement about what is important for the community is, therefore, inevitable.

It is desirable to describe relationships in the most simple and direct terms possible. It is most valid to use data that are as close as possible to the unit of analysis so that minimal inference is required. Some inference always is required when discussing how individuals are related to social structure. Reporting how individuals feel about satisfaction and
planning involves a simple inference about what kinds of shared social characteristics in space they want. In this research, people spoke of what they liked and disliked about what they believed and felt about the community. They said what they believed was satisfactory or unsatisfactory about the services and the natural and constructed environments. They said how they were involved in personal relationships since those were crucial to their personal satisfaction in the community. They were also asked about their beliefs concerning planning in order to understand how their satisfaction with services, the environment and their personal lives were associated with their perspectives about planning.

Whether people believe a community is healthy depends on the contexts from which it is perceived. A community may be seen as healthy at one point in time by nearly everyone, even though they consciously are doing little to facilitate its future existence in that state. Those people, the homebodies, are intent on living now. In a slowly changing context, they and their community can be healthy. It is when rapid change occurs that the notion of planning or participation in planning becomes relevant. The recognition of how relevant comes from experiencing other contexts and recognizing alternatives. People who have such recognition are the zealots of planning. Experts in community development often assume that participation in community planning is desirable. In a smoothly functioning, unchanging community, participation may be both irrelevant and troublesome. On the other hand, just because many people actively participate is no assurance of a pleasant or smoothly functioning community. A high rate of participation may be related to strong negative feelings, as persons struggle to gain control for its own sake. When stakes are real and there is high participation in conflict over a terrible destructive change in their community, which is out of their control, the community can disintegrate. The author observed such catastrophic dissolution of rural agricultural communities in eastern Montana as coal mining was developed. The proponents and opponents of energy development polarized intensely. Even in locations that ultimately experienced little actual development, people stopped talking to each other. The areas that developed were amply rewarded with improved facilities and services. Even so, no amount of planning for improved roads, schools and human services seemed to compensate for the loss of sharing among neighbors and friends that had existed for decades prior to energy development. Community satisfaction depends on how effectively a community provides three structures: services, human relationships and environment. Problems of relationships are less likely to be seen as a responsibility or community concern for decision makers than are services and the environment. Human relationships and social interaction are seen as the problems of individuals. Yet, the human relationships are affected by what happens to the environment and services.

People in our research who reported that everything was great usually lacked perspective. They opposed planning because they trusted the natural occurrence of community. People who were relatively satisfied sought to ensure services or to preserve the natural environment in essentially their current state. Most people assumed that getting what they want now will make it better for the future. While current choices may be inconsistent with future desired effects, they may be the best that are available for most rational people. Finally, there are those residents who are dissatisfied and disillusioned with the community. These residents, too, ranged from locals who had no experience with change to some who were cosmopolitan. The dissatisfied in either case were unlikely to attain what was seriously missing in their lives. For some, it may have been a good job; for others, good relationships. Those who opposed planning, the disenfranchised, often blamed the planning that was in effect for their failure to have a decent job in the community. The perspective of those who had more experience, the disillusioned, soon guided them to move away.

Chapter 3

Theoretical Orientations about Why People Stayed or Moved Away from Southwest Montana

MORAL AND ETHICAL CONTEXTS OF GENERAL SOCIAL THEORIES AND COMMUNITY PLANNING

Many social theories are so emotionally loaded in their underlying assumptions that they make analyses of human behavior suspect to everyone but the theorists. Both conflict and functional theories are driven by such assumptions. Conflict theory assumes that a struggle for resources between the haves and the have-nots defines the society, directs its activities and stimulates its changes. Functional theory assumes that an optimal distribution of resources prudently establishes a society of the able and the inept, which accommodates necessary changes. Both theories rely upon similar mysterious forces thought to reside deep in the nature of humanity. The struggle for existence in a world of limited resources allows this human tendency to create a social system at any point in time. Once created, the social system pursues a preordained destiny. Conflict and functional theories are especially attractive because they address why contemporary social systems exist. Both of their answers include exploiting the environment and surviving conflict in evolution toward a better world. Marxism has a utopian vision. Functionalism has no such vision. Functionalism assumes that, over a long, long period of time, after many failures and cul de sacs, a functional system is always evolving. Both theories designate heroes and villains who are responsible for the operations of the system. Both functional and conflict orientations are sophisticated evolutions of moral theory. Both lack the value neutrality of scientific theory. Therein also lies their strength and merit to social science. Each provides interpretations for social policy that are built into the theory itself.

The two other major social theories, symbolic interaction and human ecology, are value-neutral in their fundamental forms, although each has been, on occasion, interpreted through both functional and conflict perspectives. Each fundamentally assumes that humans are ordering creatures who adapt. Interaction theory stresses the social-psychological mechanisms and characteristics of adaptation through social interaction and organization. Human ecology emphasizes sociodemographic evolution in space. Their common weakness, for practical purposes, is value neutrality. Neither intrinsically defends the desirability of the social systems they describe. Instead, to make practical use of human ecology or symbolic interaction for policy purposes, it is necessary to posit some humanitarian grounds for justifying action, such as planning, before drawing upon the observations and explanations generated by the theories. For example, some goal of optimal use of resources or optimal development of the individual must be assumed to be desirable before a desirable symbolic or ecological system can be designed. This separation of theory from morality probably makes these theories less attractive to persons who seek to give a scientific aura to social policy decisions.

As far as I know, all social science thought is built upon some assumption that people behave rationally. Rational Man theory, as the underlying notion was originally called, is traced in the literature to several British and French philosophers and budding social scientists referred to, respectively, as British Empiricists and French Philosophers. These theorists argued and haggled around intellectual issues that continue to capture contemporary minds. For example, Jean-Jacques Rousseau (1911) passionately believed that society is a corrupting influence without which people would live in a blissful state of nature. The appreciation of traditional societies by modern peoples illustrates how Rousseau's ideas captured a thought that modern people continue to cherish. The move to a more natural setting and personal community mirrors this thought. Rousseau's antagonist, Thomas Hobbes (1991), was equally assured that society as expressed in the spirit of the law, distinguished humans from beasts. The social contract, the Leviathan, is a condition of being human. It optimizes the good all may share in exchange for some individual freedom. Human selfishness is exchanged for rationally agreed upon rules that elevate humans above their beastly nature.

Rational Man theory became clearly refined in the works of the early British economists Adam Ferguson (1973) and Adam Smith (1992), who insisted that individuals use a mental calculus, weighing costs and benefits of their choices. Since all people engage in this process, the social world is a composite of the essentially infinite decisions regarding the objects of the material world and the actions of the social one. In the cruder lexicon of modern economists, this refers to jobs and income to procure goods and services. The invisible hand, an economic metaphor for what had been attributed to Nature or to God by earlier sages, was posited to distribute the greatest good for the greatest number. To Smith and Ferguson, rational decision making was more than a characteristic of individuals: it was the guiding force for society. Each individual made choices based upon what was known and available to him or her in order to maximize his or her desires. However, no individual had more than limited knowledge and resources. The invisible hand alone manifested the infinite wisdom for distributing resources through the limited rational choices of the universe of interacting individuals. Marx believed that the bourgeoisie used the notion of the free market to establish a privileged and protected structure for themselves and to the detriment of the proletariat. While the poor are as rational as the rich, the capitalist system, according to Marx, becomes inequitable by preventing their equal participation in the market of goods and services. Unlike the British Empiricists, Marx believed people were intrinsically rational, if only they could be freed from the chains of oppressive society. Marx rejected the transcendent notion of the invisible hand. He maintained that people could achieve an efficient and equitable society through planning based upon the principle of the greatest good for the greatest number.

Social scientists have two general strategies for explaining why some people act beyond the limits of acceptability, beyond what most people regard as the limits of rational behavior. One explanatory strategy is to maintain that the deviants, who seem to be irrational, are rational. They are responding to conditions just as anyone would under similar circumstances. In his classic treatise, Durkheim (1933) illustrated how suicide, which seems so irrational, may be partially explained by understanding the social systems surrounding people who commit suicide. Single urban men are categorically likely to lack supportive social groups. They are especially likely to kill themselves because of the egoistic isolation or the anomie in their lives. Conversely, war heroes, such as kamikaze pilots, have been so effectively socialized that they are willing to heed the request of their society to altruistically sacrifice their lives.

This general explanation runs through most theoretical traditions in sociology. It assumes that people are socialized to do what they do, even if what they do is socially unacceptable. Whether behaviors are regarded as socially unacceptable is a matter of debate in itself and has been thoroughly discussed by social theorists (Rubbington and Weinberg, 1995). Certainly, moving to a beautiful rural setting would not be considered deviant to most people, though giving up family, friends, loved ones, a secure and promising job and significant investments might be considered a little deranged. However the boundary between deviance and acceptability are defined, this orientation of social theory explains the behavior as normal in the sense that other people socialized in the same way and experiencing the same conditions would do essentially the same thing.

A second general strategy for explaining deviance pathology is to locate the cause of the deviation in a pathology in the person or in the group, culture or society of which they are part. The logic for this strategy is that something internal to the individual — a personality quirk, idiosyncracy, an organic psychosis, a genetic malformation — accounts for why she or he behaves differently than others do in similar situations. Or, some quality or condition external to the individual which is clearly aberrant, like an addicted society, affects the person. This pathological orientation also assumes a rational system of operating. Whereas the functional strategy of social learning assumes that the deviant is behaving normally under the circumstances, the pathological strategy maintains they cannot behave normally. Even so, their deviance is explainable from the rational system posited by the theorist. Both strategies for explaining deviance, then, are built around rational decision making theory, in much the same fashion as are theories explaining conformity. Both assume that there is a rational, although possibly out of balance, system. Both assume further that someone, sometimes the people themselves, always the theorists, can make empirical sense of their behavior; that is, their choices can be interpreted as optimizing solutions for gains over losses.

It is doubtful that any causal theory of free migration based on deduction can be accurate and inclusive. The best that social science can hope to develop are probabilistic statements regarding how a few important determinants are associated with migration. This is a useful contribution that gradually has been refined since Ravenstein (1885, 1889) proposed his laws of migration. Causal theory means knowing precisely how an independent variable, whether a swinging metal ball or differential job opportunities, causes a dependent variable, the reaction by another metal ball struck by the pendulum or migration from a place with few low-paying jobs to a place with more higher paid ones. The example from physics is much closer to causality than the example from social science. Pockets of poverty persist since their unemployed residents refuse to move. And many people move to the Rockies despite terrible job opportunities. Rational Man economic theory fails to account for many aspects of migration, though it may explain more than any alternative explanation.

The realization that there can be no causal theory of migration or, for that matter, any social behavior, has been periodically recognized. The anthropologist Radcliffe-Brown (1935) rejected functional theory because he believed that the continuous introduction of new influences on social structure made precise recognition of linear cause impossible. From his perspective, though he recognized the immense importance of social institutions such as religion and family, the social structure could not be a stable cause (Radcliffe-Brown, 1952). Any social structure was so large and dynamic that each had to be understood on its own grounds, through a culturally relative perspective. Similar thoughts led Robert Merton (1949) to suggest that sociology should examine the relationships between variables in a more modest fashion than grand causal theory (pp. 38-72). He advocated theories of the middle range, analyses of a few variables, under particular conditions and, I would add, for limited times.

There can be no rational causal theory of migration, let alone a more general theory explaining any human behavior for all time. In the social sciences, there are too many variables and their interrelationships are too complex for any substantively meaningful hypothesis to explain more than a fraction of behavior for very long. Admitting that social science cannot give entirely causal explanations is not merely a matter of technology. It is a matter of fact and of logic. Faster, larger computers allow more rapid and more precise calculations, but they cannot make explanations more causal. As more variables are introduced into causal equations, an optimal causal sequence, considerably less than perfect predictability, is achieved. The Heisenberg principle is disarmingly simple. There is simply not enough energy to analyze the relationships among all of the facts. At best, social science can simultaneously consider the empirical relationships among a few variables for short time periods. Beyond a brief initial period, the precision essential to causal theory breaks down. The theory demonstrates these limitations for making long-term forecasting in a variety of contexts (Tsonis, 1992).

However disorienting, the realization that attributing causality in social science is impossible frees social scientists from the responsibility of explaining the universe, the great System. It also provides some security because it directs social scientists to study what they can within those limitations. Causal explanations and rational thought are essentially inseparable. Rational thought, whether by people in general, migrants more specifically or social scientists offering explanations, looks for causal sequences, usually optimal casual sequences. People, including migrants, want to believe and want others to believe that their behaviors make sense. Similarly, social scientists believe that there are rational explanations for human behavior, including that of migrants. Social scientists also want to convince others that their explanations are rational on the basis of empirical evidence. If social scientists attempt to explain essentially irrational or random behavior, their explanations violate the tenets of science. The hubris of sociology, according to Dennis H. Wrong (1961), occurs when social theory is overgeneralized to account for more behavior than can fit within the theory. The error is due to sociologists imputing rationality acquired through socialization to the people being studied when the causality simply isn't there.

THE FREEDOM TO MOVE

People who move to beautiful places generally choose to do so because of the natural and social qualities of such places. The immediate reaction to the above statement is: "Well, of course, people almost always choose where they want to live in a free society." Many, perhaps most, people do not live in the type of community or the type of environment in which they would most like to live. Approximately one-third of the migration among employed people, for instance, in the United States is attributable to job transfers (Sell, 1983). Although these moves are based on choice, the choice involves wanting to remain employed in an organization rather than selecting a preferred community. The former choice precludes the latter. For many people, retirement presents their first opportunity to move and stay where they most want to live.

The study of the migration of middle-class people to small towns is inescapably a study of culture and society. It may be more a study of culture with a small and pervasive "c" than the study of higher forms of art and philosophy. Despite the promise it holds, moving can be an intense experience that wrenches people from one location and social system to another. Migration, for the middle-class, is largely a volitional experience, reflecting the facts and illusions of the society at large and the more specific groups of which the individual is a part. It is common, yet intense; hopeful, yet disturbing; new, immature and yet uniquely experienced. Migration is among the most powerful social actions which is highly associated with disruptive emotional states and deviant behavior.

Migration typically is analyzed dispassionately. Migrants and those emotionally attached to them experience extreme ranges of emotion, as existing ties unravel and new ones are woven together. It is an emotional and social juggernaut that affects all people in modern societies. It analytically passes largely unnoticed and unanalyzed, save by a few pensive demographers and data-sensitive administrators. Most awareness by the public generally pertains to problems associated with ethnic minorities crossing borders. The powerful and subtle effects of internal migration are rarely considered except by residents of areas that are rapidly changing because of migration.

Job transfers frequently take place against the wishes of family members who like where they are living. Family members are an important category to consider for reasons other than the number of migrants involved. They warrant special consideration because they do not choose to move in the simple linear pattern that the phrase "choosing to live where they want" usually connotes. Instead, some make an early commitment to let their work decide their choice of where to live into a distant future. To fail to do so would be considered deviant (Blau, 1960).

Eight percent of migrants in our sample had been transferred to Bozeman and were different from other migrants for reasons other than not really choosing to live there. Their valuation of economic and job security showed through more clearly than among most respondents. They also frequently had a "stiff upper lip, this is just part of the job" attitude that was shared by both spouses. They did not feel that the Gallatin Valley was a unique and desirable place. Several of the most critical and unhappy people in the study were wives of husbands who had been transferred in this modern form of mandatory migration. With only two exceptions, job transfers among married couples involved the transfer of husbands, most of whom seemed to have accepted employment with a corporation as a basic premise in their lives. Most were minimally aware of or concerned about the qualities of the community or the surrounding area.

The unhappy wives of transferred husbands were keenly aware of the differences between their husbands, who had colleagues at work and friends in associations, and themselves, isolated in an environment they disliked. One of the most disconsolate respondents was married to the local director of a Statewide distribution and supply firm. She was in her mid 40s and had debilitating arthritis. Unable to drive, she was isolated in a tidy modest home while her husband spent several days on the road each month. After four very unhappy and lonely years, she developed a close friendship with a neighbor and began to express some satisfaction with Bozeman. They were to be transferred again in another year, a move she had been looking forward to since arriving in Bozeman.

Another of the most unhappy initial respondents was a pregnant 30-year-old woman with two preschool children. Her husband had been transferred to a Bozeman branch of a speciality firm that was owned by his family. They had come from the Denver area where both had grown up in close extended Italian Catholic families. Their lovely native rock and redwood ranch-style home had an enormous panoramic view of mountains and the valley. However, their subdivision was located eight miles from town, which magnified her loneliness and isolation. They moved back to Colorado as soon as he had endured the perfunctory on-site branch training required by his firm and a position opened up at the corporate headquarters.

Career conflicts between spouses who have both chosen work-dominated lifestyles are becoming increasingly common in the United States. As more women have entered the labor force and become committed to their work and their employer, potential conflicts regarding where the couple will live have multiplied. Since people who moved to Bozeman were rarely job transfers, there were few opportunities to observe how a successfully employed person who followed a transferred spouse felt about it. One woman quit her corporate career in order to follow her husband who had been transferred to Bozeman. She felt cheated and was particularly annoyed by the absence of job possibilities. She was similar to most men who had been transferred in that she was disinterested in the characteristics of the town, the natural environment and the people. She anxiously wanted to return to a more urban setting where she could return to corporate work, salary and associations.

Other women married to men who had been transferred to Bozeman usually saw Bozeman as just another town. They tended to see it in the same light as the places they had left. Those who were homebodies blended in quickly. More socially active women became involved with local organizations and, within a few months, were actively participating. Collectively, these organization wives projected the other-directness that Riesman (1953) described in his landmark study of modern organization men. They were pleasantly adaptable and blended into the local social scene much as a chameleon matches color with its physical environment.

The wife of a local utility executive expressed her enthusiasm about Bozeman by praising its progressive businessmen, sophisticated tastes and active social life around the country club. She (and her husband) had quickly established a weekly routine of bridge and golf and had become active in the local chamber of commerce. As they boostered Bozeman, they simultaneously praised all of the towns in Montana where they had previously resided. Each, according to them, had only good qualities which they had enjoyed. Yet, they expressed no sorrow at leaving any of them. This couple immediately mentioned that the husband occupied a publicly visible position and that they wanted to project a friendly and cooperative image. As representatives of the corporation, they wanted to make the corporation seem to be a friendly neighbor with a conscience. It would prosper and they, in turn, would be rewarded by their public presentation of selves. Having made this benign Machiavellian declaration, they eagerly qualified that they really believed in what they were doing, as if to assure their personal authenticity about what might otherwise be interpreted as manipulation in bad faith.

The partner in the couple who was swept along usually was a woman. There were only two men who had followed their wives. One was a transcontinental truck driver who loved to hunt. He was delighted with the transfer. His occupational opportunities were not reduced much by the move. He still drove long hauls for a trucking firm. When home, he was able to spend days in the mountains or gardening. He could hardly have been more satisfied. He was the disappointed partner when his wife was transferred after four years in Bozeman.

Another serendipitous finding occurred during the introductory telephone calls to the randomly selected sample of potential respondents in the early 1990s. They were much less inclined to be respondents for the project than people who had been called during the 1970s and 1980s. The unwillingness of residents in the 1990s to cooperate clearly identified them as different from earlier residents. The difference is certain. What it means for the research is unclear, however, because the reasons why so many didn't want to cooperate are unknown. The people who had moved in during the late 1980s and 1990s may have been more cosmopolitan and aloof, not wanting to be bothered, in comparison to more personal and cooperative residents in the past. Discussing this with colleagues suggested that the lower response rates may have occurred because more of the late arrivals were wealthy, wanting to protect their status and privacy.

Another possible explanation is that, by the 1990s, many people had become isolated and independent as a result of essentially knowing no other way to be. This pessimistic explanation assumes that the pervasiveness of industrial society has made the latest generation of residents somewhat jaundiced against participation. The explanation also smacks of sour grapes tasted by the researcher who feels neglected by the failure of people drawn in the sample to join the study. A more practical explanation is that, by the 1990s, people in the Gallatin Valley, as elsewhere, had become saturated and were fed up with being surveyed or invaded for any purpose. The proliferation of surveys has made many people opposed to participating. Certainly, people do not move away from the city to fairly remote rural areas in order to be interviewed. These explanations are entirely speculative. The reasons for the reduction in participation rates by the 1990s cannot really be ascertained for this project.

The difference in response rates is more than an interesting anomaly. The difference poses the difficult question of how similar the samples are from one year to the next. Statistical data analyses are designed to measure differences in behavior due to observable characteristics, such as higher occupational status being related to participating in voluntary organizations, as occurs in Bozeman. If that relationship changes, the change might be due to some intrinsic factors that affect respondents in the sample, such as the members of the sample growing older, or people in general joining fewer organizations. The older people may have achieved higher occupational status. These changes, which imply that reliable differences are occurring, can be explained by theory. On the other hand, it is possible that the people and their behavior are no different than in the past; that is, that the occupational status structure is the same as it had been, and upper status people continue to participate more.

When response rates decline, the validity of responses for making generalizations declines. It is possible to compare samples over time by demographic characteristics. If they remain similar, then the validity comparability of the samples goes up. If some people who are systematically different refuse to be interviewed, as happened during the 1990s, it is possible that their occupational and participation characteristics are not truly representative of residents. The percentages of men and women and families with children remained similar throughout the decades, which indicates that the sample respondents were similar. On the other hand, the fact that more new residents moved from the West Coast during the 1990s indicates differences between the samples. Resolving the problems of analyzing data created when people refuse to be part of the project is difficult.

The hope among social scientists for perfectly comparable samples, to permit perfectly measured statistical associations, is a hope that becomes increasingly difficult to realize as the years go by during a longitudinal analysis. Former participants drop out for various reasons. Most move away, some die and a few don't want to be interviewed anymore. It is difficult to know, across the decades, whether people in a sample are dropping out for the same reasons. The people, community and the literal universe change, making assumptions of sample similarity tenuous indeed, even when response rates remain constant.

Matters regarding the interpretation of participation and responses become even more complex because of questions of epistemology, that is, questions of whether the questionnaire and responses to the questionnaire mean the same thing as time passes. People in the 1990s had lived in a different world than did those in the 1970s. Their experiences may have altered the meaning of questions and responses, even when the wording of the questionnaire remained unchanged, and even where the geographic coordinates were identical. Time, and the complex experiences that accompany its passing, introduces challenges to comparability that challenge the investigation of different people over different periods.

An analogy drawn from sailing when navigating by compass may put this problem of explanation into perspective. After sailing a considerable distance, the compass reading has to be corrected because of changes in the location of magnetic north. Over the years, a correction factor also has to be introduced for any location. No such precise natural correction factors exist for social samples. As the craft sails from one location to the next or returns to the same course year after year, the shoreline changes. New houses and docks appear, familiar forests are cut down, navigational aids are developed. These important visual features all become part of the sailing experience, just as the recognizable changes in the Northern Rockies tell much about what has happened there. The people change and their impacts on the place make it different, although the range and township stay the same. I have returned to rapidly growing places with which I had been very familiar, such as Aspen and Santa Fe, only to find them almost unrecognizable and unnavigable.

This excursus is a cautionary tale about the specific comparability of data gathered across the various years that are reported here. That caution is advised for all longitudinal social science data. Many historians sensitive to the complexities and nuances of comparability of social phenomena over time prefer to simply report the facts within their intellectual limitations. One hopes that the important landmarks are identified and clear, the course is accurate and the craft doesn't run aground. These difficulties with accuracy are more of a problem in uncharted seas or during a first trip, which partially describes this intellectual voyage.

The methodology of the research is also designed to measure the differences between individuals in the samples at any given time, such as 1980, and across intervals, such as from 1980 to 1990. The sample difficulties for accomplishing this have been explained. The methodology also measures how each individual changes. Each respondent surely is the same person: they have the same body, the same mind, usually even the same name. Or do they?

Over the years, some respondents were scarcely recognizable physically or socially in comparison to who they were the first time they were interviewed. Wrinkles, lost hair and gained weight were three of the more visible horsemen of aging although participants generally matured gracefully and handsomely. Aging, with growing responsibility and diminishing alternatives, often was accompanied by caution and conservatism. A few of the respondents had spun a half circle, from relatively unrestricted lifestyles in the early 1970s to serious devotion to work, home and community 20 years later. Some had switched from being philosophically liberal to much more conservative orientations. Strong threads of consistency were woven into the lives of most.

Migrants who die are often neglected in analyses. Because this study followed the same people for so many years, we became aware of many major personal events, including death. Preparation for death, deciding where to move to die, was relatively uncommon, although it was mentioned by two or three retired people. Several participants in the study, both long-time and recent residents, died during the course of the study.

No record of deaths of participants was kept. Their deaths usually came to our attention in one of two ways. First, some participants were so familiar to the author and their deaths so publicized that their deaths were noticed. More frequently, deaths became known when telephone calls were made to make appointments for another round of interviews. Family members answered the phone and told us the person being called had died. Between 1972 and 1976, only two of the original sample died. By 1992, very few of the original list of long-term residents were left. We can only wonder whether those who were 50 or 60 years old when they were first interviewed had stayed in the area until they died. One of the first participants in the study, a local native and beloved character, died in 1991 at the age of 97.

In a few cases, a tragedy was especially apparent because death occurred just when the promise of what the person wanted out of life was being fulfilled. Alice Weinstein moved to an expensive subdivision outside of Bozeman in 1981. Recently widowed at 49, she was starting a new life in a new place. Alice was independently wealthy through inheritance from her family of origin and from the estate she received following her husband's death. In Bozeman, she soon became active in voluntary organizations devoted to preserving the natural environment and supporting educational opportunities and cultural preservation among Indians.

During the course of interviews, Alice confided that she had found who she was and where she wanted to be. She continued to travel for two or three extended holidays each year to visit friends, family and exotic places. She sailed to Bali, trekked in Nepal and canoed in the Amazon. When she came home, she was incredibly busy, and revered. She had lived in the Gallatin Valley for nearly six years when she was diagnosed with cancer, which ultimately was fatal. Before her death, she established a general trust fund to perpetuate her interests in helping others.

The characteristics of the community and of the respondents are not all that changed during the course of this research. I also have changed both personally and intellectually. Personal changes, physical aging and social experiences have made me more aware and sympathetic to a wide variety of respondents. The research was initiated when I was 30, married with two small children, living on a small sheep farm on the top of Bozeman Pass. I was zealously devoted to alternative lifestyles during the 1960s. I now am in my mid-50s, divorced and remarried. My children are adults. I live in a small university town in Australia. I still find deep peace along a trout stream and ski touring, but spend much less time in outdoor recreation than I did 25 years ago. I rarely encounter very Bohemian situations. Through this maturation, this transformation, I have realized how limited and shortsighted my earlier self-assurance was about the right ways to live and the correct ways to interpret social behavior.

The intellectual changes that I have experienced across those years also have affected how this book is written. The initial research projects were clearly conceptualized, accurately measured and amenable to straightforward quantitative analyses. There are so many data, so many factual relationships that could be analyzed, that they could occupy a team of researchers for a decade. Meanwhile, I have grown more interested in the whole, the qualitative relationships between the natural and social environments and the respondents. I now believe that the data transcend the precoded categories for respondents and their responses. Those data remain crucial and important for examining and resolving specific details and questions, but they are too limiting for telling a broader story.

The methodology, then, has changed over the course of the research. The project was conceived to test hypotheses. The location was a sample that was appropriate for testing the hypotheses. Gradually, the methodology became grounded in the data that were emerging. The data were, in effect, determining the hypotheses, which is the premise of the grounded theoretical approach. The method, which had been initiated as a sociological survey research project, had become more similar to that of an anthropological field analysis. The instrument changed. The trip that had begun guided by a compass, became a longer trip navigated by a Geographic Information System (GIS). Over 25 years, the trip had become a voyage. Only now at the end, the instruments are a sextant and constant sensory attention paid to watching the coastline, feeling the currents and the winds.

LUCK

The author knows of no methodological descriptions in the analysis of migration that consider luck. As used here, luck refers to the unanticipated consequences that affect outcomes, after reasonable effort has been made to anticipate what typically would occur. Cliches, such as "People make their own luck" and "Good luck is the result of a lot of effort," undoubtedly are folk knowledge. They also neglect luck. Luck is a major component in how satisfactory a move proves to be. Some newcomers, who carefully investigated information to help ensure they made the right decision, failed in their plans for reasons somewhat beyond their control. Serious illness and death are occasional examples of bad luck that forced people to change. Successful marriage, the birth of a child or an unanticipated inheritance were examples of good luck that led to change. Newcomers who invested in small businesses were especially likely to fail even after carefully investigating the needs of the local market. For some, their conclusions about what business Bozeman needed may have been naive and overly optimistic. Others were hurt by the bad luck of an unforeseen recession.

One middle-aged couple without children invested tens of thousands of dollars to open a fresh fish market. They had collected information regarding the potentially high profit margin of fresh fish markets. They anticipated a national trend away from red meat. They investigated the demographic characteristics of Bozeman and felt that the population was sufficiently cosmopolitan enough to guarantee customers. They also had worked out an intricate network of suppliers on each coast with rapid airline connections to Bozeman. They went broke within four years, blaming the lack of sophisticated taste among local residents for their failure.

An enormous number of reasons could explain the failure of this business. The most important factor was a misinterpretation of local consumer needs. Two other similar fresh fish markets had gone broke during the 1970s. The local demand foreseen by our respondents simply might have been overestimated. But the increasing national demand for fresh fish throughout the early 1980s was also occurring in Bozeman, just as their extrapolations projected they would. What they did not foresee was that supermarkets and mobile fish markets would simultaneously increase the supply of fresh fish at costs much lower than their expensive speciality market. Perhaps their criticisms of local tastes were accurate. Perhaps other outlets did not provide the quality product their shop did. If no alternative for fresh fish had been created, our entrepreneurs probably would not have gone out of business. They might even still live in Bozeman. Another reason that potential customers did not frequent their market was that the couple were chain smokers. Still another reason might be that, as proprietors, they vehemently expressed their disillusionment to customers. They left feeling disillusioned, in spite of their efforts to make decisions based on sound information. They largely failed due to misinformation and a changing market which was difficult to predict — bad luck. Their expressed initial motives had been to live in a quiet, small, peaceful town and to hunt upland game birds during the fall. Their business was described as a means to those ends. It never became possible to know whether their expressed motives were valid since the shop occupied so much time they never went hunting.

A clearer example of bad luck occurred to a family that opened a "homemade" ice-cream parlor. They, too, had studied the local market and found it ripe for their business in a new shopping center. What they had not anticipated was that, simultaneously, another family was making the same plans at an even more visible street front location downtown — and that a major ice-cream chain was opening a shop in the same new shopping center. The fact that the shop of our respondent went out of business in a few months can also be attributed to misreading the local market, but it also involved factors beyond their control or their knowledge. The other ice-cream shops prospered.

Luck worked to favor success in other instances. Terry North became the franchised regional distributor for petroleum additives. Although he was an experienced salesman in automotive products, he relied primarily on his intuition that his product would fulfill a demand rather than on documented market research. He was extraordinarily successful where other newcomers who started their own businesses failed. Terry, a close neighbor, told me, "I can't believe how much profit there has been in this business. I only go on sales trips two times a year. They provide enough orders to make headquarters happy. From my years operating a (gas) station, I suspected this was a profitable product, but I never dreamed how profitable it would be." On the other hand, Terry was an extremely honest, nice guy, which undoubtedly helped his sales.

Luck, or serendipity as it sometimes is described, is important for two reasons when analyzing migration satisfaction. The first is to make clear the immense element of unknown and unknowable qualities that surround the universe into which people move. Entropy makes perfect knowledge unavailable under any natural condition. Some places are easier to make accurate predictions about than other places. But many predictions by even the most astute predictors still turn out wrong. Bozeman and other scenic recreational towns are especially difficult to understand because they appear to be stable and integrated places to inexperienced observers when they are not. People who try to predict what they are like are likely to be inaccurate and disappointed.

The second reason luck is conceptually important is that rational, individual decision making models generally assume that people who think logically about their goals and substantiate that logic with sound evidence are likely to be successful when others fail. This over-rationalized conception of humans as predictors is itself suspect in real-life contexts. Rational predictions are likely to lead to erroneous conclusions, whether they involve expectations regarding a business venture, environmental quality or marriage in the context of a new community. This second problem, then, pertains to the limitations of individuals as processors of information.

If the predictions people make are inaccurate, then what is the most accurate model that can be used to explain their behavior in terms of the motives they give? The rational model remains the reliable choice. At least the information the rational model uses is subject to test. After all, a model that explained behavior on the basis of luck would have to be built around a typology of who is lucky and who is unlucky and then predict their success or satisfaction based on which type they were. Such a model is probably best left to soothsayers and fortunetellers, as it has been for millennia.

The rational model is a superior, but limited approach. No one is entirely rational in a finite sense, but many become more rational with time, as they adopt concepts that are more factually based. For example, married men who were attracted to the area to hunt and fish gradually spent less time in those pursuits as the importance of work and family activities became more pressing. The concepts they used to evaluate their satisfaction expanded, became more complex and competed with the fewer and simpler ones that had dominated their perspective.

Most newcomers to the Gallatin Valley initially felt that people in the area were especially friendly. They were responding to their expectations that people in small towns are friendly and to the cordial style found in Bozeman. After a year or two, many respondents had changed their opinion and said that, behind a facade of smiling faces, most people in Bozeman were aloof and closed to friendship. Their experience led to rational reconstruction of what the community was like in comparison to what the original prediction had been. The respondents were becoming more rational in the sense that their beliefs and feelings had been more empirically founded.

The challenge to the reliance upon economic explanations can be clarified by comparing cost-benefit analysis with Kant's discussion of value (Kant, 1934). From a cost-benefit explanation, a person has certain wants, all of which can be converted into economic units, which are weighted. The rational economic person chooses to live in the location that enables optimally achieving those wants. Kant, on the other hand, asserted that individuals have values which, unlike wants, have moral valence. Some values are more moral, more right and true, than others. The economic metaphor assumes that all migrants are following the single reality of optimizing costs and benefits. Other realities, which some people may value more than the economic metaphor, are not easily incorporated into this orientation. For some, the intrinsic worth of close, meaningful interaction with friends and relatives transcends other values. For others, the value attributed to community or environment may be most important. Most commonly, these values, as metaphors for life, are mixed as well as frequently being reordered.

While all choices can be assigned economic costs and benefits from an economic perspective, assigning such economic costs and benefits perverts and cheapens the value from a Kantian position. People have acquired the values attributed to kin and friend, nature and community, as well as the rational and sometimes competing notion of economic exchange. Each cultural value creates an independent reason for migrating and, incidentally, identifies different types of migrants attracted through those values.

People believed their reasons for moving were more valid than those of people who moved for other reasons. Economically motivated migrants frequently ridiculed those people who had moved without guaranteed employment for being "so foolish." Those with stable employment often maintained a superior air, as if they had mastered the secret of community satisfaction. People who moved for noneconomic reasons frequently expressed disdain for people who did not appreciate and immerse themselves into meaningful relationships, community activities and outdoor recreation. The differences between these and other beliefs express some of the foundations for personal dissatisfaction and disagreements about how the community and the environment ought to be.

AN ORIENTATION FOR CONSIDERING NONRATIONAL FREE MIGRATION

As has already been discussed, scientific explanations, by definition, must be rational. The following orientation attempts to reconcile migration, a behavior that is somewhat irrational, within an explanatory framework that is rational. Fuzzy logic in engineering provides a crude analogy. Although this analogy is flawed, it does illustrate the point. In cameras constructed with fuzzy logic design, the engineering has taken into account variables that collectively are integrated into selecting an appropriate aperture setting, shutter speed and so forth for the available light, variation in image and other variables included in the multiple-variable format. The photograph comes out clear and sharp because of the effective simultaneous coordination of the mechanics based on the multiple-variable logic. Similar programs are increasingly common in yacht racing. The formula in the computer integrates several complex navigational variables (wind direction and speed, current direction and speed and potential changes) and then recommends an optimal course.

Fuzzy logic programs are constructed on known variables and expectable conditions. The alternative to computer programs is faith in oneself as an artist. The individual photographer or skipper who decides not to rely on computer programs, in fact, takes similar variables into consideration. The outcomes are measured by aesthetic perfection or milliseconds. The difference is defined as acceptable or unacceptable, victory or defeat. An Australian boat in the Americas Cup qualifier rounds sank for unknown reasons that were beyond the variables included in its computer formula. It probably would have sunk without a computer.

Explaining social behavior is infinitely more complex than taking a photograph or sailing a boat. Erving Goffman used a photographic analogy, frame analysis, in his later social theory (1974). The sociological objective, according to Goffman, was to provide as many important and definitive images of a social situation as possible. These include the private, usually hidden, backstage social experiences as well as the public aspects of how people want their audience to see them. An honest photographer of a wedding would take pictures of the tensions of family conflicts, economic worries and immoral seductions deliberately hidden from the public eye, as well as the carefully staged wedding rehearsal dinner, walk down the aisle, tossing of the bouquet and camaraderie of the reception. Much of my time has been spent backstage looking at realities that the people being studied didn't really want most others to see.

After interviewing the same respondents over the years, it often became apparent that some aspects of the first-year interviews were an onstage facade. For example, several single persons and couples who conveyed an initial image of being energetic, active and committed eventually said that they had been frenetically living the lives of alcoholics or addicts. Some individuals claimed that they recognized their earlier pattern of presenting an artificial and constructed image of themselves. Some apologized for presenting what they believed to have been a false image. Those who made these confessions usually said that they were relieved to have realized the false and destructive pattern in their lives. As researchers, we had to rely on what people told us, what their version of the truth was. We could not surmise that they had been living in denial, as some claimed.

The problem I face in attempting to provide a clear, sharp sociological image is exactly the opposite of fuzzy logic technology, which is constructed around the interaction of a few precisely defined variables. Most sociology, quantitative or qualitative, uses such logic, but it is inadequate. The variables are too few, their interactions unclear and their time span too short. Of course, the complete image would require perfect understanding of infinite variables and perfectly observed interactions throughout eternity. What the sociologist can do is assemble the images, limited though they inevitably are, with as much care and thought as she or he can muster. While the image may seem clear and sharp to the readers, it actually is a construction of a much foggier reality by the sociologist. The analogy with photography may not be so removed from social reality. A sharp, clear photograph from a fuzzy logic camera actually is based on the idealized and conventional conception of the camera makers. The program is one of many that might be constructed.

Theory seeks to explain what can be explained. Much human behavior, certainly the decision to migrate or to stay, can be described, but not entirely explained on the bases of measured information. The nonrational aspects of behavior are among those that cannot be explained. Nonrational behavior certainly cannot be explained through any literal interpretations of the reasons that migrants provide for moving. For some few people, both descriptions and explanations are given for situations that, in the opinion of outsiders, might appear logically contradictory or so erratic that they seem crazy. However, such cases are considered rational if their unique circumstances provide a credible explanation for their actions and their actions are consistent with their explanations. Much of what is interesting about migration to the Northern Rockies is that it can be described, but not totally explained. My fascination is as much with what cannot be explained as with what can be.

Philosophers of science, including sociologists, have generated sophisticated explanations regarding how to be sure what is claimed to be fact is fact. This concern is a bit different from finding the meaning of truth, since that concern is examined through deduction, logic. The relationship between facts and accurate explanations falls more into induction, inference. The facts of migration are collected in terms of categories. They include categories for the migration itself, such as where to or from where a move has occurred, how far it was and when it took place. There also are categories of migrants that affect how likely they are to move. These are social categories such as, age, sex, occupation and education. They can include many other categories such as psychological indicators of personality, IQ and temperament. At particular times, religious or political factors may explain why most people move. For example, the partition between India and Pakistan led to mass migration on extremely short notice. Their religious beliefs determined their nation of choice.

The facts are logically integrated into theory in roughly one of two ways. The categories are treated as indicators of structure or process. An example of a structurally oriented theory is one that hypothesizes that cohesion and integration in the community will determine how out-migration occurs. The characteristics of migrants, their age and gender, among others, reflect that integration and their relative likelihood to move. Young single adults move more because they are less socially integrated into where they live than are middle-aged couples. Process-based theories draw upon how people act as a consequence of some process. One example of a process-oriented theory is that people who move frequently are predicably more likely to move in the future. Another process-oriented example is that people with higher expectations for income will be more likely to migrate than those who are satisfied with their earnings. The demographic categories for listing the theory are the same as for structurally oriented theories; that is, age, gender, ethnicity and so forth are used to imply social processes rather than structures that are causing the migrations. Process can only occur in a structure and all structures have processes.

Theories of behavior also are inevitably tautological. Since the number of variables is fixed and their relationships deterministic, they explain each other. For example, absence of cohesion frees people to move. Complete cohesion may also lead to migration, as when an entire community decides to move, as occurred among some 18th- and 19th-century European migrants to America. The tautology of the process-oriented example that people who move are more likely to move is even more obvious. While empirically correct, it is like a dog chasing its tail. Distinguishing whether the tail is the attractor for the chase or the muzzle the motivator to keep the tail moving is impossible. Tautologies are logical flaws in theory that must be accepted in exchange for having a rational explanation. In a deductive sense, the inevitability of tautology makes social theory, in itself, nonrational since it presumes to offer universal explanations that, by definition, have limitations. They also may be regarded as inductively nonrational since they presume empirical relationships that do not hold up. In fact, many people who have strong structural incentives and opportunities to migrate do not migrate while few do. Many people who have been vagabonds finally settle permanently. Either the theories or the people examined through the theories are partially irrational. Maybe both are.

A SOCIAL CONTROL PERSPECTIVE OF MODERN FREE MIGRATION

Rational theories of free migration assume that people move to optimize the resources available to them. The assumption is that the migrant's cup can be better filled by moving somewhere else.

A theory of social control that assumes a less than rational calculation may explain modern free migration more validly than rational choice theory. Social control theory assumes that humans are naturally social, selfish, bio-psychological creatures who seek to satisfy their cravings through any available means (Gottfredson and Hirschi, 1990). *Except*, humans, as social creatures, have consciously and consensually exchanged some of their unremitting biological and psychological appetites for the safety and security of society. This exchange, the social contract, as Hobbes (1991) termed it, draws humans together in mutual self-interest. To the extent to which humans may act independently of society, they will do so. The extent to which they act independently is determined by the level of social control. Moreover, they will continue to give what seem to be cogent, rational, social explanations for their behavior, their migration, which is fundamentally incoherent, irrational and individualistic.

From a social control perspective, unusual, deviant behavior is easily explained since it is the natural state for humans. More problematic is the question of why everyone does not behave that way. The answer is that as social beings, they are embedded in informal and formal social systems that, reward socially approved and punish socially disapproved behavior (Gibbs, 1989). In this structure of friends, family, church, education — the host of social institutions — they come to appreciate and value shared beliefs and activities, making them want to conform to social conventions.

Free migration in modern society is functional and dysfunctional simultaneously. It is more functional at the formal, institutional level. It permits a fluid labor force. It facilitates efficient and impersonal interaction among deployable workers. It releases the pressure on locations that have more workers than jobs. It relieves pressure on locations that have more jobs than workers by allowing workers to move there. Free migration in modern society is also problematic because it destroys informal social cohesion and integration. It separates family and loved ones. It fragments memberships in social institutions in the home community. Migration creates alienation, confusion and environmental disruption in sender and host communities. Migration, then, occurs because of a failure of social control to literally keep people in their place. Migration also is a dynamic problem-solving behavior. It stimulates development and allocation of resources. It generates the formation and sustenance of communities. And it leads to considerable personal satisfaction for many migrants.

The quality of the social contract is determined by its ability to prevent problems. The rules must be flexible. They must discourage migration when it is disruptive and encourage it when it is beneficial. Since migration is simultaneously disruptive and beneficial, the rules, the social and personal logic of migration, become ambiguous, fuzzy. In some situations, migration is clearly beneficial even to local, informal situations despite the suffering associated with it. A natural disaster, a local recession or a divorce are strong and sufficient reasons to move away just as economic windfalls and new love are powerful incentives to relocate. Even so, many people who would potentially benefit by migrating refuse to do so because of social controls that encourage them to remain where they are. In other situations, out-migration is of little benefit to the home community or to those who leave it. If pure rationality were operative, there would be a strong association between what migrants and communities gain and lose as a result of migration. Among most migrants to scenic recreation areas, there is little connection between what they say they expect and what they get; hence, their rational explanation is not very accurate. The simpler, more parsimonious explanation is that they are out of control.

Much of the struggle occurs between the goals vested in the formal and the informal structures of control. Formal structures, those that publicly serve the population, are organized around what are claimed to be universal and rational goals, such as studying hard for success and voting responsibly. The person who conforms to achieve these objectives is under control from the perspective of the formal political and economic structure. Informal structures, those that seek to engage people in close personal interaction, are typically particularistic and traditional. Family and friendships are among the strongest and most pervasive of informal structures. Formal structures tend to be consistent. They encourage moving when local jobs are scarce and work is plentiful elsewhere. Informal structures are more ambiguous. To the extent that they endorse the broader, formal, societal goals, they encourage young people to move to get a higher education and to find well-paying, stable employment. They also encourage people to remain supportive of tradition of family and friends. Informal controls can powerfully influence whether a person can move to engage in the rational choice of the formal structure.

There is considerable merging of the formal and informal structures and their respective controls affecting migration. While influences affecting migration in a modern impersonal urban environment may be minimal, they may be powerful in other settings. Much of the modern history of immigration to developed nations has been encouraged from traditional communities in less-developed nations. Third World parents encourage the migration of some of their children in order to benefit the family as a whole. On the other hand, families may discourage and inhibit their children from moving, even when moving might reap financial rewards for the entire family.

If people were effectively controlled, they would generally not move unless doing so would be beneficial to themselves, their loved ones and the broader society. Travis Hirschi (1969) has identified four dimensions of social control: attachment, commitment, activity and belief. Attachment refers to the emotional concern that individuals have for each other, particularly in families and other personal and intimate institutions. Commitment means having something to lose from the repertoire of rewards acquired or promised as a member of a community. Activities refers to engaging in shared community events. Belief refers to sharing a common belief system. Attachment, that is, caring for persons in personal, face-to-face institutions, such as, family, friends and neighbors, is primary. These dimensions of control effectively determine behavior because they connect the individual to these primary informal systems.

The reason for the disjuncture between what migrants say and what they do is that the social system is fractured and disjointed. Many people, especially lifestyle migrants, are no longer integrated into permanent, dependable supportive groups, most notably family, neighborhood, church, community. They are out of the control of a community. This absence of control frequently is called freedom, free to do what one wants and go where one wishes as long as it does not harm others. As has repeatedly been demonstrated, many migrants do hurt others. They also hurt themselves as they tear themselves apart from others. They lack the internal control, the conscience and the values to commit and stay put. They cannot even be consistent in following through with what they say they are going to do. This discussion is limited to free migration in societies that claim to value permanent community. Migration means fleeing beyond control. Ironically, history is filled with examples of nomadic communities which, despite their life on the road, keep people within the community.

Control has become a feared word in the late 20th century. It conjures images of totalitarian control exercised by government or loss of independence when the individual is concerned. The absence of control, however, is chaos. Lifestyle migrants are not in jeopardy from a regimented government. They are increasingly beyond much sustained connection with those who are personally close. Their lives are increasingly chaotic without community.

The loss of control is closely associated with migration. It is a consequence of the dissolution of community and the corresponding ascendance of society. In traditional communities, members moved in accordance with shared values and behavior which had developed as survival and opportunity strategies. When members moved, it was likely as a group, the heartbreak of separation was minimized and the opportunity for shared contributions was maximized. Individual migration occurred only in the most extreme conditions as one strategy for survival of the community. It was for a collective purpose. They knew that the move was likely to lead to a desired outcome, food, water, protection. The internal controls of the individual were consonant with the beliefs, values and behaviors, that is, the social controls, of the community. Resisting community controls was likely to lead to being exposed to a harsh and unforgiving set of natural controls, which were likely to be quick and painful: starvation, violence and isolation.

The evolution to modern capitalistic societies has increasingly allowed free migration. Economically, individual workers become free to seek work. Their employers become free of supporting them during slack times. The economic freedom corresponded with changes in political philosophy. External political controls over migration were gradually relaxed as slavery was abolished and indenturement forbidden. At the same time, the fearsome external controls exerted by the environment were reduced. Wild creatures and bandits became fewer. Opportunities for outsiders increased. Certainly, there were risks in free migration, but the advantages outweighed the disadvantages. The values, attitudes and behaviors of migrants continued to correspond to those in their community of origin. Communities begrudgingly tolerated and even encouraged their young people to seek opportunities in a distant location. Gradually, the community took on a belief in migration itself. Communities in rural America became vestigial places populated by members who had not left and those who had returned. The society encouraged the loss of informal control.

Modern migrants continue to share many values, beliefs and behaviors with their community of origin regarding why to move and where to go. The attraction of a good job and an enjoyable lifestyle are regularly sought and found. Some move to suburbs and corporate life. For many others, and migrants to scenic recreational places typify these, there is minimal correspondence between moving and what their community of origin believes is valuable. In fact, the phrase "community of origin" is likely a misnomer. It is less a community than a collective of fragmented and atomized individuals and institutions. Internal controls that make migration sensible, predictable and rational are lost. In their place is a set of articulations regarding freedom, lifestyle, work and family that make little cohesive sense in the broader life history of the migrants. Both the home community and its youth have adopted migration as the means for achieving goals. The original goals, which were based upon group cohesion and integration, have been lost. The young in such places are left with a belief in migrating and with precious little connection for achieving anything they say they want to gain through the move. They are similar to what Robert Merton refers to as ritualists, going through a routine for its own sake while articulating what seem to be rational reasons for their activities (1949, pp. 215-248). Their apparent rational reasons are only rationalizations. They are going through the motions without much connection to achieving the life quality they claim to espouse.

In the life courses of lifestyle migrants, most eventually settle down. Settling down is a relative concept. The moves most people make gradually become fewer and farther between. Having made the major step into a scenic recreation area may prove a pivotal experience for many migrants. It is likely to signify a process toward achieving more of a compromise between lifestyle and important institutions. In suburbs and small cities in the West, millions of people optimize the balance between recreation, family, work, voluntary activities and the other elements of community into a modern conditional version of the social contract. The individual ceases to be the totally selfish, migratory beast begrudgingly trading selfishness in exchange for the support and solidarity from the collective. Even in settling down, the wanderers feel pain and discomfort because they realize the opportunities they have given up. Meanwhile, complementing the nature of the beast is the social nature, constantly reminding the migrants to look for and to nourish themselves in a decent place to live.

Chapter 4

Methods

Categories in social science are artifacts of scientists, classification schemes which they hope more accurately explain relationships that previously have been explained by others. The discussions presented here follow this tradition. My faith is that the categories presented here gain validity because they articulate what people say and believe about their migration and other aspects of their lives. This grounded approach assumes that the behaviors and explanations people describe for themselves are the essential elements for understanding their lives in the context of social science (Glaser and Strauss, 1967).

In many of our interpretations, particular cases exemplify categories that are being discussed. Respondents may have used different words to describe their own experiences and rationalizations than the specific term we chose for the category. We hope that individuals reading this material will recognize themselves in the thinly disguised descriptions and will agree with how they have been classified and with the interpretations associated with the classification. Social scientists almost universally share a similar hope that a knowledgeable audience will agree with their explanations. To accept their explanation of behavior is to accept their interpretation of the motives for the behaviors they analyze. An economist analyzing the relationship between labor force changes and migration provides evidence of an association. For example, his or her findings validate more than the causal relationship between new jobs in the Sun Belt and migration to fill those jobs. They also seek to validate the motive that economists believe account for behavior, explanations which they hope will convince an audience of how the people being studied behave.

The perspective emphasized the motives and interpretations of the people being analyzed. An attempt has been made to make this reliance on qualitative analyses explicit. Essentially all research can be viewed as based upon motives imputed to the elements under analysis by the research. Physicists say to themselves, "If I know anything about quarks, then X ought to happen under Y conditions." In other words, quarks conditionally behave because of intrinsic capacities to respond under particular conditions which are recognized by the physicist. Less remotely removed from social science are ecological explanations by biologists who, for example, explain the migration of animals as a consequence of adaptive knowledge shared by the species and enacted by individual animals, presumably to preserve the species. An elk or insect is motivated to follow the annual or daily cycle of the sun. Both physicists and biologists object to the term "motivate." Their analyses are based instead on what they think their phenomena do in response to specified conditions. The findings throughout this project are sympathetic to why natural scientists omit motivation from their vocabulary. Enormous discrepancies exist between what people do and the motivations and intentions they describe to explain what they do. Most migrants don't end up doing what they said they intended to do nor do the motives they offer seem to explain what they do dependably.

Acceptance of the fact that much behavior is not rational has implications that are simultaneously freeing and frightening for the sociologist (or economists or social psychologists). It is freeing because the notion of nonrationality removes some of the terrible burden of trying to explain everything. It is freeing because it accepts that nonrational behavior is normal, common and to be expected. It also is freeing because it legitimizes and accepts the explanations from other sciences, particularly biological sciences. Biological responses among human beings may often by irrational. That, after all, is a primary assumption underlying much of clinical psychology and psychoanalysis.

The implications of the fact that much human behavior is nonrational are also frightening. The need to pay attention to other variables beyond the familiar and comfortable, but limiting, social explanations becomes apparent. If the subjects under study behave irrationally, then it remains for the researcher to rely on his or her own intellectual abilities to provide an explanation that describes a rational order despite the inability of the people being studied to rationally account for their own behavior. But, if the people being studied are unable to be rational, then why should we believe the accounts that the researcher claims are more rational? The inadequacy of assuming that any social theory can be the foundation for any completely effective plan must be rejected.

Try this: How can a plan conceived by nonrational people for nonrational people be effective? This last implication is profound across all applications of social science, from community development and educational opportunities through the processing of legal offenders. The plan may be the most rational aspect of the procedure, more rational than the people. It may be the thread that keeps the social fabric from unraveling into chaos.

Perhaps a limitation of causal analysis lies in our essentially anthropomorphic view of the world. All causal analysis may be limited by scientists' ability to conceive of causality only in motivational terms, because they are human. Equally plausible is that such a view is no limitation at all. The operation of the empirical world may correspond to the view that we apply to it in our analyses, whether physical, biological or social.

Social scientists have an opportunity and an advantage, of course, because quarks and elk cannot speak of their motives. The ability of humans to talk and consequently for migrants to express why they move is not entirely a blessing. After listening to an especially long-winded respondent hold forth for three straight hours, the curse becomes apparent: quarks and elk don't take up your time. A less selfish and more analytic problem is that verbal information provided by respondents is beyond any clearly established exclusive positivistic system such as that imposed by physicists or biologists on their subjects. People say one thing and do another. Quarks and elk are not self-contradictory. For this research, the challenge has been to ferret out the different systems of motives used by respondents to accurately explain what they did even when their actions varied from what they said. Why, for example, did some people who said they loved being outdoors essentially fail to go there? Culture provides many explanations that are taken on by societal members as sensible and desirable ways to behave. People believe in these ready-made, diverse and sometimes contradictory terms.

SAMPLING AND INTERVIEWING

The first longitudinal project was initiated in 1973, when a random sample of heads of households in Bozeman were interviewed (Table 4.1, A and B). The respondents still in the area in 1976 were reinterviewed along with a new random sample. All of these remaining respondents were reinterviewed in 1980, along with a new random sample. Many of the questions developed for these early surveys were retained, enabling valid comparisons with later interviews during the second longitudinal project. The few participants who were still living in Bozeman in 1991 were contacted one last time to be interviewed in 1991. These included 29 (8.7%) of the respondents (N=333) from the 1970s and 75 (14.6%) from the 1980s.

The second project was started in 1981. Between 1981 and 1983, 390 households were interviewed within six months after they had arrived in Bozeman and a surrounding 15-mile radius. In 1991, another sample of 46 new households was drawn. New samples were drawn in June of each of these years by comparing the two most recent telephone directories and creating a pool of newly listed names. A systematic sample was drawn from this pool. Persons in the sample were called to request their participation. In all but the 1991 sample, respondents were told that an initial interview and an annual follow-up interview would be conducted. Anonymity and confidentiality were assured. Most persons in the 1980s (81%) were cooperative and agreed to an initial interview. That cooperation dropped to 46 percent a decade later.

Table 4.1
Sample Numbers and Percentages for Survey Years and Selected Demographic Characteristics

A. Numbers in Original (1970) Panels for Each Set of Interviews

	Interviews				
Year	First	Second	Third	Last	Total
1972	146				146
1976	107	60			167
1980	80	31	17		128
1992	45	42	33	29	149
1972-92	378	133	50	29	590

B. 149 Respondents First Interviewed during the 1970s, 1981-83 and 1993 still in Sample in 1993

	1970s	1980s	1990s
1972-80	333		
1981-84		390	
1993	29 (8.7%)	75 (14.6%)	45

Initial interviews conducted at the respondents' home usually required about 45 minutes. Interviews were scheduled to allow both spouses or partners to be present among households with couples. Follow-up interviews averaged one-half hour and also were conducted with both spouses at home, when possible. A few especially verbal respondents required more than two hours to complete their interviews.

Initial and follow-up interviews were identical except for personal background information that was collected only once unless marked changes, such as death or divorce, had occurred. Early (1981) respondents were told that, if they moved away, they would be sent a self-administered questionnaire. The questionnaire sent to people who moved away was developed from the interview format and provided comparable information regarding the thoughts respondents had in retrospect regarding their Bozeman experience. It also asked questions about why they left Bozeman and why they chose their new location.

Together, the interviews and questionnaires yielded consecutive data from one measurement period to the next. In the 1980s' study, those measurements occurred every year from 1980 until 1986, from the year respondents arrived until they moved to another location. Measurement enabled comparisons from one decade to the next between the 1970s and the 1990s. Time series case study survey data have several advantages over other types of data used in social science analyses. They are superior to actuarial data, such as are produced by the census, which are collected for universal and frequently unspecified theoretical purposes, for two reasons. Time series case study data record the actual experiences and perceptions of people across dimensions the respondents regard as important. Actuarial techniques force people to respond in terms specified by the instrument. Long-term case studies document a continuous process. For example, they allow looking at the size of several places in which people say they prefer to live to see whether there are distinct processes of how they come to select a town the size of Bozeman. The case study approach to individual respondents also allows the gathering of more varied and intensive information concerning respondents than is feasible in general population surveys. For example, the changing level of satisfaction with local services and the amount of participation with local organizations can be examined to see whether they affected whether people stayed or moved away.

There are some disadvantages to long-term case studies. Creating an instrument for a particular research purpose and administering it to a specified sample over an extended period is expensive, which by practical necessity prevents using a large sample. A second disadvantage is that the scope must be limited for time series case studies. It is not feasible to use the method for very many cases or time periods. Within two decades, most of the initial residents in a high-migration community move away or die. Comparisons and generalizations must be made with caution. In this research, there were simultaneously two levels of cases: (1) the individual respondents and their households, who were followed throughout their years of participation in the project; and (2) the community, the whole, which also was changing over time. A third disadvantage is that the meanings of ideas and of references change over time. Questions about the beauty and solitude of the area meant something quite different in 1972 than in 1991. A final problem is that long-term case studies generate so much information that it defies analysis by a single author in one publication.

Time series surveys also have advantages over conventional case study techniques. Case study is a clinical, that is, a qualitative approach. However accurate the observations on each case may be, the inferences that can be made from the data are limited. Each case study becomes a unique observation. The survey of case studies over several time periods allows categories of cases to be compared and inferences to be made about the sample represented by the cases. Instead of a single example of, say, the experience of an unmarried father, this type of case can be compared to other types, such as married parents and single persons without children. The experiences of each can be interpreted as representative of a larger population because they were randomly drawn for the sample.

In the 1970s, we wanted to know which factors were linked to satisfaction, quality of life and how satisfaction was associated with planning future development in the area. By the early 1980s, we wanted to know about the people who were moving away. Although practically all respondents said they expected to be living in Bozeman permanently, about one-quarter of the 390 households had left within a year. One-half had relocated within five years. All 1981-83 respondents had agreed, when first called to participate, that they would notify the staff if they decided to move before the project was completed. They agreed to fill out a mailed questionnaire sent to them at their new residence. Fifty-three (39.3%) of the out-migrants failed to return useable questionnaires. The most common (72%) reason for lost participants was the lack of an accurate forwarding address. Most left abruptly without notifying neighbors, employees or the local post office. A few (16%) others replied that they no longer wished to participate or provided insufficient information to add to their file. One woman checked "divorce" as her reason for leaving and answered no other questions on the schedule.

Eighty-three households that had moved away returned completed questionnaires. The initial interviews of these cases were compared with cases that did not return questionnaires. No significant differences were found regarding the sex, age, presence of children, education, income or occupation of those who returned a questionnaire and those who did not. No further follow-up questionnaires were mailed to respondents who had moved away. Because of the similarities among people who stayed and those who moved, the decision was made to treat all out-migrants as one group when comparing them to persons who stayed in Bozeman.

Longitudinal analyses also allow putting findings into contexts that are external to the respondents and the questions asked. They make it possible to see what kinds of people stay and leave, or feel a particular way, in conjunction with local and national influences, such as economic and population growth cycles.

The first project, initiated in 1972, interviewed a random sample of 146 full-time, permanent Bozeman residents. Students, military personnel and other temporary residents were eliminated from the sample drawn from the most recent city directory. The 60 willing respondents who were still residing in the county were interviewed again in 1976. At that time, a new sample of 107 residents was drawn, interviewed and compared with the original sample. This procedure was repeated again in 1980 and 1992. By 1992, only 29 of the original 1972 respondents were available to be interviewed. The same questions were asked for consistency so that reliable comparisons could be made.

A combination of open-ended questions and forced-choice questions were asked. Open-ended questions, such as which three aspects of Bozeman the respondents liked and disliked, permitted enormous leeway in their answers. Systematic ways of categorizing their responses were developed after the sample had been interviewed. The Likert design forced-choice questions required respondents to say how strongly they agreed or disagreed with each statement. The responses ranged from strongly agree to strongly disagree. Most questions were substantive and specific, such as How do you feel about local sign ordinances, traffic, and subdivisions? A few were more general and theoretical, such as How do you feel about planning?

The second project was designed to understand migrants and their adjustments and satisfaction within the Gallatin Valley. A random sample of recent in-migrants was drawn in 1980 by identifying names that did not appear in the 1979 telephone directory. The telephone company at that time estimated that 4 percent of residents had unlisted numbers. This sampling technique permitted interviewing newcomers who had moved to the area during the previous six months. People in the first (1980) sample were asked only open-ended questions, that is, they answered the question in plain English. There were no ready-made answers for respondents to check yes or no or strongly agree or disagree. Categories for the forced-choice responses were established following completion of the interviews in 1980. The same sampling procedures were followed in 1981 and again in 1982. And each respondent was interviewed each year, over and over again, until 1985. The remaining 1980 respondents were interviewed five times, the 1981 respondents four times, and the 1982 respondents three times. Finally, a new sample of 23 newcomers was drawn in 1992.

This final sample, along with all the respondents who had been interviewed initially during the 1970s and in 1980-1983, were interviewed. This project permitted close and frequent examination of newcomers as they spoke of their origins, dreams and discouragement.

Much of the strength of these projects lies in the interview process. A personal interview each year was the source of all data. For some respondents, the same interviewer conducted the interview several years in a row. I interviewed many respondents four or more times. A few, quite incidentally, became friends and neighbors. The depth of information from this procedure cannot be obtained through any other method, short of clinical analysis. The thousands of interviews provide a large number of data for quantitative analyses. They also combine into oral histories rich in nuance and detail, humor and tragedy, tales of success and failure. They are the words of people who live in small beautiful towns, those who stay and, more commonly, those who leave.

The descriptions in this research are of several different stages of residence among participants. Some were long-term residents from the first time they were interviewed. Most were respondents who were first interviewed shortly after arriving in Bozeman, while their recollections of why they left where they had lived and how they felt about leaving were still fresh in their minds. Both old-timers and newcomers were reinterviewed systematically for at least eight and as long as 20 years.

The possible number of comparisons that can be made over time, between newcomers and old-timers and across several demographic characteristics, made reporting statistical differences cumbersome. To avoid inundating readers with nearly infinite detail, data analyses were deliberately kept to a minimum. Most data are reported as percentages and proportions, statistics that are familiar to most people. Some use is made of two other types of simple statistics, dispersion and association. The likelihood ratio chi square (L) is a measure of dispersion. It measures whether the way the data fall into the matrix, the table, is random. If the ratio is significant, the data could not be expected to have become organized in that manner randomly. Gamma (γ) is a proportional reduction in error measure that indicates the strength of association between two variables (Costner, 1965). These are interpreted as correlations, ranging from -1.0, which means every person behaved exactly the reverse of what had been predicted, to 1.0, which means everyone behaved in the expected fashion. A zero means there is no correlation at all between the two variables. Associations of .20 begin to merit attention, those of .40 clearly indicate that the variables are strongly linked. Those over .60 are worth shouting about, providing that the variables share some theoretically interesting properties and the nature of the dispersion is significant.

Serious analytic limitations are inherent in such a simplified approach. Other, more sophisticated statistics can more accurately indicate the causal relationships between three or more variables. Such analyses will be left for professional journals. Another limitation is that the few measures reported here are designed for particular types of data, referred to as levels of measurement. The statistics are sometimes reported for variables which are not of the same level as the statistic. Gamma is designed for nominal variables, such as men and women, old and young, rich and poor. When gamma is used for the most elementary 2 x 2 table, it is equivalent to Yule's Q (de Vaus, 1995).

Other more precise statistics could have been calculated for measurement and analyses. For example, Tau b is designed for ordinal data. As ordinal implies, these variables are ordered, such as annual incomes over $50,000 dollars, between 50 and 30, and under 30. For some variables, such as older and younger, the data are drawn from ordered data, which in this example is the age of participants. When that occurs, the measures are so similar that the difference between nominal and ordinal data are a matter of where to make the statistical cutting point in the division between older and younger or richer and poorer. Most nominal variables in this research have an underlying order, making both statistical measures appropriate. For a few, such as gender, there is no agreed-upon underlying dimension of order. Inclusion of all of the appropriate types of statistics for all of the data that could have been compared in this research would have made the text unmanageable. These statistics are not specifically designed to answer whether one variable causes another. Some critics maintain that causal analysis is not possible. Most social scientists try to explain what they can about how independent variables act on dependent variables. I draw upon the statistical data as just one type of information to explain what is happening to the people and their community. When what seems to be a causal process is evident, it is mentioned. Otherwise, readers are left to their own imaginations to account for what is causing what.

Respondents were not reminded of what they had said in previous interviews. Most retained some recollection of what they had said and many commented when they had made a major epistemic change in interpretation between one year and the next. A few seemed oblivious to the contradictions between the two. When respondents were aware of the changes, conscious reality testing of their conception occurred. This awareness permitted respondents to decide what was valuable to them, whether they liked or disliked what they discovered and whether they wanted to leave or stay.

The people who obviously shifted from loving the place to hating it effectively bypassed subjecting their illusory conception to test. Rather than saying "Was I ever mistaken!," they were very likely to move on without seriously considering whether they had been correct, or why they were incorrect. We called this category of out-migrants "unconscious romantics." They seemed to hold the place objectively responsible for their error in judgment, almost as if the place had changed during the interim rather than their interpretation of the place. These people did not modify their interpretation to become a richer and more valid conception of the reality of the town and its residents. They shifted from one invalid image to another.

Jim and Ruth Cardoza, mentioned in Chapter 2, exemplify unconsciousness. The first time they were interviewed, they described the town, the area and the residents in the most glowing terms, largely without empirical foundation. Their neighbors and local residents were friendly, even though they did not know them. The environment was beautiful, even though they had not spent time in it. And the community was progressive, although they did not say how. Their final interview, three years later, was a reversal of the first. Neighbors and residents were unfriendly, the environment distant and cold and the community archaic because the county attorney opposed bingo and gambling machines. This switch occurred in the minds of the Cardozas, who belonged to no organizations, did not visit the natural environment and, as far as the author could determine, rarely left the house except to do essential shopping. Their stated motives for coming to the Rockies where they could enjoy the outdoors in the friendly ambience of a small town obviously were not satisfied.

At the beginning of the two projects, no institutionalized persons were interviewed. This omission probably led to a slight underrepresentation of older people. During the course of the project, some respondents moved into retirement facilities, which alerted us to having omitted them in the first place. The intention had been to analyze only separate and independent households that decided to move or stay because of choices made by its members. We felt that free household migration was the most common and most universally important type. We also suspected that other types might be so different that they would deserve special consideration beyond the capabilities of this project.

By the 1990s, the aging and maturation of people who had been interviewed 10 and even 20 years earlier led them naturally to retirement homes. Four former respondents had moved into retirement facilities. One had Alzheimer's disease and was no longer mentally competent to be interviewed. One no longer wanted to be interviewed. A third lived alone following the illness and death of her husband. And one couple remained intact, energetic and alert. The number of cases was too small to enable many generalizations.

RELATIONSHIP BETWEEN SAMPLE RESPONSES

There is no simple, singular way to describe the responses people made to interviews and how those responses changed over time. A brief example about how people reported changes in their levels of satisfaction may give an inkling about the complexity of describing change over time. Satisfaction is only one of several dozen different indicators of changes that were measured in this study. Fifty-eight persons interviewed in 1976 were reinterviewed in 1980. Generally, their 1976 satisfaction was less than that of persons who had first been interviewed in 1972. Still, they reported higher satisfaction when first interviewed in 1976 than did the respondents first interviewed in 1972. And people first interviewed in 1980 reported the highest satisfaction of all first-year respondents.

By the 1990s, this trend toward higher satisfaction had been reversed. Among both recent arrivals and long-term residents, there was less satisfaction than there had been for comparable groups during the 1970s and 1980s. Several factors might account for these waxings and wanings of satisfaction. First, experimental bias might have been induced, leading persons who had been interviewed and then reinterviewed to report their level of satisfaction in successive interviews because the instrument had somehow sensitized them or because self-selection occurred in successive subsamples. A second explanation is that the town had changed in ways that led people to accurately respond earlier that the area was a better place and later that it was less desirable. A third explanation of potential experimental bias is that people who remain in the community regard it more positively over time. Experimental bias is difficult to disprove. The instrument was regarded as neutral during the pretest in 1972. How people interpreted it may have changed over time. Self-selection may have favored those persons more favorably disposed to the place. However, differences between the number of years people had lived there was much more significant than differences between samples in either 1976 or 1980. This indicates that research-induced influences were negligible in comparison to changes in perception attributable to accurate evaluations of actual changes in the community or increasing aggrandizement among those people who remain in the community.

AN EXCURSUS ON RESEARCH METHODS AND THEORY

Our interpretations about migration are based on different types of methods: survey, secondary data analysis and participant observation. Good science requires multiple approaches. Some social scientists wage relentless battles with each other about which method is best. Over the years, all methods have generated interesting, useful and accurate knowledge. $E = MC^2$ enjoys a stable reference the likes of which are nonexistent in social science. Social sciences, while able to incorporate methods (not measures) derived from physical sciences, lack the definitive quanta for incorporating all meaningful causal variables.

The core data for this analysis came from two longitudinal survey research projects conducted in the Gallatin Valley. Longitudinal means that the data were collected over an extended period rather than a single point in time. Trends can be observed. For example, changes in the characteristics of newcomers or of the differences between newcomers and old-timers can be observed.

Sociology requires clarification of the phenomena being discussed. Clarification does more than define the concepts to be studied and the ways they are operationalized. It also delineates the units of analysis that are specifically being studied. The general phenomenon studied here is how people interpret migration, particularly to small towns in beautiful rural areas of the West. The units of analysis are the individuals who move and stay, their households and the broader community. These are very different social units, separate yet interrelated. They usually are discussed independently to avoid confusing the reader and to lend more order to the text. Since individuals and community are interrelated, changes in one leads to changes in the other. For example, the marital status of individuals affects what people want as a community. Keeping these units of analysis clear and independent is an impossible or sterile luxury when discussing dynamic, complex, interrelated social phenomena over time.

When the study began in 1972, the individual was the primary unit of analysis. Individuals were considered to have demographic attributes such as being single, poor and educated. These attributes, it was assumed, would affect what residents wanted and liked about their community. What individuals wanted and liked regarding the community were also considered to be attributes. The community was conceived as a separate objective entity with its own attributes such as small size, natural setting and being home to friends and families. Keeping the individual and the community separate became increasingly difficult as each new sample was interviewed. The most complicating aspect was that people sometimes changed their attributes, conceptually becoming different people. Some returned to school. Others got married, divorced and remarried. Some changed economic status. While they were the same individuals, they became more difficult to analyze as part of a single category.

Thinking of people as distinct individuals was further complicated because of their involvement with others, particularly the family. While families are composed of individuals, they usually move and live as a group. The needs and satisfactions of one affect the other family members. Family members think of their families as units and they are regarded as units by others. Changes in the status of the individual as a unit may change the nature of the household. For example, when an individual gets married or divorced, has a child or has a child leave home, the family household unit changes. The family often is considered as a unit of analysis.

A household is different from a family. One person living alone is a household just as much as is an extended multiple-generation family with a dozen members. The definition of a household is the occupants of a single dwelling. Our discussions of family often consider other important characteristics such as whether children are present or people are married. People who live alone, while not technically a family, are discussed in the same context as a family because they have an attribute, such as being single, that is crucial for understanding the importance of the family. In fact, what is meant by a family is both confusing and contentious in the late 1990s. This study evades serious moral arguments regarding whether unmarried partners are a family or single parents with children who live with someone else are a family.

Community is the third unit of analysis. Community is more difficult to clearly define than is the individual person. Generally, it is the area in which residents collectively reside, obtain their goods and services, interact with each other and share a common identity. In the eastern half of the Gallatin Valley, several small towns are intermixed with rural neighborhoods, suburban-type subdivisions and isolated farms and ranches. Each of these has some or all of the characteristics of a community. For the purposes of this study, the entire study area is subsumed into the concept of community. Considering this differentiated area as a community has been done largely for convenience, to establish a single landmark and concept. It is not an entirely satisfying or accurate use of the concept. It does not correspond to the ideal of gemeinschaft. Yet, some portions of the study area approach that ideal much more than do others. Ranchers near Maudlow are close to the ideal. The intensity with which established residents of Belgrade share activities, have common interests and identify with their town and each other is much greater than most subdivisions in the area. A few outlying suburbs were discovered to be bleakly impersonal and asocial, with especially high mobility. In the course of five consecutive years of interviewing, some of the residences in these areas because the homes of a new household of respondents. The original randomly drawn respondents had moved away, replaced by new randomly drawn respondents. Such places usually had many For Sale signs and visible problems such as weed growth and no visible human activity.

Gemeinschaft is an ideal way of considering community. There are no pure gemeinschaft in the study area because of rapid mobility and the constant influences from urban life. For lack of a more precise and succinct word, "community" is used. Most residents comfortably use the term in this general manner. A few restrict their discussions of community to a small, exclusive group with which they share especially important activities, such as close neighbors and devoted members of a congregation.

There also are practical purposes for treating the notion of community at a general level. Residents vary enormously in what they see as the boundaries of their community, each defining it according to where they live and how they define it. Except for specific locales, it would be impossible to get common agreement on what they mean or even where it is located. Practically, the residents live in a real world which has unique geographic space and features. Residents determine what happens to that place and what kind of place it is and will become. How the spaces and special features of the area are exploited and preserved, in turn, influence who is attracted to the area, who is likely to be satisfied and who stays. Concern with esoteric meanings of community can distract attention from the objective and concrete impacts that people collectively make on the area they commonly occupy. Their common presence and activities in the natural area define what kind of community it is.

The most concise and predictable way of knowing how something causes something else is through the experimental method. The causal factor is termed the "independent variable" and the response is called the "dependent variable." Experiments attempt to carefully control for, that is exclude or nullify, any other influences that might cause the response, except for the independent variable. There are diverse methods for excluding and nullifying external influences, such as random sampling, which was used in this study. The experimental method is a luxury that is rarely applicable to real-life conditions where the independent and dependent variables are complex phenomena. The method is sufficiently precise and sufficiently applicable for more limited questions, such as those asked in market research regarding which new product is favored by consumers. Even so, as the Coca Cola Company belatedly discovered, even carefully controlled experiments may not fully explain consumer preferences. Several experiments indicated that consumers preferred a new formula for the Coca Cola Company. The fact was that, for a variety of reasons which were not controlled in the experiments, customers wanted to keep the old formula, which is now called Classic Coke®.

This research is not an experiment, but it does investigate causes and effects. On a very practical level, in-migration is an independent variable that causes changes in the community, a dependent variable. On a more theoretical level, satisfaction is an independent variable that influences decisions to move. People are presumably less satisfied with where they used to live than they hope to be after moving to a scenic recreational place. Satisfaction is based on expectations, what people want from a place. Satisfaction is further complicated by the consideration of alternatives. As long as residents think about the relative advantages of living somewhere else, they will be somewhat dissatisfied. They potentially may move if the level of that dissatisfaction becomes sufficiently uncomfortable. Or residents may try to make their lives and their community better, more satisfactory, thereby reducing the tension they feel by comparing home with somewhere else. Unfortunately, from a scientific perspective, satisfaction is a dependent variable, partially determined by their quality of experience in the community. A tautolology exists. Being a migrant decreases the quality of the experience, which causes dissatisfaction.

During the earliest phase of this research, the community, more precisely the physical and social characteristics of the community, was one independent variable. The community was experienced by the residents with their demographic and social characteristics. These characteristics are an intervening variable. The dependent variable is resident satisfaction across a host of personal, social and environmental dimensions with the area and community. The dependent variable includes support for planning to preserve and develop their idea of the good community. These independent and dependent variables are useful for organizing information, for understanding changes and for focusing attention on preserving and creating a good place to live.

As the analyses became more complete, as I lived in the area longer and studied the region more intensively, migration emerged as a concept that demanded special attention. It seemed to be a key to understanding the characteristics of residents, their satisfaction, the impacts on the community and how that community was being rapidly changed without much activity to preserve what was most attractive about it. However, the variables interact with each other. Satisfaction affects the characteristics of community. Changes in the community affect satisfaction. It is a classic chicken-or-egg problem. The independent variable, community, was also a dependent variable that was influencing who moved and whether they stayed. What had started as a simple empirical and conceptual analysis of cause and effect had become complex. The types of people who moved in were creating a new and different kind of place which, in turn, was making it more attractive to still different kinds of new people. The rapidity with which these changes and their mutual effects were occurring was modifying the very meaning of the variables being analyzed. The phenomena which had been of research interest were themselves changing.

Random samples from all projects were selected for individuals, as their names appeared in directories. The selected telephone number was called and the interviewer introduced him- or herself and described the nature of the project. Screening questions were asked. If the person was a full-time resident who had no intention of moving away and was not a student or in the military service, they were requested to become part of the survey. During the 1970s and early 1980s, most people were cooperative, actually eager to be interviewed. In 1972, only 8 percent of the people who were contacted declined to participate. By 1990, many more did not want to be bothered, though they were only being asked for a single interview. The early respondents had been told that they would be interviewed several times over the years, that the project was interested in examining changes in their lives and how they felt about the community. They also were asked if they were part of a couple. If they were, the interviewer requested that both members of the couple be present for the interview. An appointment then was made to meet them at their residence.

While sampling and interviewing are mechanical procedures, they require sensitive personal skills. Interviewers were selected because they had demonstrated both practical and social skills. Most were advanced undergraduate students who had taken several courses from me before they began interviewing. Over a 20-year period, only eight interviewers, including myself, collected over 90 percent of the data. In 1972, the first interviews were collected as part of a class project. The interviewers were marvelous: friendly, cheery, efficient and dependable. Years later, respondents often asked about previous interviewers. Early in the project, there were many forgotten or neglected appointments by people in the sample. Since their residences were often 10 or 20 miles from town, a missed appointment posed considerable inconvenience. With experience, interviewers learned to call in advance to be sure the respondent was at home. There was not a single harassment or complaint throughout the 20 years and thousands of interviews.

The first few minutes of the interview were designed primarily to reassure the people to be interviewed. They were given a one-page summary of the research proposal which included the telephone numbers of the project director. They were asked if the head of the household was the person who was listed in the directory. If it was not, then the person who they said was the household head became the unit of analysis, the primary interviewee. However, exact detailed information for the other adult also was collected. Consequently, the number of individuals interviewed was actually half again as many as the number of listed cases. In addition, many questions were asked about other household members. Their responses gave a much more complete, and sometimes opposed, perspective of how the family was finding life in the area. Thus, while the individual was the primary unit of analysis, data for the household also were collected and interpreted.

SERENDIPITOUS HINTS OF POPULATION INSTABILITY

Data generally are thought of as information deliberately collected to be analyzed. Occasionally, data appear which had not received much thought, which were not previously intended to affect the analyses. Such serendipitous data unexpectedly began to show up early in this research and continued to provide important information 20 years later. The first surprises showed up in 1976 as telephone calls were made to arrange the second round of interviews with people who had been respondents in 1972. About half of the sample interviewed in 1976 had moved away! Remember, the sample was composed of people who regarded themselves as permanent residents. That unexpected finding was to become definitive of the instability of residents in the area. The community structure was more like sand than rock. Despite their intentions to remain in a stable community, most residents were quickly moving on. By 1980, just eight years after the initial interviews, nearly four out of five of the original sample had moved away. In fact, the turnover of population was undoubtedly even higher. Since the samples were composed of people who were still residing where they were listed in the directory, only the more permanent residents were in the sample. People who had moved on without ever having a listing, and those who had moved away since being listed, were not interviewed in the first place. Yet they were more permanent at that moment in the Gallatin Valley than anywhere else. The level of residential instability, then, is greater than the more conservative yet still very high figures reported for respondents.

It is important to return to the consideration of pervasive theories of migration, particularly economic or other single prime variable explanations of migration. Practically speaking, all migration can be examined via a single perspective, although much richness and detail is lost in the exercise. Once the single-minded examination is complete, much remains to be explained. Philosophically, mathematically, the conversion cannot be done because of analytic limitations.

In effect, these broad generalizations, combined with specific examples, are a social application of the Heisenberg Principle. A rigid empiricist could claim that any of the variables being considered by a potential migrant could be converted to economic or psychological units. The Heisenberg Principle says that more energy would be required to collect the data and make the conversions over an infinite number of variables, which the scientist might consider, than exists in the universe. Researchers carefully pare down the number of variables and the number of categories per variable to a size that is manageable and, hopefully, valid and reliable. Even if this is done, the attempt to convert variables, which are more essentially political or social or biological than economic, into economic or some other quantitative terms is inefficient. To do so obfuscates the fundamentally complex nature of the variables of life and likely lends a scientific aura to an essentially metaphysical operation.

The notion that human behavior cannot be understood outside its milieu is sacrosanct in sociology (Small, 1916). Meaningful interpretation of any particular social action requires familiarity with the immediate social system and the zeitgeist of its actors (Park, 1952). So much abstraction is introduced that interpretations are scarcely recognizable to someone familiar with the "real life" setting. Small declared that, "many people get so interested in the tools that they forget all about the work which the tools are expected to do. The common problem of the social sciences is to understand people, past, present, and maybe future; but we get so wrought up in championship of our favorite method of approaching people that we may omit to deal very intimately with the people themselves" (1916, p. 220). Error is less in the specific methods they use than in what they omit. However sloppy, conceptually simplistic or incomplete these data may be, I trust my general conclusions. I doubt that any other competent sociologist, given the same exposure I have had, would disagree with them.

THE USE OF CASE STUDIES

The case studies are reported as exactly as possible in the words of the participants, but altered to assure anonymity. Specific names and states of origin and destination have been changed. The names of adjacent states have been substituted in order to retain a similar profile of where they came from and where they were moving. Specific occupations also have been changed. For example, the owner of a flower shop might be described as the owner of an antique shop. Professional occupations are described with few changes.

Most of the observations from case studies are my own. I administered the questionnaire and recorded the responses myself. A few of the case studies also include observations by other interviewers. I read each questionnaire shortly after it was handed in by the interviewers. We frequently discussed cases. We were especially sensitive to rapid changes in respondents' satisfaction with the place, whether they were becoming more pessimistic or optimistic and whether they were considering moving. These discussions also gave us a chance to check our hunches, our gradually evolving theory. These discussions provided many valuable insights and opportunities to gradually modify explanations about who would stay and why. Another valuable aspect of these discussions was that they were lively opportunities to assert, challenge and resolve observations and issues with others. Disagreements about what we thought was happening in the lives of participants were infrequent. When we had disagreements, they usually had to do with underlying differences in our respective interpretations of why respondents said or did something.

As the years passed, the number of disagreements declined. The length of the project made it possible to resolve our disagreements by simply waiting for the answer to appear. In most cases, we didn't have to wait long: a year or two or three. A longitudinal study, despite its difficulties, is a luxury in social science because so many tangible questions are answered during the research project. Patterns began to emerge that we collectively recognized. For example, we initially assumed that economic failure was a more common reason for feeling dissatisfied and moving away than it actually was. This became apparent for a variety of reasons. Many poor people stayed and were happy. Many relatively wealthy people became dissatisfied and moved. As these observations accumulated, we watched other influences even more carefully.

At the end of each year, all data were tabulated and cross-classified. These data provided another more actuarial source of information. By looking at these data analyses, it was possible to get a more general sense of how the aggregate of our subsamples and the sample as a whole were behaving. Patterns we had suspected on the basis of literature review and individual interviews began to appear. Younger participants were more likely to move away. People who had originally moved with the stated intention of finding a better job were more likely to move again, giving the same reason for their subsequent move.

Patterns that filled a void in research or challenged the observations of others began to appear frequently, as had been hypothesized. For example, women were significantly more likely than men to move to a small, safe, slow-paced town.

For years, social researchers have argued the issue of whether induction or deduction is the appropriate perspective for their sciences. The arguments seem naive to us now. While our research may have been consciously conducted as retroduction, the interaction between induction and deduction, a similar process probably is nearly universal, project by research project, science by science. Constantly drawing inference from facts and then testing inference from more facts seems inevitable.

Jonathan Turner has termed sociology a "multiple paradigm science" (1991). Variety and complementarity are as common to methodology as they are to theory. The procedures followed in this project are a combination of techniques that have origins in both inductive and deductive orientations. The project was initiated around a clearly stated theoretical perspective. Measures of each variable were carefully operationalized, following conventional survey research techniques for a panel study. However, the project was also a case study of both the migrants who move into high-amenity areas and the process of migration and its effects on the area itself. This distinction is not hairsplitting. Individual respondents are one unit of analysis and the community is another.

Intensive interviews with the same people that extended over several years form case studies rich with interpretation of behavior provided by the respondents themselves. They are the flesh around the bones, the visible content around the less visible normative structures that both guide behavior and theories to account for behavior. They give intensive accounts of how and why people think they move. Each of these case studies complements the statistical analyses.

The survey and case study approaches stimulated and complemented each other throughout the project. Each became a validity and reliability check of the other. Initially, the open-ended questions in the interview directed respondents to consider a broad set of issues about their migration history. Following the first year of interviews, a protocol was developed to code responses. The protocol was constructed out of categories provided by the respondents. For example, respondents gave nine different types of reasons for moving to the area in order to use the natural environment. These categories formed the basis of the coding that was used in all subsequent interviews. Content analysis was used to establish the initial response categories from open-ended responses provided by the respondents. We then generated many of the more general variable names, such as income or social environment, from sociological forms and from our observations. The first research project had shown that the primary reasons people moved involved income and occupations, family and friendship ties, the physical and social characteristics of the town and the natural environment. These categories were retained throughout the analyses.

The interviews of the first year of the early 1980s project also stimulated new kinds of observations that would be collected in subsequent years. For example, it soon became apparent that many newcomers were indeed conforming to one of our underlying assumptions. Many were perceiving Bozeman and the surrounding area to be almost flawless, denying the place much depth and reality. These effusive respondents were also the most likely to speak with unmitigated enthusiasm about their future. They seemed self-assured that they had a clearer vision of the special qualities of the area. They were especially determined to take advantage of these qualities. Some focused on the aesthetic visual qualities, as if they were going to become one with them. Others said that they were going to immerse themselves in outdoor recreation or community activities. During the first-year interviews, these self-assured statements of what they were going to do sometimes seemed to make little sense. Many of the respondents who made them seemed to have little background for what they were saying was going to be a major purpose in their lives. Even as they spoke of hiking every weekend or experiencing community, many people had yet to be outdoors or participate in any local organizations or activities.

Respondents who said they were going to find satisfaction through behaviors in which they were neither currently engaged nor had much past experience in, prompted us to start making casual guesses about their probable future satisfaction with Bozeman. Interviewers did not begin making guesses until they had been interviewing for several weeks. The newness of their job, the intrinsic interest of talking to people about their lives, kept their minds occupied. During the first few weeks, they would come back to the office and say something like "I just interviewed the Johnsons. They were so enthusiastic about living here. Both of them have lived in Cleveland all of their lives. They are happy just to be here. They haven't done much yet except move into their house and relax, but they say they will start doing a lot after they get settled." Later, the interviewers started making observations beyond what the respondents told them. They began to say things like "He talked the whole time about how great it is to be out of the rat race. She never disagreed with him, but she didn't seem to have much reason to be here except to be with him" or "They kept bragging about the house and neighborhood they had had back in San Antonio. They didn't really give a clear statement about why they had moved here. They seem like people who would be happier in a big city" or "Mr. Dark is an enthusiastic big-game hunter. He talked about all the hunting and fishing he used to do. It's funny. He didn't really look like a outdoors man and he hadn't been out camping yet. I hate to say it, but he is so overweight that he looks like he could have a heart attack at any time."

Volumes have been written about systematic approaches to qualitative analyses of social behavior. C. Wright Mills (1959) believed that the sociological perspective is intrinsically interesting. He cherished curiosity that led sociologists to look for answers to the question of why people behave as they do, as social beings. I believe a system is endemic to the process of longitudinal case study analysis as long as the interviewers are energetic and intelligent and the information interesting. The interviewers were beginning to conceptualize the information provided by the respondents. They were recognizing that what some respondents were saying was not consistent with what they were doing or seemed likely to be doing in the future. This gradual process of listening to what people said and then evaluating whether we agreed with their predictions prompted us to formulate a set of intuitive evaluations that were made at the close of each interview with new respondents after the first year. Respondents never saw these comments and questions.

These evaluations served several purposes. They made the initial interviews a little more fun and exciting. At the end of each interview, formulating these impressions gave the interviewer a chance to agree or disagree with what the respondent had just said. We were able to note whether we thought the respondents' expectations were too high or too low for what they were likely to experience. We could judge whether the respondents were experiencing a traumatic change in their lives that might affect their satisfaction. If we felt they were, we characterized the nature of their trauma. We also recorded whether they were likely to move away within five years, and we speculated what would cause them to move.

The intuitive evaluations also provided an incentive for paying attention to and recording information provided by respondents. They stimulated interviewers to pay attention to details that might explain what was influencing the perceptions and behaviors of respondents. They encouraged interviewers to go beyond the established limits set by the protocol of the main section of the questionnaire. The interviewers were challenged to reflect about influences to migration that had not been anticipated through the review of the literature or our categorization of responses developed to reliably codify and data and to validly encapsulate the behaviors and beliefs of respondents.

Methodology is the study of methods. The contribution of valid and reliable methods for social research can scarcely be overstated. It is so important as to be a shibboleth, a sacred cow around which endless rites of purification of the discipline occur. New offerings for how to achieve a better method for arriving at truth are advocated. Obsolete, usually simpler methods fall into disfavor. As time passes, such approaches often are rediscovered and resurrected. A continuing battle between case study and more actuarial techniques is waged. This research has been conducted with an eclectic perspective on methods: it is a case study of case studies built around panel survey techniques.

MOVING ON — AGAIN

The relatively rapid out-migration among people who had moved to the Gallatin Valley has been the most recurrent theme in this research. Although some categories of residents were more likely to stay than others, or stayed longer than others, most people eventually moved away. The questions of where did they move, why they chose those places and how they felt about Bozeman when they left were an integral part of this research.

During the surveys conducted in the early 1980s, participants in the research agreed to notify the research project office if they decided to move. Few participants actually called the office. There are more pressing matters to attend to than talking to the local sociologist during the final days before moving. Several didn't really know they were moving almost until they drove away.

Their absence was noted during the preparation for the next round of interviews the following year. They were immediately sent a follow-up questionnaire. The questions were almost identical to the original interview questions except that people were asked about their reasons for leaving the Gallatin Valley, for choosing their new location and their satisfaction in both places.

The most general and unsurprising finding was that most people who moved away were leaving for nearly the same reasons they had left their previous hometowns. They were also moving to their new locations for remarkably similar reasons to those they had given a year earlier for having moved to the Bozeman area, with one notable exception. They said they wanted the security and friendliness of small-town life combined with the cosmopolitan atmosphere and the diverse opportunities of the city. They were moving to metropolitan areas, small suburbs near major cities.

The move to Montana had established a legacy which sometimes was played out in the migration away from the study area. For example, among married couples, if one objected to the move to Montana in the first place, they were more likely to move away within a year. The objecting one was usually the wife. Men without children said they had enjoyed living in Bozeman more than did the single women or couples who moved away. Single people who had met with objections were no more likely to move away than those who had come to Bozeman without any objections from others.

One of the most noticeable differences among the out-migrants who moved out of the State of Montana (and almost all of the out-migrants left Montana) was how critical they had become. They listed significantly more criticisms on the mailed questionnaires about the Gallatin Valley than they had given about where they had moved from a year earlier. The experiences of moving, especially to and then away from their dream, seemed to have made them more aware of qualities in the social and natural environments where they had lived previously.

Chapter 5

Newcomers and Changes in Lifestyles

Descriptions in this and in later chapters are based on interviews collected at different stages in the process of becoming a resident in the area. Some were collected shortly after respondents had arrived in Bozeman while their recollections of why they left where they had lived and how they felt about leaving were still fresh in their minds. Comparisons of newcomers usually are made between initial interviews conducted shortly after they arrived. Newcomers in the early 1980s are compared with those who arrived a decade later. Other descriptions come from old-timers or with newcomers who had weathered a few years in the area.

Many respondents were eager to try to convince others or to receive validation of their reason for moving. During the first-year interviews, they zealously articulated what sometimes verged on a worldview about why they came to Bozeman. They spoke convincingly about what they were expecting to find and how that was going to occur because they knew what was right and they believed this was the right place to get it. Their views of what was right varied broadly. For some it was a Christian community, for others an ectopia and for others a place to make a decent living. In later interviews, disconsolate respondents tenaciously held to their worldview of what was right and, therefore, what was wrong with the area once it failed to fulfill their expectations. For these respondents, the worldview based on hope was so real that they forgot the essential truth about the place. The Gallatin Valley was real even if the schools did not throw out books offensive to some religious groups. Its air pollution and suburban sprawl were real, however much they offended the environmentalists and the economic opportunities were few, despite the belief that, with hard work, good ideas and investment, there would be financial success for those who wanted it.

Towns are composites of myriad factors that create their idiosyncratic characters and allow them to function. Planning, as a profession, ostensibly considers all factors in helping towns adapt the unique features and conditions of an area to the preferences of residents, albeit within statutory constraints. In fact, this visionary orientation is likely to be only partially achieved, particularly in rapidly growing scenic and recreation areas. Planning in these areas spins around a vortex of development, leaving planners precious little time or creativity to do much more than enforce codes and resist the most blatant attempts to destroy local natural and social environments. Realistically, planners are doing a commendable job if traffic flows on the roads, the garbage is collected and there are enough police officers, fire fighters, school teachers, administrative personnel and facilities to perform essential public services. Provision of public services becomes the de facto rationale for planning. This is no mean task. However, the level of tension and the insecurity of the job increase geometrically when planners attempt to go beyond this narrowly conscribed assignment into ethical and aesthetic considerations of how to preserve precious and desirable qualities of the natural and social environments.

CHARACTERISTICS OF NEWCOMERS

The new settlers to the Gallatin Valley come from throughout the United States (Table 5.1). Among 1980s newcomers, one-fifth had been born in Montana, although many of those had lived in another state before moving to Bozeman. By 1990, that number had nearly doubled. During the 70s and 80s, more (7.5%) had been born in California and Minnesota than other states. By the early 1990s, those coming from California had doubled. Others were more likely to have been born in high-population eastern states, such as New York, Pennsylvania and Michigan, or in nearby North Dakota. The rest were primarily drawn from the Midwest and the West. Few had been born in the South.

Most newcomers were experienced movers. Their move to Bozeman was a first for very few migrants. About 40 percent had moved three or more times during the previous 10 years. The state in which they had most recently resided was quite different from their birthplace. One-third of the newcomers came from some other location in Montana. Only California (8%) and Colorado (7%) had been home for more than 5 percent during the 1980s. California became by far the most common state of origin during the 1990s. Nearly one-third (32%) came from the Pacific Coast, almost all from California. Since California had nearly thirty million residents, it would be expected to be the primary source of population for the region. Few came from the southern Midwest, the South or New England. Those areas have their own rural recreation centers with natural attractions, as well as regional identity. As a result, rural New England, Appalachia and the Ozarks have acted as magnets within their respective regions. They have retained people who otherwise might have headed west. Westerners who have acquired a taste for open spaces and mountains look toward the southwest and the Northern Rockies to find more of what they are looking for. Westerners also may have fewer established

Table 5.1
**Geographic Origins, Frequency of Migration and Residential Ownership Reported (%)
by Newcomers in Early 1980s (N=390) and Early 1990s (N=45)**

Marital Status	(%)	(%)	γ
Single	(27)	(29)	.05
Married	(73)	(71)	
State of Birth			
Montana	(19)	(33)	.14
Mountain	(9)		
Pacific	(11)	(25)	
Other	(61)	(42)	
State of Most Recent Residence			
Montana	(32)	(7)	.20**
Mountain	(16)	(40)	
Pacific	(18)	(29)	
Other	(34)	(24)	
City Size of Most Recent Residence			
Under 10,000	(30)	(24)	-.08
10,000-999,999	61	43	
1,000,000+	9	14	
Residential Location			
Country	13	17	-.04
Small town	33	34	
Outer suburbs	27	19	
City	27	30	
Years Lived in Most Recent Place of Residence			
-3	34	36	.07
3-10	48	36	
10+	18	28	

Table 5.1 *continued*

	(%)	(%)	γ
Number of Previous Moves in Past 10 Years			
1	24	15	.31*
2-3	37	43	
4+	39	43	
Ownership of Recent Residence			
Rented	43	43	.07
Owned	51	43	
Living with parents	6	13	
Household Income in 1980 Dollars			
Under 15,000	26	56	-.53***
15,000-49,999	53	37	
50,000+	21	7	

*.05 level of significance
**.01 level of significance
***.001 level of significance

social bonds to anchor them, because most of their families had migrated within the past generation.

Most migrants to small towns in other parts of the United States originated in larger cities. About half of the newcomers came directly from a city or a suburb in the early 1980s (54%) and the early 1990s (49%). People moving to the Gallatin Valley more frequently had moved directly from towns the size of Bozeman or smaller than occurred in other rural areas, although they may have once resided in a metropolitan area. In the 1980s, 13 percent came from farms or villages with fewer than 2,500 residents. Another 33 percent came from towns with 2,500 to 10,000 residents. In the 1990s, even more came from such small places (51%). Most frequently, newcomers came from places with 10,000 to 50,000 residents. In the 1980s, fewer than 10 percent came directly to Bozeman from cities of 1,000,000 or more. By the 1990s, the percentage had increased to almost 15 percent. Their most recent move makes newcomers appear to be less metropolitan than they are. When asked about their previous three residential locations, most indicated they had recently lived in cities.

Metropolitan and nonmetropolitan categories distinguish densely populated urban counties from those less populated. The distinction also implies that there are urban people and rural people, types of people who categorically differ from each other. While these categories may accurately describe extremes, they are of limited value for distinguishing the new nonmetropolitan migration.

There are rural people who live their entire lives in the country and big-city residents who never leave the metropolis. But there are enormous variations among most people that make classifying them as metropolitan or nonmetropolitan difficult. Even if they remain in the same place their entire lives, they may have lived in both the country and the city. The places where they grew up or lived are likely to have increased in size. By 1960, over four-fifths of the U.S. population lived in standard metropolitan areas (SMAs). Many nonmetropolitan areas became metropolitan between 1950 and 1980.

Most people did not stay in the same place. Americans typically change residence every five years. Migrants, like the people who moved to Bozeman, move even more frequently. Over one-third of Bozeman newcomers had lived three years or less in their previous location. Roughly three-quarters had lived there less than 10 years. Only 10 percent had lived there 20 years or longer. By the 1990s, a slightly higher percentage of people (28%) who moved to Bozeman had resided in their previous location for 10 years than had occurred among the 1980s newcomers (18%). Most live in cities some of the time and in town or the country at other times. While they were born metro or nonmetro, their migration patterns reflect diverse experiences through which they become neither one nor the other, an urban restlessness.

Creating a sociodemographic profile of the average newcomers is tempting. They are primarily young and early middle-aged, white, college-educated adults, more likely married than single. Beyond these characteristics, a profile would be misleading. They correspond closely to the characteristics of turnaround migrants in New England and the North-Central and Northwestern states. They share characteristics with massive numbers of modern migrants, save the exodus of retirees who moved to the Sun Belt. They are old enough to be independent from their families of origin, yet young enough to have become consciously restricted by concerns like paying for childrens' education, optimizing retirement programs and taking advantage of low mortgage payments. They also have sufficient education and training to acquire satisfactory employment once they move. Their incomes are notably low, given their education. Whereas most (53%) 1980s newcomers fell into the middle income category, many (56%) 1990s newcomers were near or below the poverty line. Late middle-aged persons do not feel they can afford to risk economic losses for quality-of-life gains, while many among them may have optimized a balance between the two and decided not to move until retirement.

Migrants to Bozeman were largely young and early middle-aged adults (Table 5.2). Their profile, though, resembled the aging face of America (Lichter et al., 1981). The percentage of newcomers over 55 years of age nearly doubled, from 8 percent to 15 percent between the early 1980s and the early 1990s. In the early 80s, 50 percent were under 35. Ten years later, this figure had dropped to 49 percent. The gender, educational and occupational characteristics of new arrivals remained similar between the 1970s and the 1990s. Women's ages average about two years younger than men, which is about the difference in their ages at marriage. There

Table 5.2
Gender, Age and Number of Children of Newcomers to Gallatin Valley during Early 1980s and Early 1990s

	1980s % (N=390)	1990s % (N=47)	γ
Gender			
Single man	10	11	.03
Single woman	17	15	
Couple	73	75	
Number of Children			
None	48	36	.30**
1-3	49	49	
4+	3	15	
Age of Female Respondents			
Under 35	61	49	.24
35-54	31	38	
55+	8	13	
Age of Male Respondents			
Under 35	54	28	.45*
35-54	59	56	
55+	7	16	

*.05 level of significance
**.01 level of significance

were about 10 percent more women under 25 than men. At the other end of the age spectrum, there were a few more women over 65, indicating their greater longevity combined with the propensity to move as they near retirement. Women outnumber men by about 4 percent in all of the samples.

Newcomers to Bozeman tended to be highly educated, as could be expected for a college town (Table 5.3). Throughout the entire study period, over three-fourths had attended college and most had graduated. Men were slightly more likely to have higher overall attainment. Thirty percent reported graduating from college and another 30 percent had done postgraduate study. The occupational characteristics of people who moved to Bozeman are consonant with their

Table 5.3
Education and Occupation Characteristics of Men and Women Newcomers to the Gallatin Valley during the Early 1980s and Early 1990s

	1980s	1990s	γ
Education of Women Respondents			
High school	25	13	.11
Some college	27	37	
BA or more	48	50	
Education of Male Respondents			
High school	19	19	-.12
Some college	21	29	
BA or more	60	52	
Occupation of Women Respondents			
White collar	51	49	.05
Blue collar	49	51	
Occupation of Male Respondents			
White collar	77	50	.53**
Blue collar	23	50	

*.05 level of significance

educational achievement. About three-fourths of the men and one-half of the women were employed in white collar work. Among women, the most common occupation was housewife. Nevertheless, most (56%) were employed outside the home.

One migrant to Bozeman in 17 (6%) was setting up their first household since living with his or her parents and consequently had neither owned nor rented a house. About one-half (51%) had owned or had been buying the house they lived in before moving to Bozeman. The remainder (43%) had rented.

WHY THEY LEFT THEIR PREVIOUS LOCATION

People consider many diverse and idiosyncratic factors when they are thinking about moving (Table 5.4). Respondents were asked to describe and rank the importance of their reasons for deciding to leave where they used to live. Reasons related to work and income accounted for nearly 60 percent of the responses. These

Table 5.4
Considerations about Leaving Their Previous Location Reported (%) by Newcomers to the Gallatin Valley in Early 1980s and in Early 1990s

	1980s % (N=390)	1990s % (N=47)	γ
First Considered Moving			
Days before leaving	4	11	-.04
Less than one year	48	39	
More than one year	48	50	
Reason Wanted to Leave			
Job	61	61	-.04
Social ties	18	26	
Constructed environment	17	9	
Physical environment	3	4	
Who Decided to Leave			
Man	35	29	.15
Woman	24	20	
Equal	41	51	
Did Anyone Object to Leaving?			
No	56	77	-.45*
Yes	44	23	
Reasons for Objection to Leaving			
Job/work	16	17	.07
Social ties	79	75	
Constructed environment	3	-	
Natural environment	2	9	
First Reason for Choosing Gallatin Valley			
Employment	54	45	.21
Social ties	26	19	
Constructed environment	12	28	
Natural environment	7	9	

*significant at .01

included being out of work or disliking the work they had, as well as anticipating professional advancement or higher income somewhere else. Diverse, usually negative, reasons related to social ties were given by another 18 percent. These involved wanting to get away from a divorced spouse, an abusive family and memories of a loved one who had died. About the same number felt that their previous location had an unacceptable social environment. Overcrowding, crime and pollution were mentioned most frequently. Reasons related to the natural environment, such as being too isolated, lacking natural areas and poor climate, were mentioned less often (3%) as the primary reasons for deciding to leave.

While questions of work and income were the most important reasons for leaving their previous location, nearly 40 percent of the sample did not even mention them. Once mentioned, they were not frequently mentioned again. Only about one in 10 respondents mentioned work or income factors as a second reason and fewer than one in 10 mentioned them as a third or fourth reason for leaving where they used to live.

The alternative reasons for leaving express the noneconomic motives of the migrants to Bozeman. About one-fourth mentioned undesirable situations with family and friends or social ties as their second most important reason for leaving where they had previously lived; a similar number mentioned these as their third and fourth reasons. They alluded to their own change in lifestyle, away from previous friends and companions. Several respondents said that they had wanted to get away from the heavy drinking and drug use of their former companions. Nearly one-third reported that they had left because they didn't like their former community. The most common reasons involved environmental problems, such as pollution and overcrowding, although a few objected to its size or inadequate services. Another one-fourth mentioned social characteristics of the community as reasons for leaving. These were as diverse as "All that the wives thought about was cosmetics and clothes" to "They didn't care about quality in the schools, the police, the way the town looked . . . anything." Fewer than 10 percent reported that the second most important reason they had left was because they didn't like the natural environment. However, the environment exerted an ambient influence on decisions to move away. Nearly 40 percent mentioned it as their third or fourth consideration.

These figures indicate that people moved for many reasons and that the intensity they felt regarding their reasons also differed. Although they mentioned economic factors initially, most later mentioned noneconomic reasons. The absence of family and friends became progressively important, as did their dislike of the physical characteristics of their community and its surrounding natural environment.

Among married couples, both spouses (41%) or husbands (35%) usually wanted most to move away among newcomers. More old-timers (51%) had been egalitarian in their choice. Many people experienced some objections to their move. Old-timers (23%) recalled significantly less opposition than did newcomers (44%). Other members of their family usually did not object. About 9 percent of the wives and children did not want to move away. Four percent of the husbands felt that way. People out of their immediate family, other relatives and close friends, objected more frequently. The loss of these close personal ties was the primary objection to moving. Only 44 out of the 390 newcomer households in the 1980s objected to moving away because of employment or income factors. Economic factors were pulling at very few migrants to stay where they had lived. Only a few regretted losing economic opportunities.

The decision to leave a place and the decision to move to another place are separate yet somewhat interdependent choices (Roseman, 1984). Newton's second law of thermodynamics says that everyone has to live somewhere. The logical relationship between leaving and arriving in space leads to a number of intriguing social questions. The first question is how consistently the motives for leaving one place are related to choosing the next. A second is whether different types of people have different motives for making either choice. Especially interesting is how their satisfaction in a place is related to what they are looking for and whether they find it. This question involves how people's expectations about a place are satisfied and whether they adjust their expectations if they are not satisfied. Finally, the question of how satisfaction is associated with deciding to leave a place provides an indication about the process of searching for a home.

The most general reason for people moving away was that they expected much more than they found. People who moved away because they felt disappointed usually either accepted responsibility for their error in judgment or blamed the community for not being as they had expected it to be. People who accepted responsibility, sadder but wiser, philosophically accepted their error. The costs of wisdom were frequently high: a nest egg and a dream. These people most frequently referred to their choice as a mistake. Many were good-natured about it and were looking forward to moving on to a more realistic and suitable way of life. Most would move to a city in the Northwest. One of the few big-city easterners who headed straight back to Manhattan after a year in Bozeman said,

For five years, I had been imagining what the perfect life in Bozeman would be like. After being here for six months, I was bored. I was still traveling half the time. I left close friends who are vital and interested in their work and what is happening in the rest of the world. I realized I am just as compulsive and crazy as they are and I will be happy to get back with them. I even missed the traffic and the noise. I have met a lot of really nice people in Bozeman, but they lack the inflexible determination of the professional people back home. I will still come back to fish on my time off for a couple of weeks every summer, like I did before I moved here. I'll leave the laid back pace for somebody else. But I never would have known if I hadn't tried it.

People who blamed their failure on attributes of the place presented an angry or bitter contrast to those who accepted the failure as their own. Although some readers may cringe, failure is the appropriate term, the word used by the angrier and more bitter respondents. They frequently spoke in terms of a conditional "if": "If only the business climate had been more progressive," "if the winters were warmer," or "if people here could only understand how precious the area around here is. . . then I would be happy and stay here." People who blamed the community were adopting a passive position by blaming external causes rather than admitting an error in their judgment. They were more likely to move on to some place that they imagined would have all the right attributes. They didn't seem to learn very much about themselves as people who were incompatible with the place. Instead, they were inadvertently saying that they were right, they knew the right way to live and the rest of the community was wrong.

WHO DECIDED TO MOVE?

Free migration occurs because someone wants to move. When a person lives alone, that wish is more easily or with less complexity translated into a choice. The presence of a spouse usually involves his or her feelings being taken into consideration. The feelings of children are less likely to be given much weight. A near majority of married couples in our study reported that they shared equally in their decision to move to the Gallatin Valley. Only 2 percent of parents reported that their children had shared in the decision. The right of parental authority to make major decisions was clear.

Reflective of traditional rights to make family decisions was the relative influence of husband or wife. When a spouse unilaterally decided to move, the other spouse was forced to acquiesce or respond in some other manner to the person initiating the move. Husbands were far more likely to decide unilaterally than women. The likelihood of this disproportionate imposition of the husband over the wife, as opposed to the wife over the husband, was 6:1 in the 1980s. By the 1990s, the ratio had declined to 3:1. Perhaps more important, though, was the increase in sharing the decision. More families, about 88 percent, had made joint decisions. It is possible that the person who did not participate in the decision cared so little about moving and so much about pleasing the spouse that participating in the decision seemed irrelevant. This is perhaps the most traditional division of labor in a marriage, acquiescence to the husband's wishes along with the attendant belief that a wife's happiness will follow from her husband's decisions. This tradition even assumes that men have the predominant needs as well as the ability and right to decide what other family members need. Occasionally, there were reversals of this tradition. During the 1980s, wives made the unilateral decision to move in 6 percent of the married households. Although proportionally more by the 1990s, that percentage had dropped to 3 percent. When wives made a unilateral decision, the pattern conformed to neither a traditional nor an egalitarian ideal, claiming their right to make primary decisions. Whatever slight change in power this assertiveness might imply, it seemed to be minor in comparison to the increasing expectation for sharing the decision to move.

The question of who decided to move is closely linked to whether anyone objected and who that person might be. Unilateral decisions were more likely to meet with objections than shared decisions. Wives who objected were far more frequent than husbands, primarily because husbands made a unilateral decision much more often than wives. Just because a spouse agreed to follow a decision made by his wife or her husband did not mean that he or she liked it. Some believed that their objections were a rejection of traditional marriage expectations to cheerfully accept the decision, along with an affirmation of their marriage. The wife of a senior government official from Washington, D.C., who had taken early retirement to join a local law firm, spoke quietly and directly about her sadness and resentment at having to leave her former life. She had left a group of friends who were also wives of government officials. She and her friends frequently had lunch together, offered emotional support to each other and even took vacations with each other. A "deeply Christian woman," by her own description, she accepted her suffering as part of her duty. Her articulation as a martyr was an extreme. She divorced her husband three years later, returning to the Midwest where she had grown up.

LIFESTYLE CHANGES

As men initiated migration over the objections of their families, the nature of those objections became apparent. The rest of the family was being forced to give up their family and old friends, jobs and neighborhood. Only about 5 percent of the spouses objected for economic or employment reasons. Among those, half were being asked to interrupt their own career. The few who objected for other reasons were scattered. Fewer than one in 20 objected to their lack of knowledge of the area, the quality of services, the population or the natural environment. They objected almost solely because of the loss of social ties and, secondarily, because of economic factors, rarely mentioning any other reasons.

Moving to Bozeman was associated with occupational changes among most people in the sample. More women (46%) than men (26%) reported no change in occupation, primarily because so many women were housewives. Most people who were transferred said the relocation was a step up (44 out of 50). Men who were changing employers or employment often obtained work before moving. Thirty-five percent of the husbands had obtained work before arriving compared to only 20 percent of the wives, indicating the primacy given to the occupation of husbands in comparison to wives. Since so many women arrived without secure employment, this implied that more women would be looking for work once they arrived. Sixteen and 20 percent of the unemployed husbands and wives, respectively, were able to find work within a few weeks after they arrived. Women had a more difficult time finding satisfactory employment. Seventeen percent said they had not yet been able to find a satisfactory job, compared to 6 percent of the men at the time of their initial interview. Satisfaction is a relative matter, though. Jobs that seemed satisfactory during the initial glow after recently arriving soon became unsatisfactory.

The sample of 1990s newcomers was about equally divided between households that were renting (48%) and buying a home (52%). This figure was close to that for newcomers first interviewed in the 1980s. Buying a home was one indication that respondents were planning to stay in the community. It also indicated that they had sufficient financial resources to at least begin the purchase. More persons would have bought a home their first year in the area if they had had a down payment and were certain of their future. Several respondents who were renting prudently said they wanted to learn more about what the real estate market was like before buying. Even though temporarily renting means remaining unsettled and moving one more time, it often leads to more satisfactory housing at a lower price. Jumping into a purchase without information may lead to a regrettable choice. Most of the longer term residents had moved into a house (70%) that they were buying (68%).

Table 5.5 summarizes the types of housing and locations in which newcomers and longer term residents lived in the early 1990s. Since most of the longer term residents had once been newcomers, the comparisons between newcomers and old-timers reflects the kinds of choices that people who settle in were more likely to make. People who have lived in the area for more than six years were clearly more likely to live in single family dwellings in subdivisions outside of Bozeman on larger acreage. To some degree, these choices may reflect more settled, economically capable and socially committed people who had moved to such places with their initial choice in housing. More frequently, however, they indicate a thoughtful and gradual acquisition of houses on larger lots out of town.

George C., a 33-year-old bachelor, was first interviewed in a solitary mobile home he rented four miles from Bozeman. He had requested a transfer from his job as a transport supervisor in Salt Lake City in order to gain the solitude in nature that he found in southwestern Montana. There, with his dog, a motorcycle and vintage pickup truck, he described how happy he was with his decision to move.

Table 5.5
Type of Dwelling Unit and Location of Residence Among 1992-1993 Newcomers (N=47) and Longer Term (at Least Six Years) Residents (N=109)

(156) N	(47) Recent Arrivals %	(109) Longer Term Resident %	γ
Type of Dwelling			
Mobile home or apartment	43	30	.17
Single family dwelling	57	70	
Location of Dwelling			
Bozeman location	86	74	-.35*
Outside Bozeman	14	26	
Residential Location			
Subdivision	51	67	-.31*
No	49	33	
Size of Acreage			
-10 acres	98	92	-.33*
10+ acres	2	8	

*.05 level of significance

He planned to purchase more remote acreage when he found a "perfect" place he a could afford. Two years later, he had found it on eight acres at the end of a country road north of Belgrade. He also had found a lovely wife and her child to share it with him. George migrated almost entirely to obtain a romanticized lifestyle. He was extremely cautious, realistic and patient in obtaining what he wanted. He appears to have found it during the 18 years since he moved to the Gallatin Valley.

Doris and Tom Gretcher were almost mirror opposites of George. They were first interviewed drinking beer on the deck of their subdivision ranch-style home about four miles from downtown. They marveled at the low cost of housing in comparison to California where they had been living. They felt they had made a bargain buy. A bridal path passed near the subdivision, which pleased the Gretchers, both being horseback riders. They expressed how they appreciated the combination of town and country living. The subdivision into which they moved had several visible for-sale signs. It was one of the residential areas that became familiar to interviewers during the research because of its high rate of in- and out-migration. The more out-migration from a location, the greater the likelihood that newcomers would be drawn into the sample.

Three years later, I interviewed Doris on the patio of her apartment in town. Recently divorced, she said that she appreciated the convenience of being in town. She and her former husband had moved to Bozeman with the hope of saving their failing marriage. He thought that, if they moved to a small town where they could share family life and outdoor recreation, they might become happy again. Her children now out of high school, she reported finding happiness alone. Tom had moved back to central California. Reflecting on her recently vacated home, she mused that, in retrospect, it had the disadvantages of both town and country. Their acre was so far out of town that it was inconvenient, but not large enough to escape the difficulties of neighbors.

Selecting a residence involves many of the same considerations as choosing a community. Economic factors place limits on choices that represent preferences to life in town or to take advantage of natural amenities. Even in towns the size of Bozeman and Belgrade, choices are necessary for most people. Few locations exist with in-town convenience and out-of-town amenities at a price most people can afford. Most residents knew their primary consideration. The most important considerations for nearly half (48%) of the households were economic. People who were primarily concerned with price were divided between those who said that the house they bought had been the only place available within their economic limitations (22%) or it was the right price (26%). Economic factors diminished after the initial consideration. Practical factors were the second most important primary considerations for selecting a home. Twenty-three percent wanted to be conveniently near schools and services or right in town. Most others based their decisions primarily on environmental considerations. They liked their scenic view (8%) and living in or near the country (12%), being away from congestion (6%) and falling in love with the house at first sight (6%). Noneconomic factors became even more important as secondary considerations.

Most people in the sample (83%) lived in the Bozeman area. Fourteen percent lived in or near Belgrade. The remaining 13 households (3%) lived around Gallatin Gateway. Newcomers were more likely to move to Bozeman (86%). The longer they lived in the area, the more likely they were to move out of town. Nearly two-thirds (64%) lived within the city limits. Twenty percent lived on one acre or less out of town. Only 1 percent lived on acreage with more than 40 acres. The most common rural lot was from one to 10 acres (11%) in size. Fewer newcomers (2%) than old-timers (8%) lived on more than eight acres.

A few migrants dream of some degree of self-sufficiency. For them, the attraction to country living involves a rich amalgam of land ownership, relative privacy and a quiet refuge. These people are capitalizing on the unique features of the natural environment. They prefer using space, as one aspect of their lifestyle, in a manner impossible in more urban locations. Although they lived out of town, almost all identified with the town community.

No migrants in our study were full-time farmers, though some might argue with our surmise. Their preference for rural living was aesthetic rather than agricultural. Two very wealthy young couples bought large, more than 1,000 acre, remnants of cattle ranches within a year after they moved to the area. The cost of operating the ranches undoubtedly was much greater than any income generated through agriculture. The van Pelt's hired a ranch manager to run cattle on a small portion of the original piece and a realtor to subdivide the rest. Only the O'Neal family owned and lived on a working cattle ranch. However, the ranch was managed by a professional ranch manager. Mr. O'Neal was a realtor. His wife had received a sizable inheritance from her family. Though their ranch was a full-time ranch, they were not ranchers. She liked rural life and horses. He disliked both. They divorced eight years after moving to Bozeman. She stayed on the ranch with their young daughter. He moved to town.

The largest landowners were usually hobby farmers who chose to farm or ranch because they enjoyed the operations of land management and animal care. A few townspeople, largely those who did not own their own home, said they wished they could afford to buy a place in the country. Among people who lived in the country, there did not seem to be much desire to acquire more land, as would be typical among real farmers. They had chosen their parcel because it suited their wishes for living a rural nonagricultural lifestyle.

Karen and Jerry North were among the larger hobby farmers in our survey. They had two sons, ages 8 and 10, and a 16-year-old daughter when first interviewed. They had been raised on Midwestern farms and liked running a small operation, although there was no financial gain to be made. After living in Billings for a few years, they had found their acreage outside Bozeman. Karen devoted herself to being a mother, homemaker and caretaker of her beloved Jersey cows. Jerry ran his franchise out of his home and traveled frequently. When at home, he and his sons maintained the farm machinery, baled hay, plowed snow, hunted and shared work activities and social life with neighbors. More typical respondents living on smaller acreage were less involved with agriculture than the Norths. Most had a vegetable garden, but few raised farm animals. They wanted to live out of town rather than work the land.

SATISFACTION AND CHANGE WITH LIFESTYLES

Practically everyone who moved to the Gallatin Valley was cognizant of changes in their lifestyles (Table 5.6). An open-ended question asked respondents about lifestyle changes and what they meant by lifestyle. Only 6 percent of newcomers said No when asked Whether you have experienced any changes in your lifestyle since moving to the Gallatin Valley. Old-timers either had few changes in lifestyles or forgot what they had experienced, since over one-fourth (27%) said No. Twenty percent of respondents said they had experienced as many as six changes in lifestyle. Twenty-eight percent described at least three changes. Their responses indicated three things. First, respondents were able to apply the ambiguous concept to their lives. Lifestyle had inherent validity from their perspective. Second, they focused upon several dimensions that corresponded to the four categories of evaluative variables used throughout these analyses. Third, lifestyle was perceived to be a relatively unidimensional variable for some persons and a complex multidimensional variable for others.

When asked about changes in their lifestyles, respondents most frequently described economic changes (Table 5.6). Fifty-two percent described both positive and negative ways that their lives had been affected by economic factors. Most thought their lifestyle quality had improved (64%). However, few (28%) people reported being happier with their income than reported being poorer (28%), out of work (28%) or suffering from a high cost of living (20%). Significant differences distinguished newcomers from people who had lived in the area several years. Looking back, not many (27%) old-timers said their lifestyles had changed since they arrived. Most (94%) newcomers reported such changes. Some changes were negative. Nearly five times as many newcomers (28%) as old-timers (6%) had not found work. Family satisfaction was lower for one-third (34%) of the newcomers, but only 17 percent of the old-timers.

Other changes were reported to be significantly more positive by newcomers. Most newcomers said they were enjoying their life quality (64%) and cultural (61%) and physical (71%) environments comparatively more than where they had previously lived. These included such diverse activities as attending outdoor concerts and spending more time in outdoor recreation. Their glowing comments about these qualities far exceeded those of longer term residents. Longer term residents seemed to take such factors as part of life rather than as qualities that were rapidly changing. Only one person, a woman with severe arthritis, felt that her life had been negatively affected by the harsh climate, compared to four who felt that theirs had improved. The remaining initial responses related to how the community had changed their lives. Only 4 percent of these were negative, including unfriendly residents, poor cultural amenities, more housing maintenance and a conservative political climate. The remaining 18 percent felt that their lives had improved because the community had a lack of status consciousness, a relaxed pace, better cultural amenities and was a better place to raise children.

Table 5.6
Changes in Lifestyle Reported by Newcomers (N=47) and Longer Term Residents (N=109) to the Gallatin Valley, 1992-1993

	Newcomers %	Old-Timers %	γ
Lifestyle Change			
No	6	27	.71**
Yes	94	73	
Financial Situation			
Same or worse	72	52	-.49**
Better	28	48	
Employment			
Haven't found job	28	6	-.63**
Other	72	94	
Family Satisfaction			
Less	36	17	-.42*
Same or more	64	83	
Lifestyle Quality			
Better	64	37	-.50*
Other	36	64	
Lifestyle Culture			
Same or fewer	39	68	.54*
More	61	32	
Lifestyle/Environment			
Same or fewer	29	54	.64*
More	71	46	

*.05 level of significance
**.01 level of significance

Economic changes in lifestyle, once mentioned, were rarely mentioned again. Fewer than 10 percent of the respondents mentioned job or income after their second reported change in lifestyle. People who mentioned one negative economic effect were also most likely to mention further negative economic effects. People who thought about economic factors as hurting their lifestyle tended to have a narrowed and more economic definition of lifestyle than other respondents. A few more respondents mentioned increased (15%) and decreased (9%) interaction with friends and relatives, as a second consideration, but that was rarely mentioned again.

The other changes in lifestyle that people reported to be most important occurred in relation to the community and to the natural environment. Between 40 and 50 percent reported that their lives and activities had been changed because of the community, the human environment. These changes were generally favorable, although a few felt that local people were unfriendly, local culture too provincial or the amount of home maintenance too great. The percentage of people who experienced lifestyle changes because of the new natural environment around them hovered around 20 percent. These changes were almost completely positive. Two women, for example, attended the same weekly downhill ski day organized by the local women's activity group. "I started going just to get out of the house and meet some other women. It was so much fun, I built my schedule around it. I take the kids up on the weekends, even if Fred can't go," said one of these new devotees.

NEWCOMERS WHO LEFT

The participants in the 1980s sample who moved away before the project was completed were the most moving among a group of movers. They typified characteristics of migrants even more than the rest of the sample. They were younger and more likely to be single. They were much less likely to be parents. And they had earned significantly less income during the previous year than had the stayers. There were no differences between their educational achievement or occupational statuses. Thus, they had as much or more to gain by moving on as did the people who stayed.

Being young and single without children offers the opportunity to be relatively commitment-free in industrial society. However, childless young singles were relatively unlikely to give up a high-paying job in order to migrate away from the Gallatin Valley. Conversely, perhaps their more low-paid counterparts felt an economic incentive to move away when they would have liked to stay. About one-half (51%) of the newcomers' households with earnings their first year in Bozeman of less than $15,000 (1980 dollars) moved within five years. High earnings were no assurance that people would stay. Over one-third (28%) of those earning over $50,000 moved away. The most settled people were those with incomes between $20,000 and $36,000. High income, it appears, may provide economic freedom to move rather than an incentive to stay. The wealthiest persons represented the groups with perhaps the greatest freedom to follow their dream to the destination of their choice.

The comparison of people who were independent, young and had low incomes with people who were wealthy compares one freedom against another. Higher income and wealthier newcomers also were usually older with children, in contrast to young, childless, single persons who had the least restraint to remain where they were. A few newcomers were young, childless and had high incomes. These were people with the economic option to live almost anywhere. One, a brilliant and ambitious entomologist, moved to a prestigous university at a much higher salary as soon as his wife completed her doctorate at Montana State University, where he was employed.

Ultimately, the decision to migrate was likely to be made because of how satisfied residents felt with the place, although their feelings may reflect stage of life and economic security. Migrants varied widely in satisfaction during their first year. Most (60%) people liked the Gallatin Valley better than they had expected and even more (80%) liked it better than where they used to live. One-third felt that it was about as they had expected it would be while the remainder felt it was worse. Level of satisfaction was strongly associated with whether people stayed or moved on. Slightly more than one-half of the newcomers who felt Bozeman was worse than they had expected moved away within three years. About one-third of those who liked it better than they expected moved away during the same interval. The people who were least likely to move were those who felt it was about like they expected. Less than one-fourth of these people moved away in five years.

The question of liking a place better or worse than had been expected is abstract and subjective. A more substantive, but more subjective question is how well people like a place in comparison to a place where they had lived. When asked how satisfied they were in comparison to where they had previously lived, nearly three-fourths of the respondents who liked it better were likely to stay. People who thought it was worse were the most likely to move away within five years. Sixty percent of them moved, in contrast to slightly fewer than one-half of those respondents who felt it was neither better nor worse than the place they had left. Remembering and realizing how bad a previous place was made their new community more acceptable.

Involvement in meaningful social activities is an important aspect of community integration. The more integrated people in our sample were, the less likely they were to move away. Respondents were asked three types of direct questions regarding integration, only one of which was significantly related to their out-migration. People were asked how friendly they regarded people in the Gallatin Valley. This measured the quality of friendliness people attributed to the people in the area. Only one respondent in 10 felt that people were not very friendly. Those who felt that way were significantly more likely to move away quickly. The least likely people to move were those who felt that local people were friendly and open. Respondents also were asked about the degree of friendships they had established since moving to the Gallatin Valley. This measured their subjective interpretation of their personal experiences. People who stayed were no more likely to have well-developed friendships than those people who moved away. The questions about friendship probably were superficial measures of friendship. Respondents may have been responding to less intense familiarity, like being friendly or cordial, instead of developed friendships. The young and restless seemed to form an instant cadre of friends. People who deliberately held back from forming friendships were, in fact, more likely to stay than those with friends. Those who held back may have been giving a deeper meaning to friendship. The third measure of community integration was their degree of organizational involvement in Bozeman. Respondents summarized the number and types of organizations to which the adults and children in the household belonged, as well as the frequency of their participation. Level of participation was more important than membership. People who stayed were no more likely to belong to organizations, although those who devoted more time to organizations were more likely to stay. The quality of their involvement, whether in friendships or in organizations, established the more secure anchor.

"I had this dream for years," related Steve K., the former department head of a state welfare department.

I wanted to just leave Olympia and go teach English at a junior college in Lander, Wyoming. Hell, I didn't even know if there was a junior college in Lander. I had been there with my parents when I was in high school. I wanted to get to some beautiful little town in the Rockies. Practically any town would have been acceptable to me. I'm glad to be away from my jobs, which I hated, and my relatives, whom I disliked. I am relieved to be in a place with a few nice uncomplicated people. I really think the way I imagined Lander is pretty accurate. Bozeman is a compromise. It has most of the qualities Lander has, while offering more job opportunities for me and cosmopolitan activities for my wife and daughters.

When asked how their lifestyle had changed, he replied,

The main difference is how I feel. Just being able to look out at the mountains is worth a lot. I am out from under the pressure of my former job. Our family is a lot closer. We are spending more time together. People here are much friendlier and energetic than they were in Olympia. Olympia is the state capital. . . . We still are just enjoying each other right now, but I'm sure we will develop friends when we want them. After we finish settling in, I'll begin looking for something [a job] more permanent. Carol has started part-time at the hospital [as a nurse]. We haven't skied for years, but we can hardly wait for winter so we can start again.

Two years later, their house was on the market. He had not found a suitable job. They were planning on returning to the Northwest.

No single universal statement described or explained why people stayed or left. No linear relationship occurred between how much money people earned, whether they were married or had children or how satisfied they felt about the area and whether they stayed or left. Each of these factors exerted some influence. The complexity of the influence of the relationship between these factors is noteworthy because they challenged the notion that one or another of them, particularly economic factors, was the only important influence.

Many people behaved in ways that were somewhat independent of any structured qualities that might typify them. People also acted independently of their internalized impressions. Wealthy persons or religious adherents sometimes behaved more like poor persons or heathens. When their feelings were not consonant with their experience, people were more likely to act out of phase with the character they thought they were. Social scientists, like the people they attempt to predict, follow certain trains of thought which they consider to be rational explanations. When economists predict that people move if there are economic rewards, they assume that the people they are analyzing will respond as rational economic persons. Real life offers sufficiently important economic rewards for most of the people much of the time for many of them to crudely conform to the economists' model. That conformity, under some conditions, ignores enormous levels of nonrational activities, that is, those activities that do conform to the economists' prediction. The same logic that leads to inaccurate predictions also is applicable to the explanations of scientists using quality of environment among turnaround migrants, the desire for political freedom among political refugees or the presence of intimate family and friendship networks among migrants seeking social ties. Whatever the variable that social scientists use to explain behavior, it is only accurate to the extent that persons take it seriously enough to behave in the way the scientists expect.

The foregoing discussion does not imply that people behave only in accord with conscious considerations. But, conscious or not, they must be acting according to influential variables, if social explanations are to be useful for describing their behavior. People occasionally become aware of factors about which they had not been previously aware because that factor had not yet pressed itself into their consciousness.

I became reasonably certain that many people were giving honest and authentic descriptions of and explanations for their feelings regarding their move, even though their interpretations were inaccurate. When recent young childless refugees from a large city recited a litany of the perfect qualities of friendliness, natural environment and community spirit at the same time that they spoke of moving to Bozeman instead of to another beautiful and trendy nonmetropolitan area, my initial private response was You are romanticizing this place. The more extreme their romance, the farther removed from reality they were and the more likely they were to be disappointed. Their limited initial knowledge about small beautiful places heavily influenced their conception of how things ought to be.

Ebullient newcomers often expounded on how they were going to spend the rest of their lives there. My silent response then was "You are in for a disappointment, because this place isn't like what you expect." Generally, I was correct. The more extreme their optimism about Bozeman, the more likely they were to become more negative later on. Their negativism involved more than a regression toward the mean expected of people with extreme positions. Rather, it often involved a realization that their interpretation had been wrong, that their romantic image had been inaccurate. Environmentalists often were irate to discover that the mass of kindred souls they expected to be living in Bozeman intent on preserving wilderness simply were not there, or their changed optimism might involve a recognition that they had left out a necessary crucial consideration during their first glowing interview. Couples experiencing marital discord before moving frequently confided, in later interviews, that they had anticipated being happier once they moved to this new and better place. While this strategy may have worked for some who did not mention it during their interviews, it certainly failed for many of those who had brought their problems along with them.

Not everyone we studied was a newcomer. The 1972 sample was randomly drawn from the entire population of Bozeman. While many people in the 1972, 1976 and 1980 samples for the initial panel study were newcomers, most were longer term residents. The most distinct differences among the panel samples were, obviously, that residents were more likely to have grown up in Montana (Table 5.7) and, by definition, that many had been living in Bozeman for more than 15 years. They also were more likely to have been raised on a farm or in a small town. Nearly three-quarters were married. We cannot conclude why old-timers in Bozeman were more likely to have origins in rural Montana. Although it is tempting to conclude that married rural Montanans had been socialized to become permanent residents, their primary reason may have been that they never left or, if they left, may have settled back in, essentially as natives. The greater likelihood that rural natives become long-term in-state residents probably can be found in most rural settings for all states.

Our conclusion is that the more realistic people were in deciding to move to the Gallatin Valley, the more likely they were to adjust and remain. And the more realistic in their interpretation of what the place was like, providing they did not object to the place, the more likely they were to remain. We also learned to distinguish between what people said and what they did. When people said they

Table 5.7
Selected Demographic Characteristics in Percentages for Each Panel

		Panel Year		
Characteristics	1972	1976	1980	1993
Grew up in Montana	63	53	61	51
Raised on farm or small town	63	65	68	58
Lived in Bozeman 15+ years	47	68	65	56
Married	71	75	75	70
College graduate	39	44	46	51
White collar occupation	53	51	38	56
Children away from home	21	35	51	49

loved the area and were going to become active in it, that did not mean they would continue to like it or become active. Whether they would stay or leave was determined more by whether they were already becoming active and engaged with the area and its people. Those who were already attached with family and friends, who were committed to people, who shared beliefs and activities in common with them, were the people who were likely to stay. Otherwise, they were likely soon to move on. Even so, many very realistic people who liked the area moved away.

Chapter 6

Economics and Migration

INCOME, EMPLOYMENT AND SATISFACTION

Economic measures were among the most consistent and powerful indicators of satisfaction among residents and the length of time that they would stay in the Gallatin Valley. Economic factors formed a rough foundation for survival and for acquiring a level of satisfaction in other dimensions. Although important, they were but one serious influence. It is important to avoid applying an economic metaphor as the sole explanation for why people move and whether they find happiness if they think they have found the pot of gold at the end of their rainbow.

Earning a low income is an important factor in in-migration. However, some people would prefer to be poor in one place than another, particularly when that one place has qualities that these particular poor really like. Poorer people moved more frequently, but they did not seem especially eager to move from the Gallatin Valley merely because of low income. Those who wished to get out of a continually financially insecure life seem to have moved quickly from Bozeman. At the same time, many low-income people traded their relative poverty for the mountains, streams or ambience of the community, at least for a few years. Meanwhile, many financially successful immigrants were dissatisfied where they had lived and continued to be dissatisfied following their move. Most of their dissatisfactions were not financial.

George and Harriet Howard moved to rural Gallatin Gateway from the Boston ˙ area. Recently divorced from his previous wife, George (46) had been an executive in a chemical corporation and had also owned a small fabric and drapery retail store. Harriet had "bloomed late," returning to graduate from college in computer science at 29. Following his divorce, George married Harriet, liquidated his assets and headed west in their new four-wheel drive pickup truck. He had among the higher reported incomes reported by respondents the year before moving to the Gallatin Valley.

We spent a few weeks looking at towns and talking to people about where they thought the nicest places to live were. When we heard about a beautiful place that seemed interesting, we went there. We didn't want to live in Utah because of the Mormons and we never made it to Oregon, but we saw lots of places in Colorado and Idaho we liked, especially the area around Ketchum.

We bought this place (a log cabin on a bluff above the Gallatin River) and did nothing but relax and enjoy life for six months. We love it here. I keep remembering the rat race around Boston. I have better fishing in a one-minute walk than exists in any stream in the Northeast. We planted a garden, cut wood for the winter, canned fruit and vegetables, and sat by the wood stove and relaxed with friends. The people here have been so helpful.

This spring, we decided we better start making some money. We know it won't take much. Harriet read several books on self-employed work. We wanted work we could do together and which would not force us into an eight-to-five routine, but which would bring in enough cash to take care of our needs. I have always loved crafting wood, so we settled on making cabinets at home.

Two years later, they had modified their business to furniture and cabinet rebuilding.

We are getting so much business that we aren't having enough time to play and relax. I don't want to lose what we moved here for. This August, we are not taking any more orders for eight weeks. How much money did we earn last year? Less than $15,000 — that is less than a quarter of what I made the year I quit my job — and I feel richer now than I have at anytime in my life.

The Howards had a low income, but high satisfaction. At least for this limited period of their lives, they had balance between what they wanted and what they had. Eight years later, a terrible public tragedy occurred that destroyed their lives in the area. Even given their relative and temporary satisfaction, their happiness was unstable. The tragedy cannot be described in detail because it would potentially identify the Howards.

Sam (age 48) and Dorothy Harris (age 46) said that they had been drawn to the area for essentially the same reason as the Howards. The Harrises had two sons in college. The youngest son was a junior in high school when they moved. Sam, a relatively high-ranking federal official in Washington, had grown weary of the stress and wanted to spend his late middle years skiing and enjoying other outdoor recreation with his boys. He said he never wanted "to be an administrator again." He joined a local law firm where a classmate from law school was a senior partner. His retirement income, when added to his law practice, was more than he had earned before moving to the study area. Dorothy openly suffered from his decision. A deeply religious, "painfully shy and retired" person by her own description, she had left a supportive group of church members in order to move to Bozeman. The Harrises were financially secure. Their elegant home was as richly and elegantly furnished as a Manhattan salon. They lived on 20 acres next to a trout stream in one of the most prestigious locations in the area on the road to the ski hill.

Interviews with the Harrises were somber. He described how he would be fishing, hunting and skiing with the boys during vacations. They had not joined the country club in Bozeman because he was interested in purer experiences in nature. She had never cared for the country club, she reassuringly added. In each subsequent interview, she described her continuing loneliness. Despite membership and activity in a local congregation, she had not been able to regain the personal, spiritual and communal satisfaction she felt she had known in Washington. After three years, Dorothy Harris filed for divorce. The house was sold. Sam moved into a condominium in town. He said he felt great with his change in life, free to do what he wanted and free from the sadness of living with his wife. During her last interview, she confided her hope to save her marriage by moving to Montana with Sam. He also mentioned his hope. Each had very different wants and needs somewhat exclusive of the other, a gap greater than the move could resolve. Their move to Bozeman and her move away had essentially nothing to do with employment or income.

Economic well-being was strongly associated with whether people stayed in the Gallatin Valley or left. The higher the income a household had been before moving, the more likely that they would stay in Bozeman ($\gamma = .40$). Slightly more than one-fourth of the households earning over $36,000 moved again during the study period, which was about the same as one-fourth of the medium income households that left. Nearly one-half of the lowest (under $15,000) households moved. The poorer a household was before moving to Bozeman, the more likely it was that they would move on. Perhaps the more crucial issue is whether their income after coming to Bozeman had affected their likelihood to stay. While people who reported low incomes after their first year were more likely to move than people in the higher brackets, the association is neither as strong ($r = .19$) nor as significant as their income before moving to the study area. In comparison to each other, then, the more economically secure newcomers were not much more likely to stay than those with low incomes.

Household income showed essentially no relationship with whether respondents felt more or less satisfied than they had expected. A few more low-income women found the area worse than they had expected than did women with higher incomes. The lower the income, the greater the out-migration was among dissatisfied respondents. Nearly three-fourths of the lowest income people with the worst evaluations of Bozeman had moved, whereas three-quarters of the higher income people had stayed, even if the area was worse than they expected. Higher income people were no more likely to stay or leave based on how their expectations were satisfied. One important reason for high-income dissatisfied people staying was that they were in effect trapped by their employment. Ralph and Sharon Talmadge stayed in order to earn their income. Sharon was the only child of aging parents who owned a lucrative retail franchise. They returned to Bozeman to inherit the business and to take care of Sharon's parents. They were unhappily doing both, 12 years after first being interviewed. People who were dissatisfied and poor, who lacked the luxury of being trapped by wealth, quickly moved away.

THE RELATIONSHIP OF ECONOMIES: LOCAL, REGIONAL AND NATIONAL

There is a tendency to explain success and failure on the basis of individual decision and behaviors. We also recognize the influence of the largest macrostructures, politics and the economy, on the system of society. For example, newcomers typically wanted to credit themselves for moving to Montana. At the same time, several should have mentioned that, for example, the failing economy where they had been living had been an incentive to move away. The economy is closely related to the likelihood that people will move and stay.

The national economy is a complex system which does not rise and fall equally and simultaneously throughout the United States. One location can prosper while others are depressed. The economic well-being in outside areas effects whether people will move to another area, which has its own local economic characteristics. Making matters even more complicated are the differences in how households are prospering within the local economies. Economists have precise concepts and sophisticated theories that explain the relationship between local, regional and national economies and the characteristics of residents and migration. My comments are based on observations and interviews that communicate how migrants consider and respond to economic influences.

The Northern Rockies frequently have been out of synchrony with the state of the national economy. During the 1970s, many areas in the region prospered while the rest of the nation wallowed in a severe recession. During the 1980s, when the rest of the nation boomed, most of the Northern Rockies was an economic disaster area, although several recreational scenic locales continued to grow rapidly. Local, regional and national economies and migration characteristics were rising and falling in very different patterns throughout the study period.

The economic and population growth of regional small towns, the regions and the nation have often been out synchrony, although their differences may be synchronous at a larger systemic level. However, since 1950, growth and relative prosperity have occurred in most of the study area and in the United States, in general (Table 2.3, Chapter 2). For example, Bozeman grew by 31 percent in the 1950s and 40 percent during the 1970s. Growth slowed down, but continued through the 1980s in many scenic recreational areas of the region, despite the national recession which followed the rises in oil prices in 1973 and in 1976. Even so, Bozeman grew 17 percent during the 1980s. Rural growth that swept the nation during the 1960s and early 1970s came to a standstill in most regions, but not in the beautiful areas of the Rockies. The 1970s were lush years for development in mountain towns from New Mexico to Montana. The long lines of vehicles at gas pumps that plagued most cities never occurred in most scenic recreational areas of the West. Jobs were relatively plentiful throughout the region. Massive rapid development of oil and coal reserves created boomtowns. Agriculture generally prospered. America discovered the beauty and desirability of small towns in the mountains while the Rust Belt was decaying. As Bozeman grew and diversified, the extreme economic domination of the university became less pronounced. Although education levels remained very high, there was a gradual shift to more blue-collar newcomers, as illustrated in Table 6.1. Nearly 80 percent (79.2%) of newcomers in 1981 had been in white-collar occupations. That figure had dropped considerably (62.2%) by 1993.

The 1980s reversed these general trends. The prosperity that was heralded throughout America was something that most residents in the Northern Rockies only read about. The energy boom had passed, a severe drought had devastated regional agriculture and urbanites were too busy making money to consider moving to the country. Even in most beautiful mountain towns, growth slowed to a trickle. Jobs became scarce, businesses closed and real estate stagnated. For sale signs, an uncommon sight during the 1970s, appeared on almost every street for weeks at a time.

Tim Rogers (28) a building contractor, arrived in Bozeman during the rapid growth of the early 1970s. He developed an excellent reputation for building quality spec houses. By 1985, he had been forced to lay off most of his crew. He survived by taking small remodeling jobs in addition to building an occasional new residence. His crew had tripled by 1988. There was more new construction than he could accommodate. He was not able to hire enough skilled craftsmen to accept more new projects. Tim was among the fortunate tradesmen who survived the local economic decline dictated by external forces. He was successful partially because he had arrived early enough to establish a reputation for doing excellent work at a fair price and for being easy to work with. A former, self-declared "old hippie," he and his wife had lived on a shoestring and avoided debts. Contractors who arrived between the late 1970s and mid-1980s were rarely successful, whatever their aesthetic and technical skills.

Tim deserves credit for his organizational abilities as well as his technical and aesthetic sense. He weathered difficult times through thrift and foresight. Still, the failures of most other contractors, shopkeepers and restaurant owners was a consequence of the vagaries of the local, regional and national economies. While some people undoubtedly had special insights and wisdom about how and where to live, their successes may be due to being in the right place at the right time. Tim and his wife, Nola, had left their hometown, a small city in Minnesota. Both had been employed at a factory that manufactured framed windows. He learned many

Table 6.1
Occupation of Recent Migrants: Male White or Blue Collar

Cohort	1981	1982	1983	1993	Total
White collar	57 (79.2%)	87 (79.8%)	87 (71.9%)	28 (62.2%)	259 (74.6%)
Blue collar	15 (20.8%)	22 (20.2%)	34 (28.1%)	17 (37.8%)	88 (25.4%)
Total	72	109	121	45	347 (100%)

of his fine cabinetry skills while working in the factory. Nola had been a clerk in the payroll department. In Bozeman, she eventually worked for the local branch of a national firm that specialized in preparing taxes. She also managed the books for Tim's slowly expanding construction business. She had held several minimum-wage clerical jobs before landing her job with the tax firm.

For every success story like Tim's and Nola's, three or four households moved away during the 1970s and four or five during the 1980s. Some left because they found the location and its style of life unpleasant or unsuited to their tastes. Many left because of strong economic incentives. The local economy in recreational towns is rarely lush. Most of the time, living in such places is comparable to a recession for the half of each year when the tourists are away. Few decent jobs are available for the large number of educated, talented, energetic newcomers. To make matters even more painful, as in a depression, the goods and services for the privileged and the tourists are constantly visible and available, even when the local economy is stagnant. Excellent restaurants, shops filled with cutting-edge athletic equipment and automobile dealerships are constant reminders to local wage earners of their own financial difficulties.

I conducted this research from the vantage of a privileged resident. The comments made by respondents have not been selected to express sourgrapes that I harvested from the local vineyard. I loved Bozeman and Montana. My position was stable and relatively well paid by local standards. Faculty in the Montana universities were paid very little compared to colleagues in other states, save the Dakotas. Within the Gallatin Valley, tenured university faculty earn dependable incomes well above the local average.

University and other positions sponsored by local and state governments exemplify how varied the quality of jobs and incomes were within the area. Broad differences are typical in all regions and localities. In scenic and recreational areas of the Northern Rockies, the local standards of income were low and remained low. Other rural areas, especially in the Black Belt and in the Southwest, also have legacies of poverty. Their poor incomes and occupational opportunities reflect low levels of education among indigenous minorities scarred by poverty. The modest local incomes in scenic recreational towns in the Northern Rockies occur in spite of high human capital: educated, cosmopolitan young people from advantaged backgrounds.

ADVANTAGE IN GALLATIN VALLEY

The state of the Gallatin Valley economy was only partially related to the earnings and styles of spending money among residents. A small, fortunate minority of residents was economically independent of the need to earn a living where they lived. Some were retirees with comfortable incomes from retirement programs and investments. A few were employed in lucrative occupations such as airline pilots and successful performing artists, living in the Rockies while working somewhere else. A small number of residents resided and worked in the area, selling their labors to the national marketplace. A handful of designers and artists with national recognition lived in the area and remained independent of the community for their income. Finally, some residents had varying levels of independent wealth and did not depend on their own labors for an income. These categories were not entirely independent. Some invested in local businesses. The very wealthy regarded managing their investments as work. Many people had a variety of simultaneous income sources, some from working locally and some from independent wealth and retirement incomes. What they all shared was a common desire to live in the rural Northern Rockies.

There are financial advantages to living in rural areas, especially relatively obscure ones. The study area was no exception. Costs of land and labor were low, at least until the mid-1990s. It was possible to buy a quarter-section of land for the cost of an acre in major cities. The wildlife, mountains and plants came at no extra cost. When the urban economy was declining, the rural areas of the Rockies were attractive, particularly if people could sell their urban real estate before moving. The apparent advantage of moving was an incentive to relocate during such times. Most urban refugees in the study, unless truly financially independent, found that sustaining themselves at the level to which they had grown accustomed became impossible as time passed.

There are several continual advantages of living in such places even for the poor, providing they are content to stay poor. There was a constant influx of people, mostly young, who were eking out a living through manual labor and minimum wage service jobs. One primary attraction was having an informal, comfortable, safe, friendly place devoid of pressure to perform and produce. There also was a strong attraction for some to be part of the serious local outdoor recreation cadre: skiers, kayakers, hunters, mountain climbers, fishermen, hikers and other outdoor recreationists. Many in our sample were devotees whose lifestyles and identities were tied to one or more of these activities. A few of these people juggled responsible work and even families with their devotion to play. A few had varying support from parents or inheritance. Many devotees made just enough to buy superb equipment and to use it almost continually.

Among recreational devotees, the levels of their skill and dedication to their sports were important sources of recognition within their group. The few extreme devotees who were able to earn a living through their recreational activities were held in awe by less skilled and less favorably employed devotees. Guides, sporting goods shop owners and ski patrol members were broad examples, although some had more specialized competencies, like being a snow ranger or an elk biologist. Many recreational zealots wished they could earn a living in their favorite types of recreation. Such jobs were few and competitive. In our samples, there were many examples of this dedication to recreation.

The particular type of recreation was less important for distinguishing devotees than was the dedication itself. Two of the luckier examples were Michael Singleton and Ron Walsley. Michael was the reclusive grandson of a wealthy Chicago industrialist. His sole occupation was managing some of the family fortune which, on a few occasions, made him a silent partner to local businesses. Married with two children, he and his wife, Anna, built a small mansion on 80 acres with a spring-fed creek teeming with trout. Anna was active in the local opera guild. Michael was fascinated by guns and hunting. He spent days working alone in his private machine shop, developing firearms. He traveled several times each year to go hunting. His name was well known among local serious firearms enthusiasts, although few would have recognized his face.

Ron Walsley was an assistant crew boss for the Forest Service. His passions were bicycle racing and cross-country ski racing. Devoted to serious outdoor recreation since youth, he threw himself into training and competition after moving to Bozeman from New England, via a small town in western Montana. He became a state champion in bicycling during the research project. Ron's work was a perfect blend of responsibility and physical exercise. It provided a 12-month salary that made it possible for him to pursue his dedication to racing. His athletic pursuits were encouraged by his wife who stayed home with their daughter who had been born a year after they moved to Bozeman. There were three national champion athletes in our samples.

There was a nearly constant supply of young men and women who were at the center or on the periphery of the recreational devotees. Most arrived casually from outside the region and as students to attend the university. They seemed to come independent of the national economy. They came to the area because of its specific attractions rather than through calculating economic incentives and disincentives. Once they made the decision to immerse themselves in a recreational lifestyle, the choice was where to most enjoyably pursue it in spite of the poverty that often accompanied it — Park City, Jackson, Whitefish, Bozeman — to name just four of the dozens of towns in the region. Many circulated from one to others until they balanced livelihood and recreation at a level of comfort for themselves. Most left the cadre to do something else, like going to work in Albuquerque or to school in Seattle.

THE PERSISTENT SHADOW OF ECONOMIC RATIONALITY

Young people who have never been bitten by the recreation bug may be more economically rational in their considerations. Agencies and corporations may be filled with employees who never seriously considered moving to the Northern Rockies or other recreational meccas. The state of the regional and national economies may be a prime determinant of economically rational movers. It is possible to conceive of how the broader economy even affects the choices of young recreational migrants to the Northern Rockies. Certainly, an absence of any really attractive and lucrative jobs would seem to make being poor while fishing and hunting preferable to being poor without them. However, the most ardent outdoor recreationists never said, "There were no jobs anywhere, so I decided to come here to climb and ski until more lucrative work became available elsewhere." They were likely to say that they didn't want to work in a conventional job in a city. An occasional introspective respondent would say that this was a time when he or she had the luxury and freedom to live for recreation and a composite lifestyle. The middle-aged and retired devotees believed they already had earned the right to a life of recreation and leisure. As a former executive who had retired at 49 remarked, he had paid before he played.

These decisions sometimes did seem to involve an economic calculus based on what opportunities existed at some other location. I say seemed to because people said they had considered their motives and investigated places before moving. They "seemed to" weigh their alternatives according to criteria that had been thought about by comparing reasonable information. They "seemed to" conform to what social scientists describe as rational. Based on watching migrants, I am not sure what rational is, other than "seeming to" be rational from their perspective and having that perspective correspond with what a professional also deems as rational. If the perspective of the person, the perspective of a professional who evaluates their rationality and the empirical facts of their life roughly correspond with each other, they might be considered rational. Often, no more than one or two of these factors for testing rationality are present. Does that mean that people are, say, one-third rational for, say, one-third of the time? Perhaps the answer is in becoming. They may be becoming more rational.

Total awareness of all possible places and their respective opportunities, of course, can never exist nor did any respondent claim to have been so informed and rational. Once in the Gallatin Valley, though, most became increasingly economically rational. During the local recession of the 1980s, people moved away a little more quickly than in the early 1990s when temporary, part-time and unskilled jobs were easy to find. Even so, the number of new people moving in from the outside largely determined the number that would flow through and then move away. The longer most people resided in these scenic recreational places, the more apparent the economic costs became. People had more years of experience from which to compare the economic costs. As they grew older, people also became more economically dependent. Some married, had children, bought cars, houses and insurance and developed the sundry and almost inescapable economic burdens of maturity. A few made a pact to stay, effectively closing off alternatives.

Local, regional and national economies, then, had some influence on whether people moved to this small town in the Rockies, whether they stayed and for how long. The external forces of these economic influences were filtered through the residents who had their own personal formulas regarding who they were and what variables were important to them. These formulas were themselves being continually revised. As they matured, the conscious optimization of economic considerations usually increased. Most, especially the young, eventually contradicted statements which they had made about the primacy of living there whatever the local economic conditions might offer them.

WEALTH AND THE APPEARANCE OF WEALTH

Scenic recreational areas commonly convey an image of economic success and prosperity. Compared to the economically flat agricultural towns in the region, towns like Bozeman, Jackson and Kalispell seemed to be growing and prosperous. In one sense, the successful image was accurate because construction and population growth implied capital expenditures and expansion of services. In my travels throughout the region, residents in slowly growing agricultural areas often spoke both enviously and sympathetically about Bozeman, because of the apparent success from growth and the obvious problems that accompanied it. Most would like to have experienced an injection of outside money, although there was considerable ambivalence concerning the consequences of growth. The increased growth of the local economy was frequently, yet erroneously assumed to be due to a high proportion of economically successful newcomers. The visible wealthy few, albeit frequently temporary, outsiders easily led to the conclusion that the area was attracting financially successful residents who shared their wealth locally. The costly suburban houses and four-wheel drive recreational vehicles were tangible evidence for this conclusion.

Ironically, the conclusion was deceptive and largely wrong. A high proportion of newcomers had very modest, even poor, incomes. New and exclusive developments created a deceptive appearance of wealth. Service, construction and maintenance employees in recreational areas frequently had to live outside the area where they worked. We interviewed construction employees in the large recreational complex at Big Sky who commuted from Belgrade. This passed on the costly expenses of social services to another locale that lacked the financial well-being of the wealthy development community. Another variation was for temporary workers to reside in comparatively inferior housing provided by development. Recreational areas rented mobile homes to their employees. They were hidden from view and geographically separated from the condominiums for tourists and wealthy residents. A third style of low-income development was in private rural ghettos, as their residents affectionately call them, that were affordable to a few employees in areas near the development. The privileged movers were rural analogs to white flight in the cities. The essential work was performed by workers who frequently lived in poverty. The development that was visible and appealing, it often was forgotten, was primarily funded by tourists for tourists. Local residents simply could not afford to buy or to maintain such places.

Wealthy new residents were a small proportion of either the new residents or the total population in the study area. The meaning of "wealthy" is a subjective matter, but, by any definition, the incomes of new migrants to the Gallatin Valley were modest and had been declining. During the 1970s and 1980s, 21.4 percent of the newcomers reported household annual incomes of over $36,000 (1980 dollars). That figure had dropped about 7 percent, corrected for inflation, by the 1990s. Correspondingly, incomes under $15,000 had surged from 26 percent of the earlier newcomers to 56.1 percent in the 1990s. These differences were very strong ($\gamma = .53$) and highly significant. It is possible that wealthy residents would be less likely to participate in the study. The wealthy and the poor typically are less available for surveys. But that fails to account for why they would be less likely to participate in the 1990s than in the earlier phases of the project. Most new migrants were relatively poor. It also seems that more of the middle-class in the area were dropping toward lower-class earnings than were moving up.

It is tempting to think that wealthy newcomers contributed more financially than poorer residents did to the area. On an individual comparative basis, the wealthy in our sample undoubtedly did spend more money locally. However, most of the wealthiest people associated with the Gallatin Valley were not in our samples. They were not eligible because they were not full-time residents. Their local expenditures for housing, vehicles and athletic equipment certainly must average higher than their poorer fellow migrants. The wealthy varied enormously in what and how they contributed financially or socially to the area. Some, including the famous media and wealthy business and professional residents, owned property primarily as a quiet haven. Some of these were infamous among local fisherman because they attempted to close off public domain access to trout streams. These people were not residents since they lived somewhere else most of the time. There also are famous and wealthy residents who have lived in the area for more than two decades. A couple of them are included in the sample.

The contributions of the established privileged residents frequently were considerable, in comparison to the hideaway elite. Their annual local expenditures were greater, keeping local businesses busy. They also were often generous donors to local cultural activities and welfare causes. Wealth almost inevitably encounters some resentment. Jealousy of what another has and perceptions of the arrogance of some wealthy people were eternal themes in the region. In natural recreational and scenic areas, in-migration by people with wealth often leads to redistribution of large properties, closing those lands to public use. When large parcels of good hunting, fishing and hiking lands are closed off by new wealthy absentee owners, resentment runs high. Given that such people contribute relatively little to the economy or to the social and cultural life of the community, and that they foreclose attractive opportunities at the same time, they are seen as net detractors of the local quality of life. On the other hand, they temporarily preserve lands that sometimes would be quickly subdivided were they not kept in large blocks as hideaways.

IN-KIND CONTRIBUTIONS TO THE LOCAL ECONOMY

The contributions of the poor are also complex. While new residents earning less than $15,000 annually obviously cannot make much of an individual financial contribution, they typically do spend most of their earnings locally. They frequently spend more than that since they tap into savings or take out loans. Since there are so many lower and moderate income residents, collectively they account for most of the money circulating locally, especially during the off-tourist season. The poor also make an enormous and frequently forgotten contribution. They do most of the work for very little pay. Living in scenic and recreational towns for most residents requires making an in-kind contribution.

By working for near minimum wages, skilled, educated and competent residents were in effect paying considerable amounts by foregoing what they would have earned in similar jobs somewhere else. One resident who had moved to Bozeman during the early 1980s became the administrative assistant for a nonprofit academic society. By local standards, she was well paid for her competence, dedication and good will. Several years later, an incoming president for the society carefully scrutinized the budget and remarked, "I thought Laura was full-time!" When informed that she was, he added, "That is what *half-time* administrative assistants get at my university." This in-kind contribution exists in every strata among residents with local incomes. While reduced regional incomes affected local physicians and university faculty, they at least had relatively high-paying dependable incomes. Low-income employers contributed even more because of their relatively greater numbers. People in jobs that usually paid less than $10 per hour (1990) were often college graduates who had considerable skills.

Most lower-income recent residents were not initially concerned with income and living standards. In time, this became a standard and grating topic of conversation. At first, taking an alternative job often was fun, a chance to learn a new trade and to join the salt of the Earth. As costs mounted and the tedium of work set in, much of the fun turned to resentment. Living on such low wages implied not being able to buy a home, have children and obtain medical and dental care, let alone buying a decent car or new downhill gear.

The broader society as well as the local community also benefitted from in-kind financial contributions. Many jobs served the tourist industry, making comparable local tourist expenses lower than they otherwise would have been The tiny industrial sector manufactured goods with national and even international reputations. Custom-made stringed instruments for America's most famous guitar manufacturer were made in Bozeman. Arguably, the most rugged, well-constructed and effectively designed backpacks in the world were produced there. An international leader in computer-lottery design and manufacture was located there. World-renowned fishing and cycling equipment were or have been produced there. The net recipient of these goods was the general public. While local jobs were created and local owners profited, most employees were able to just maintain themselves. If the local wages were much higher, the production sites probably would have been transferred somewhere else, which would have been a loss for nearly everyone locally.

ECONOMIC INFLUENCES ON SATISFACTION WITH THE COMMUNITY

Satisfaction is a complex subjective state based on a variety of factors, of which occupational success and financial well-being are important. Migration involves two complex decisions: the choice to leave somewhere and the choice to move somewhere. Both choices are influenced by an enormous range of interacting influences. For the sake of simplification, the reasons for wanting to move have been categorized along four primary dimensions. The first is job-related factors. These include being dissatisfied with colleagues, the challenge of work, the opportunities for advancement, job stability, income and other economic factors. Second is social ties: family, friends, neighbors, loved ones, voluntary associations and other personal involvements. Third is the constructed environment, the scale, distribution and physical character of the location and its population. This includes local design, appearance, architecture, functional quality of the infrastructure, availability of services and orientation regarding planning, among others. The fourth variable is the natural environment: the scenery, topography, weather and the ways in which individuals evaluate them. Each of these dimensions can be evaluated positively or negatively. From the perspectives of individuals, work, social life, the size and character of the constructed environment or the natural setting may be so terrible that they can't stand it and want to leave or so good that leaving is unthinkable. Other conditions do generally mediate what individuals think and feel.

Chapter 5 described why respondents left their previous locations. They were first asked what they didn't like about their prior location. Their responses provided a list of their negative perceptions. They then were asked if anyone objected to leaving, as a counterpoint of positive reasons to stay. Identical questions were then asked regarding their reasons for choosing or opposing a move to the Gallatin Valley.

The reasons for choosing and for objecting to the choice of the Gallatin Valley complemented the reasons related to leaving their previous locations. Positively, the most common most important reasons reported for moving there were related to employment (53%), followed respectively by social ties respondents had there (25%) and its constructed (14%) and natural environments (8%). Respondents also were asked their second, third and fourth reasons for selecting and for objecting to moving to the Gallatin Valley. The most important factor that a majority of respondents felt first attracted them to the Gallatin Valley were employment factors (63%), social ties (51%), the constructed environment (67%) and the natural environment (65%). Conversely, they reported considerable dissatisfaction once arriving with their social lives (27%) and with the constructed environment (53%). The natural environment was rarely (12%) criticized.

At first, it appeared that economic factors were the primary reasons both for driving people from where they lived and attracting people to the Gallatin Valley. While economic dissatisfaction was widespread before leaving where they had lived, it became even more intense after they moved to the Bozeman area. Many of the newcomers had talents they hoped to convert into employment or a successful local business. Very rarely did those hopes materialize, as in the cases of local industries that manufactured backpacking equipment and fishing gear. Most typically, people were forced by market forces to take their ideas elsewhere to make them profitable.

An early 1980s participant in the study, Ron Sides, was a designer specializing in outdoor recreational clothing. His innovative designs have been in the catalogues of several national outdoor goods retailers since the 1970s. His knowledge had to be absolutely current with state-of-the-art materials and production systems. He also had to have immediate and familiar access to his primary clients, outdoor recreational manufacturers and retailers. Ron moved from Cambridge, Massachusetts, with a recent string of successes, optimistic that it would continue uninterrupted by his move. After three years of watching his business slowly decline, he moved to Seattle where he could be at a major outdoor equipment production and marketing center. He reported two years later that his business once again was expanding. Another outdoor equipment designer, Bob Bauman, had moved to the Gallatin Valley at about the same time. He was an acquaintance, although not a close friend of Ron Sides. Bob specialized in the design and manufacture of bicycle softwear, bags and panniers. His equipment, handmade in a garage converted to a shop next to his small house, is considered to be the most rugged, well-sewn, practical equipment of its type. Bob had just enough sales to live very modestly, earning under $15,000 a year. After five years in Bozeman, he moved to Springfield, Oregon. Three years later, he and his new wife moved back to Bozeman where they remained for less than a year. In 1989, they bought acreage near Pendleton, Oregon, where they built a house and a new shop. He now employs one full-time employee to help keep up with orders. Throughout this period, his business was slowly, but gradually increasing. His decision to move to Pendleton was based on several factors. The acreage he purchased was a bargain in comparison to the Gallatin Valley. It was an area with a longer growing season and much less winter even though it is near a major ski resort. Bob was not a winter sports enthusiast. Most importantly, his new wife wanted to live nearer her family in eastern Oregon.

Perhaps the most definitive indicator of satisfaction among residents in our samples was whether they actually stayed. Most newcomers said they were satisfied with most aspects of the Gallatin Valley; they liked it better than they expected (62%) and liked it better than where they had been living (70%). Yet, nearly one-third (32%) already had moved or were thinking about moving again within one year after arriving. The longer term residents, although not as mobile as recent newcomers, were also likely to move.

SMALL-TOWN POLITICS AND DEVELOPMENT

The local economy was interrelated with all local institutions. The relationship it shared with local political decisions was important and merits some discussion although that subject was not a primary concern of this research. Many respondents, especially business owners, over the years complained about how local and state political structures were interfering with the local economy. This is an extremely complex matter that may have little correspondence to the subjective interpretations of individuals. People, when looking for answers, often looked to politics as the explanatory mechanism, believing that politics was to blame for what was wrong and capable of making it right. The belief may have been hubris to a considerable extent. There may have been relatively little that politics could do to help local commerce prosper, given acceptable limits for protecting the social life and environment in the area. The criticism that growth was being stalled because business was being hampered by political decisions certainly did not correspond with the rapid growth and development in the area and in similar areas throughout the West.

In some respects, the division between politics and the private sector is artificial. The political structure in small towns largely administers the consequences of private decisions. Those decisions usually are made during conversations between entrepreneurs and developers and local politicians and planners. Most political planning generally hopes to slow down and direct growth for the short run in order to stimulate development for the long run. In the Gallatin Valley, most major activities were organized both by the private and public sectors. Several examples illustrate the complex mixing of formal and informal and public and private organizations. The Wally Byam Caravan Club (the International

Airstream club) was initially invited because of the private sector. Local and national members enthusiastically inquired about the possibility of holding an international rally in Bozeman. Eventually, the university, local politicians and the Wally Byam Club joined forces to organize three international rallies, despite considerable gnashing of teeth by local environmentalists. The National College Rodeo, which is held annually at Montana State University, and Big Sky, which has grown to a destination ski resort, were initiated by entrepreneurs. The local university over a century ago was the brainchild of local business people in politics. Small-town politics sometimes allows development when it otherwise would occur somewhere else. It rarely slows development. It also can function fairly efficiently and can act symbolically. But it rarely can make anything in particular happen. The private sector, especially developers, financiers and larger landowners, can initiate change profoundly and rapidly.

While liberal urban theorists espouse greater equity, rural communities are ambivalent about how to or whether to provide greater equity for people. Respondents clearly said they did not want more minorities, industrial growth or other changes that might have create solid employment. The Gallatin Valley is an escapist place for most newcomers. Newcomers probably were no more bigoted than people who lived elsewhere. They were looking for peace and happiness for themselves while not feeling particularly concerned about the well-being of others, unless others infringed on that peace and happiness.

Many respondents were skeptical, fearing that the same old business-developer oligarchy would grow and obtain additional power. They frequently spoke against local developers who seemed to use the laws to serve the rights of the financial establishment. They were perhaps even more cautious that a new and previously marginal group might attain power and influence. For example, many groused about the growing influence of environmentalists, yet generally endorsed environmental protections. They were concerned that they would have to pay a greater share for development or for some protectionist plan. They feared that someone else might get more than they currently had and at a cost to them. They often spoke of the failure of planners to provide satisfactory social services despite increases in their taxes.

The more satisfied people were, the more polarized they were toward planning. More satisfied people either strongly opposed planning or supported it. Less satisfied people generally opposed planning, convinced that it was not effective. The more satisfied respondents were, the more they opposed changes in the status quo because they liked what they had. Most people said they did not support planning, but insisted they didn't want unplanned development. When people evaluated their community as a political entity, they seemed to be mirroring their personal feelings rather than evaluating either the place, politics or the economy. The conversion of a natural resource was unlikely to be objected to unless new use could be shown to have an undesirable consequence such as creating dangerous pollution or closing a major public access. Land use controls were almost never used to prevent development, nor were they intended to be. Thousands of acres of fertile farmland in the area were subdivided with little opposition.

The presence of children in the family did not affect the levels of satisfaction reported by parents. Respondents felt about the same levels of general satisfaction with Bozeman, whether they had children or not. Most (57%) liked it better than they had expected. A few (7%) liked it less. The rest felt it was about as they had thought it would be. While the presence of children did not influence respondents' expectations, it did influence whether respondents stayed or moved away. Parents who found the area worse than they expected were more likely to move than the childless. Parents who liked it as much, or better than expected, were more likely to stay. Children added another dimension of responsibility as parents weighed economic well-being with satisfaction. The presence of children intensified how their parents responded to family obligations. While no more involved with planning parents were also more active in the community. As with other responsibilities that intervene between employment and satisfaction, the presence of children intensified the involvement of respondents. While no more involved with planning, parents were more active in the community.

Planning in small towns is fraught with difficulties and inadequacies. It also is probably the most effective existing mechanism for providing the political sector with a modicum of control. Certainly, newcomers from the cities were ignorant about what policies were desirable or necessary to protect the natural environment. For example, most of them were oblivious to the impacts of nonmetro development on agriculture because they had not experienced them where they had previously lived. Townspeople lived their lives in town except when they took to the countryside for recreation. Ideologues, whether from urban or rural environments, may have been moved to regard the transformation of agricultural land as problematic because of lost aesthetic space or lost production potential. To those few sensitive to environmental and planning problems, most planning seemed to be engaged in piecemeal correction of existing problems rather than widespread preventive measures. Such piecemeal attempts may be the inevitable reality of small recreational towns like Bozeman, where the pressures for development were intense, public support for planning was minimal and reactive and decisions were made on very personal grounds.

Chapter 7

Age, Sex, Marital Status and Satisfaction

Migration is easier for certain demographic categories. This chapter summarizes how age, sex and marital status were related to migration and to satisfaction among residents. Although conceptually independent, age, sex and marital status interacted to influence how people moved and their responses to moving. The characteristics of migrants also are dynamic over time. Newcomers may differ across periods just as newcomers and longer term residents differ. This chapter compares respondents who had moved to the study area within six months of being interviewed in 1992-93 with respondents from prior interviews, all of whom had lived in the study area for at least six years at the time of this last interview. It also compares some characteristics of newcomers in the 1990s with those in the 1980s.

GENDER AND MARITAL STATUS

Gender and marital status are strongly associated with being a migrant. Consistent with other research, nearly three-quarters (72.8%) of the adults newly arrived in the Gallatin Valley were married (Table 7.1). About 10 percent (10.3 %) were single men and 17 percent (16.9 %) were single women. The percentage of men and women, married couples and single adults remained essentially unchanged from 1972 through 1993. Most (53%) households had at least one child. Households with children had increased significantly from 52 percent in 1980 to 64 percent by 1990. Since the frequency of children increased while frequently married couples did not, these figures imply that an increase in single-parent households had occurred, consistent with the national marital trend. There were significantly more families with four or more children by the 1990s (14.9%) than during the earlier years (3.3%), a reversal of the national tendency toward smaller families. It may be that people moving to rural areas are more likely to have larger families.

Table 7.1
Percentages of Selected Sociodemographic Characteristics of 437 Newcomers to the Gallatin Valley during the 1980s and 1990s

	1980s N= 390 %	1990s N= 47 %	γ
Gender			
Single man	10	11	.03
Single woman	17	15	
Couple	73	75	
Number of Children			
None	48	36	.30**
1-3	49	49	
4+	3	15	
Age of Female Respondents			
Under 35	61	49	.24
35-54	31	38	
55+	8	13	
Age of Male Respondents			
Under 35	54	28	.45*
35-54	59	56	
55+	7	16	
Education of Women Respondents			
High school	25	13	.11
Some college	27	37	
BA or more	48	50	
Education of Male Respondents			
High school	19	19	-.12
Some college	21	29	
BA or more	60	52	

Table 7.1 *continued*

	1980s N= 390 %	1990s N= 47 %	γ
Occupation of Women Respondents			
White collar	51	49	.05
Blue collar	49	51	
Occupation of Male Respondents			
White collar	77	50	.53**
Blue collar	23	50	
Birth State for Male Respondents			
Montana	19	39	-.33**
Mountain	9	0	
Pacific	12	23	
Other	59	39	
Birth State for Female Respondents			
Montana	20	27	-.17**
Mountain	10		
Pacific	11	27	
Other	59	47	

Newcomers in the study area were most commonly under 35 years of age, although their average age had been gradually inching up since 1970. This reflected two factors. First, the American population was aging, as the Baby Boom generation matured into middle age. Second, migrants to scenic recreational places were more frequently middle-aged or older. The percentage of men over 35 jumped significantly from nearly one-half (46.5%) in the early period to nearly three-quarters (71.9%) by the 1990s.

EDUCATION

Newcomers usually had graduated from college during the 1970s and 1980s. Most (77%) had white-collar jobs. That figure had dropped to one-half (50%) by the 1990s. Significantly more men who moved to the area during the 1990s had been blue-collar workers than had been the case in the 1980s. Significantly more newcomers had been born in either Montana or in Pacific Coast states. Not one of the 1990s newcomers had been born in a state adjacent to Montana. The contrast between where residents were born and where they had lived prior to moving to the

Gallatin Valley was striking. By 1990, nearly one-third of the residents had moved from a Rocky Mountain state, although none had been born in those states. During the 1990s, practically no one residing in Montana moved to the Gallatin Valley. These figures indicate some harsh realities in the region during much of the study period. Most Montanans realized by the 1990s that they could not find work or afford to live in the Gallatin Valley. Many were native Montanans returning to their home territory, others were looking for a promised land. An especially difficult recession in California during the late 1980s made it advantageous to move elsewhere. Most Pacific Coast newcomers were from California. In most respects, newcomers during the 1990s were very similar to earlier migrants. They were equally likely to have lived in a city, town or the countryside. They had been equally mobile in the past. Only 20 percent had lived in their previous community for 10 years or more. They were equally likely to have owned their home. They had thought about moving to Montana for about the same amount of time. They also were very similar in their expressed motivations for moving to Montana and whether family members wanted to move.

HOUSING

The question of where to live is among the first important matters to consider upon moving. Over half (57.4%) of the newcomers moved into houses, the rest chose apartments, mobile homes and condominiums. Most (83%) moved into Bozeman and the area immediately surrounding it. Almost half (47.3%) lived in new subdivisions in town or on the outskirts (29.1%). Significantly more of the 1990s newcomers (48.8%) moved into the country or the older sections of town. Most resided on lots of less than one acre (76.7%). The later newcomers (38.1%) were significantly more likely to live on small acreage between one and 10 acres than the earlier newcomers (17.1%). That newcomers in both periods were equally likely to buy their own single-family houses further indicates consistent similarities over time. Larger acreages were becoming more scarce and more expensive as the population increased. Smaller parcel subdivisions were becoming increasingly developed and conveniently available, as much as changes in personal preferences for living on a small acreage.

Marital status affects the structure and dynamics of moving. The freedom of movement for single persons stood in some contrast to the commitment of marriage or a permanent relationship. The dynamics changed both within the migrating household and between the household and their broader network of acquaintances. When couples shared the decision to move to Bozeman, they felt relatively little opposition (18%), which came primarily from their children. However, the opposition nearly doubled when either the husband (33%) or the wife (27%) unilaterally decided on Bozeman, the additional opposition coming from the spouse. Single-minded decisions to move to the area were unpopular within the household.

Single people encountered little opposition to moving to the Gallatin Valley in comparison to married people. Single women who moved to Bozeman felt more opposition (19%) than men (13%), primarily because women were more likely to have children who didn't want to leave their previous home. Married couples expressed more and different kinds of opposition. The objections to moving were not so much against moving to Bozeman as they were to leaving their prior location, frequently the hometown to the children. Single men (38%) and women (29%) actually had more opposition to leaving their prior location than did married couples (24%). Singles said that their children, parents and friends did not want them to move away. "My dad was worried about our moving away from Springfield. He had grown very close to my children after my divorce. He had helped us get back on our feet," said one woman in her late thirties. "This was my first big move after college. My parents [who had paid for her college expenses] wanted me to stay at home and get a job," reported a free-spirited skier. While couples felt less resistance to their moving, the resistance was more intense. "Our parents, friends and my husband's boss really hated to see us move. They wished us well, but really hated to see us go."

Objections to moving away from where they had been living were expressed by at least one family member in over 40 percent (42.1%) of the households. Nearly four out of five objections (79%) were about losing family, friends and neighbors. Some (16%) worried about giving up a good job. Very few felt badly about leaving either the constructed (3%) or natural (2%) environments in their prior communities.

Moving *from* a place is related to, yet somewhat independent of, moving *to a* place. The factors and motives taken into consideration can be quite different, in effect, trading apples for oranges. Respondents told us their reasons for moving to the Gallatin Valley. They then ranked those reasons relative to each other. The most frequently mentioned first reason for moving to the valley in the 1980s was employment (53.1%), followed by social ties (25.4%), the constructed environment (14%) and the natural environment (7.6%). The later (1990s) migrants were very similar to the 1980s respondents with regard to having been attracted by economic, social and environmental factors (Table 7.2).

SATISFACTION AND DISSATISFACTION

The satisfaction and dissatisfaction with services in a new community are partially determined by what brought people there in the first place. Since they were attracted by particular qualities, they were more likely to seek and find them. If they hoped to find something, but did not find it, they were likely to be especially dissatisfied. We asked respondents to describe the three greatest satisfactions and dissatisfactions they had with the services and other aspects of the community. Twenty-five percent of the households reported no special satisfaction with services while 45 percent said they had no particular dissatisfaction. Many people were not very critical.

In their initial year, newcomers had little time to acquire much information about services. Their knowledge was frequently based on rough impressions. The few who had specific reasons for having to investigate what services were available were the most knowledgeable about how capable particular services were for meeting their needs. Households with particular medical or transportation needs

Table 7.2
Considerations and Objections Related to Moving to the Gallatin Valley among Newcomers during the Early 1980s (N=390) and 1990s (N=47)

First Considered Moving			
	Newcomer 1980s	Newcomers 1990s	γ
Days before leaving	4	11	-.04
Less than one year	48	39	
More than one year	48	50	
Reason Wanted to Leave			
Job	61	61	-.04
Social ties	18	26	
Constructed environment	17	9	
Physical environment	3	4	
Who Decided to Leave			
Man	35	29	.15
Woman	24	20	
Equal	41	51	
Did Anyone Object to Leaving			
No	56	77	-.45**
Yes	44	23	
Reasons for Objection to Leaving			
Job/work	16	17	.07
Social ties	79	75	
Constructed environment	3	-	
Natural environment	2	9	
First Reason for Choosing Gallatin Valley			
Employment	54%	45%	.21
Social ties	26%	19%	
Constructed environment	12%	28%	
Natural environment	7%	9%	

usually had moved there only after ascertaining what was available. The service that was most frequently praised was Montana State University. Thirty-one percent of the households mentioned that it was a valued service. The quality of local shopping was appreciated by nearly one-quarter. Only schools (11%) and local art and culture (6%) were mentioned by more than 5 percent of the respondents (Table 7.3).

Newcomers in the 1990s generally were more satisfied than newcomers during the 1980s. The 1990s respondents were more likely to answer open-ended questions about satisfaction than the 1980s newcomers had been. The later arrivals were significantly more satisfied with private and public services, transportation and cultural and recreational amenities. The 1990s newcomers were also significantly more dissatisfied with transportation services and the constructed environment than was the earlier cohort.

Satisfaction was often an evaluation of whether the qualities of their new community were as good as expected. Newcomers were generally less satisfied than were longer term residents. The longer they stayed, the more satisfactory they reported services to be. Expectations of newcomers were likely to be based on their experiences elsewhere and upon their hopes. People with extensive urban backgrounds, for example, often took services and the provision of the quality and diversity of cultural amenities for granted. Newcomers felt that some services, for example, road maintenance, should be better than they were. Most residents, including newcomers, were also more universally positive about other services such as local schools. Services which reflected care for human needs were well appreciated. Residents like to think of themselves as compassionate citizens who provide opportunities and care for the young, hence their high evaluation of local schools. More concrete services that involve constant use, such as roads and mail service, were most criticized.

Community

When asked about the satisfaction they felt with the community exclusive of services, economic factors were mentioned by only 4 percent of the residents, all of whom said they liked paying no sales tax. Nearly everyone mentioned at least once that they liked some aspect of the natural environment. Forty-nine percent regarded the clean air, the nearness of nature, the weather or the scenery as the community quality they liked most. A few (8%) interpreted satisfaction in terms of how the community affected their social life, their ties within the community and with family and friends. The remaining 40 percent responded to qualities presented by the town. They liked the small size and the slow pace most frequently. People also appreciated how attractive the town was, often describing its peacefulness and freedom from noise and the absence of crime.

Having already probed respondents about their satisfaction and changes regarding their lifestyle and services, interviewers asked about other aspects of the community. This question allowed residents to include matters that they had left out and to reiterate some they had discussed. Over one-half (58%) said the friendliness of local people was their greatest other satisfaction. Nearly two-thirds mentioned

Table 7.3
Satisfaction with Services and the Social and Physical Environments Mentioned by Newcomers, 1980s (N=390) and 1990s (N=47), with and without Prompting

	Newcomers 1980s	Newcomers 1990s	γ
Percentages of Respondents Who Mentioned Satisfaction without Prompting			
Public service	14%	34%	.52**
Private service	39%	57%	.35*
Transportation	6%	17%	.53*
Culture/recreation	51%	72%	.43**
Social ties	37%	40%	.07
Constructed environment	52%	38%	-.27
Natural environment	81%	88%	.24
Percentages of Respondents Who Mentioned Dissatisfaction with Prompting			
Public service	6%	13%	.36
Private service	36%	47%	.21
Transportation	25%	47%	.45**
Culture/recreation	5%	13%	.44
Social ties	29%	13%	.44
Constructed environment	49%	81%	.63**
Natural environment	2%	2%	.02

* .05 level of significance; ** .01 level of significance.

it as one of their most important considerations. The next most important other satisfaction was their personal lifestyle, which was mentioned by nearly one-third. Much less frequently mentioned were the lack of pressure they felt and the convenient location of the area.

Far fewer people expressed dissatisfaction than had expressed satisfactions. Dissatisfaction with services was widespread, particularly and significantly among newcomers during the 1990s. Nearly everyone was dissatisfied with at least one service. Public services, that is, schools, welfare assistance, recreation facilities and so forth, were rarely identified as problematic. Services criticized the most were private services, including shopping, professional services and transportation. Nearly half of 1990s newcomers criticized private services (47%) and transportation (47%). Together, shopping, medical and transportation services accounted for about two-thirds of all criticisms about services. Criticisms of local restaurants, schools and postal services accounted for most of the rest of the dissatisfaction with services.

Dissatisfaction expressed about the community generally focused on characteristics that other people had liked. To paraphrase my Irish grandmother, they saw a sow's ear where others had seen a silk purse. A few of the dissatisfied complained that the town was too small (3%), the pace too slow (3%) and particularly that traffic was congested (18%). Fifteen percent of the critics found residents closed to socializing or reported that their families were unhappy (3%). Critics also criticized the political process, focusing on an inept government (16%), conservative residents (20%), growth (14%) and the lack of zoning and planning to protect the community (22%).

Other dissatisfactions reported in the initial interviews were similar to antipathies reported for negative experiences in lifestyle. Among the 59 percent who reported dissatisfaction in their personal realm, most newcomers were unhappy with the poor job opportunities (55%) and financial problems they were experiencing (24%), indicating that there was considerable dissatisfaction with their economic adjustment immediately following their move to the area. Similarly, the difficulty of finding adequate housing, mentioned earlier, was mentioned by 52 percent of the critics, along with unfriendly neighbors (15%) and its inconvenient location (7%). Climate emerged for the first time as a quality that many new residents did not like (31%) although most had not yet experienced a Montana winter.

While not every characteristic in the community met with their approval, most respondents gave it generally high marks. A global satisfaction question asked whether their satisfaction was worse than (9%), better than (58%) or about as they had expected it to be (33%) (Table 7.4). Women (11%) were a little more disappointed than men (7%). A comparative question asked whether their satisfaction was worse than (10%), better than (74%) or the same as (16%) it had been in their previous community. These responses indicated that respondents initially felt generally satisfied with the community and that they had set reasonable expectations before moving. In spite of criticism made by 1990s newcomers, their comparative satisfaction was equal to the 1980s newcomers. The satisfaction of men and women was about the same for both periods.

Participation and involvement with other people in the community are important influences on satisfaction. They indicate a willingness and ability to develop relationships within the community as well as commitment to the community. Two general questions about friendship were asked. The responses to these questions show that most respondents were fairly satisfied with the friendliness of people in the area. When asked about the level of friendliness of local people, most 1980s respondents felt that they were friendly and open (37%) or that it was easy to make good friends (28%). Fewer thought they were friendly, but that it was hard to make friends with them (26%), or that people were not very

Table 7.4
Comparative Expectations about How Newcomers Liked the Gallatin Valley in the Early 1980s (N=390) and Early 1990s (N=47)

I like it ____ than I expected to (male response)			
	Newcomers 1980s	Newcomers 1990s	γ
Worse	7%	13%	.08
Same	36%	23%	
Better	57%	65%	

I like it _____ than I expected to (female response)			
Worse	11%	15%	-.03
Same	30%	26%	
Better	59%	59%	

I like it _____ than the last place I lived (male response)			
Worse	7%	10%	-.02
Same	9%	6%	
Better	76%	78%	
Cannot compare	8%	6%	

I like it _____ than the last place I lived (female response)			
Worse	13%	7%	-.03
Same	5%	21%	
Better	72%	62%	
Cannot compare	10%	10%	

friendly (9%). The perceptions by 1990s newcomers regarding friendliness of local residents were very similar to those reported in the early 1980s.

The formation of friendships was significantly different in the 1980s and the 1990s (Table 7.5). In the early 1980s, most reported having made some friends (49%) or to have close, fully developed friendships (25%). The rest said they had purposely not developed friendships yet (17%) or that they felt discouraged by their lack of friends (9%). Significantly ($\gamma = .52$) more newcomers in the 1990s (51%) said they had fully developed friendships.

The primary information collected to indicate how involved respondents had become with community activities was based on questions asking about their participation in voluntary organizations. During the first year of residence, about one-third of respondents and their household members belonged to no organizations and participated less than one hour each week. Another third were joiners who belonged to four or more organizations. Many joiners arranged much of their lives around their organizations as soccer parents and ski club parents. This implied a daily ritual of transporting their children to practices and games for several months each year. It also meant that they coached, attended clinics and organized fundraisers during the off season. "I'm married to the mob," laughed one mother.

Women were slightly more active then men, both in the number of organizations to which they belonged and in the amount of time they devoted. The most common type of organizations to which women belonged were churches (36%) and athletic clubs (16%). Sororities (11%) and service clubs (12%) were the only other types of organizations to which more than 10 percent of the women belonged. Men had similar patterns, belonging most frequently to churches (34%) and sports clubs (23%). Organizations provided opportunities to meet people and to become socially active. Many people also sought organizations, especially churches and twelve-step groups, for more direct support.

THINKING ABOUT MOVING — AGAIN

Migration is a process that ends only with permanent residence. For most Americans, each new community is a stationary stopover enroute to another. When newcomers were called to participate in the research, they were asked screening questions to ensure that they were permanent residents. Respondents had to answer Yes to the question Are you a permanent resident? While this question does not carve in stone their intentions to stay, it is a subjective statement of their current commitment. Responses to this question are presented in Table 7.6. New respondents were further asked if they had thought of moving away from the Gallatin Valley. About one-third (33.2%) said they had already thought about moving again. More than double this number would be gone in less than a decade, but the fact that so many already were considering moving on seemed to violate an ultimate level of permanence. Permanence appears to be a temporary matter for most Americans. Single adults (39%) were slightly, although significantly, more likely to have thought about moving again than were married couples (32.7%). Men and women were equally likely to have thought about moving. There were no differences between the samples from the 1980s and 1990s, in spite of the fact that the 1990s residents reported greater satisfaction.

Each year between 1980 and 1985, respondents who were newcomers were asked if they were considering moving. Relatively few people said that they were considering moving again after arriving their first year. Sixty-seven percent said, "No, I am not considering moving again" (Table 7.6). Twenty-three percent said Maybe and the remaining 10 percent said Yes. The intentions of moving among 1990s newcomers were very similar. Most (70%) said they had no intentions of moving again. In the 1980s, slightly more than one-quarter (28%) of those

Table 7.5

Perception of Friendliness, Formation of Friendships and Organizational Membership among 1980s and 1990s Newcomers to the Gallatin Valley

Friendliness of People

	Newcomers 1980s	Newcomers 1990s	γ
Not Very	9%	7%	-.03
Friendly but distant	26%	30%	
Friendly and open	37%	39%	
Developed friends	28%	23%	

Friends in Area

None	26%	6%	.52***
Same	49%	43%	
Fully developed	25%	51%	

Are Any Members of Your Family Members of Local Organizations?

Number of Organizations	Wife	Husband	Child	Wife	Husband	Child
None	31%	37%	37%	41%	45%	42%
1-3	31%	40%	27%	29%	26%	42%
4+	38%	24%	36%	29%	29%	16%

*** .001 level of significance

considering moving wanted to relocate in Montana. In the 1990s, no women and few men wanted to remain in Montana. Approximately three-quarters (79% in 1980s, 71% in 1990s) wished to stay in the West, particularly Washington, Colorado or Alaska. Only North Dakota, among states outside the West, was being considered by more than two households. North Dakota was being considered by three.

The choices of new places to live were distinctly different from the places that they had left behind. Having moved west, the migrants to Montana wanted to remain there. While some (25%) wanted to move on to suburbs of larger cities, particularly in the Denver and Seattle areas, they still wanted to live in the West. Most wanted to live in towns no larger than Bozeman, indicating their belief that small towns are

Table 7.6
"Have You Thought about Moving Again? Where Would You Move?" Responses by Newcomers to the Gallatin Valley, Early 1980s (N=390) and Early 1990s (N=47)

Have You Thought about Moving Again?

	Newcomers 1980s	Newcomers 1990	
No	67%	70%	-0.06
Yes	33%	30%	

Where Would You Move ?

	Women	Men	Women	Men
Montana	28%	28%	0	14%
Pacific Coast	25%	25%	43%	57%
Other Rocky Mountain states	25%	29%	29%	14%
Other locations	21%	18%	29%	14%

superior to cities. Even so, most of the towns they were considering were suburbs of large metropolitan areas, places like Evergreen, Colorado; Burley, Idaho; and Sedro Wooley, Washington. The very few people who already were looking to small towns in Alaska or in Montana frequently expressed their desire to find what they felt Bozeman lacked, more cohesive community, wilder natural environment, sensitivity to planning and nurturing resources. Only about 5 percent of the residents who eventually moved away chose such places.

EFFECT OF SOCIAL ROLES ON MOVING

There is a longstanding tradition in popular psychological and sociological literature which explains what people do on the basis of what they say they want. Running counter to this tradition is one that explains behavior by knowing what roles, that is, social positions, people occupy. Migration is an ideal behavior to analyze based on these competing explanations. Several comparisons between how people with different role characteristics liked the area were made. The research recorded how well men liked the Gallatin Valley, assuming that those who liked it less would move away more often than those who liked it more. Information about their family roles also was recorded, assuming that men who were single would move more than those who were married. Both assumptions were correct. Men who did not like the area and single men were more likely to move away than men who liked the area and married men. The more interesting finding was that single men who liked the area better than they had expected were more likely to move away than were married men who did not like it as well as they had expected. The importance of family role is clearly more of an influence on moving or staying than is satisfaction.

In contrast, married women were as likely to move away as single women were if they didn't like the area. Personal preference was more important for determining whether women would move more than for men. The implication is that women acted more on their feelings. Men acted more out of duty to their role. Childless couples, lacking responsibilities as parents, moved more than couples with children. Fortunately for the compatibility of married couples, married women and men generally liked the area about the same. Single women liked it a little less than single men.

Differences between married couples and singles were partially due to their ages. Single people were younger than married people, and the young were more mobile than older people. The sense of time and commitment differed between younger and older people. Older people had more concern with permanence, security and predictability. They also understood what they wanted and shopped more carefully for where they wanted to obtain it. Older couples were much less likely to move again than were childless couples in their twenties and thirties.

Finding an optimal new community is an elusive task which these people were already reconsidering. For most, migration to Bozeman was an opportunity to see how close they had come to an imaginary bulls-eye. The Gallatin Valley offered an experience to funnel those few who thought Bozeman was too big, too rapidly growing, to incapable to protect nature, to a more remote, smaller and cohesive place. Those headed to the suburbs, their curiosity about small towns satisfied, were beginning to look to brighter lights and bigger cities.

When newcomers were asked their most important reason for moving to Bozeman, about half mentioned employment. That figure held constant among newcomers throughout the project. About 2 percent had lost their job where they had been living. They and another 18 percent felt that Bozeman offered better job opportunities than where they had been. Twenty-four percent had located work before they moved and 9 percent were transferred by their employer.

The other half said that they chose Bozeman primarily for noneconomic reasons. Fifteen percent mentioned the nearby presence of family and friends or previous contact with the area. Many of these people had been thinking about moving to Bozeman for several years. Social ties and employment were the tangible primary reasons most people chose the location where they lived. About one-third of the newcomers felt that other attractions were more important than ties or jobs. Asked what their second, third and fourth reasons for moving to the Gallatin Valley were, only one-tenth of the total responses were related to social ties or work.

People were attracted to what they imagined to be the characteristics of the community and the surrounding natural environment. Nearly everyone we talked to mentioned community and natural environment as important reasons for moving there. Many repeatedly mentioned variations on these themes, especially the nearby presence of natural areas. Sixty-two percent mentioned more specific attractions to the natural environment, such as no overcrowding, the presence of Yellowstone

National Park and nearby fishing, hunting and skiing. Thirty-eight (10%) persons specifically mentioned skiing.

Many spoke of the importance of the natural environment in their life. Some alluded to the inestimable value of their view of the mountains. The recreational devotees spoke with special passion about how special the area was to them. Many made comments like this one made by a couple in their late 20s: "We moved here from Minnesota. We skied and rode snow machines there, but that was just a taste of what we can do here. We drove out to Bozeman twice (before moving here) during the winter and liked it. The skiing was fantastic compared to the Midwest area. And Bridger Bowl (one local ski area) is so close. We used to have to drive an hour and a half to ski down a foothill. Then, we stood in line most of the time because the areas were so crowded. We're going to buy season passes and ski every day we can." Though divorced, both members of this couple were still living in Bozeman 12 years later.

A professor in agricultural economics, who had left a position at a prestigious Midwestern state university in order to teach at Montana State University, described his infatuation with the area:

I love everything about the environment here. I look out my living room window and see only natural beauty. I have been scoping the hillside near my house and have seen deer and elk browsing almost every evening. My typical Saturday morning is to get up about 6:00 A.M. and go get a load of wood. I can be back home by 8:00 A.M. Then, I take my son fishing in the creek that flows through the little canyon down the road. We don't catch anything very big, but there are lots of 8- and 10-inch rainbows. It is better stream fishing than any that was available within several hours of where we lived in Bloomington. I grew up in New England and it didn't have anything like we have here — and it is practically in our back yard. I took a $10,000 cut in salary to move here even though I am still being paid more than anyone else in this department has ever received. And it is worth every cent I gave up to live here. I shot an elk and a bear with my bow last year. I feel more alive and relaxed than I have felt in years.

This respondent also was divorced during the course of the research. First interviewed in 1981, he was still in Bozeman in mid-1994. His ex-wife, who had never expressed any interest in the outdoors, had moved to Utah with their children to join her family of origin.

Most people who said they had moved to Montana because of the natural environment were more passive in their appreciation than the above cases. Their direct use was likely to be limited to sightseeing drives or occasional casual camping. But they appreciated the constant presence of the scenery, the clean air and water and the lack of crowding. The importance of nature and the intensity with which it was used were more important to newcomers in the 1970s and 1980s than in the 1990s. The number of dedicated hunters, fisherman and skiers had dropped to about 2 percent by the 1990s compared to slightly over 5 percent in the early 1980s.

However important the natural environment was for drawing people to Bozeman, the characteristics of the community were even more important, particularly by the 1990s. Newcomers were attracted for a collage of reasons, which together were mentioned more frequently than economic reasons, social ties or the natural environment. About one-quarter (21% in 1980s, 28% in 1990s) listed the constructed environment as the primary reason for their move. Collectively, most newcomers (84%) mentioned it as a reason. The two most recurrent attractions were the size of the town and the presence of the university, both of which were mentioned by about one-quarter of the sample. The common theme surrounding the size of the town was that it was convenient: "Even during rush hour, it can't take more than ten minutes to drive across town. People here complain about the traffic, they should sit an hour on the freeway. They don't know the meaning of traffic," laughed a former Philadelphian. "I can get almost anything here I could get in Chicago. It is just the right size, maybe a little bit too small. My shopping takes half as long as it did there." Newcomers who came from cities often remarked that the town was small enough to allow them to get to know people. Socially conscious joiners occasionally remarked how easy it had been to feel welcome. They did not feel excluded by local residents intent on protecting their status, as had occurred in the cities they came from. Newcomers had been asked if they had considered moving to other locations when they moved to the Gallatin Valley. The preference for small cities in the Rockies was even more pronounced for their second and third choices.

The presence of the university was the only community facility or service that was mentioned as frequently as the convenient size. Usually, people alluded to wanting to live in a university town because of its vitality and culture, although few mentioned attending university-related activities. They felt that university towns had more progressive ideas or more tasteful neighborhoods. A few others believed that the university offered special facilities or provided a stable business climate.

Except for the university, newcomers sporadically mentioned specific services. Specific reference to schools, hospitals and retirement homes were associated with the stage of life. Homes with children often mentioned schools. People with health-care conditions and the elderly mentioned medical and retirement facilities. Only 6 percent mentioned any other specific service or amenity. Most of these were referred to in very general ways. Several respondents said that Bozeman afforded the advantages of a small town along with the services and culture of a city. A few had based their decision on very realistic investigations of local services crucial to them. A couple who had moved to a small acreage after the husband retired from government services, for example, said that the presence of a comfortable and well-organized retirement home had been important in their decision to move back to Bozeman. The husband, an agricultural scientist, had been temporarily assigned to Montana State University three decades earlier. They liked the area and had developed friendships, but would not have returned had the local retirement home operated by a Protestant denomination not been there. They intended to move into the retirement home when they were no longer able to take care of their two acres.

A few residents mentioned the importance of the airport in selecting the Gallatin Valley. Three newcomers during the 1980s were airline pilots assigned to airports in Pittsburgh, Denver and San Diego. The local airport allowed them to reach their assigned locations with minimal effort. Major airline connections are rare in rural areas. One said, "I commute an hour and a half each way, every two weeks, most of my neighbors in Los Angeles used to spend that much time a day." A consultant also said that the airport was essential for his work. For these cases, the airport was a necessary, but not sufficient reason for moving to the Gallatin Valley. The small-town environment and natural settings were mentioned by all four as reasons why they had decided to live there.

People who mentioned community characteristics were rarely specific. Instead, they alluded to the size of the town, its beauty (7%), freedom from pollution and noise (10%), its location (5%) and that "it is a great place to raise kids" (4%). Such comments were rarely mentioned as the main reason for choosing the area, but were influences in their decision to move there nevertheless. That people mentioned such factors does not mean that they had investigated whether their attractions were more imaginary than real. One couple glorified the small town as having natural qualities ideal for raising children. They had not investigated how they would evaluate the schools, assuming that the place would conform to their expectations. Sorely disappointed, they moved within 18 months.

A few respondents in 1981 specifically mentioned having been influenced by a national map published in *Mother Jones* magazine, which indicated an absence of radiation danger in Montana. They were appalled to discover, after relocating, that, although there were no nuclear reactors, there were nuclear missiles scattered throughout central and northern Montana, a fact apparently omitted from the map. Living in a nuclear-free zone was important to these people and they had not tested their wish with facts. Montana was one of the most heavily armed nuclear powers, only slightly behind North Dakota.

If people mentioned a variable that was important in their considerations and then failed to investigate whether their expectations were well-founded, they were being romantic. They were anticipating a desirable new experience when investigation would have made it appear realistically unlikely. Romantics may be even less realistic than people who have not considered a factor. Both forms of ignorance are based on naive assumptions. Not having considered a factor that is likely to affect life satisfaction is based on ignorance. Ignorance is a simpler error than the error of unverified knowledge. Once people realize that a previously unconsidered factor is important, they can investigate its importance to their well-being and its presence in the place they choose to live. But when people know a factor is important in their lives and then fail to investigate it, they commit an error of greater magnitude.

Both types of errors are illusional when they lead to migration. The error of ignorance is associated with mistakenly thinking they have taken enough factors that are relevant in their lives into consideration. The error of inadequate information implies that people accept an unfounded conceptualization. Many people who made this error of conceptualization seemed almost to ignore deliberately facts rather than risk the loss of their illusion. No one could be realistic about all aspects of the place where they were moving. It came as no surprise that so few people were inclusively realistic about work and employment, social ties, community characteristics and the physical environment. Some were unrealistic about all of them, while most were unrealistic about only one or two.

Lowahna Tierney was among the most extreme cases of spontaneous migration. The week before she was to be married in May 1980 in a small Pennsylvania city, her fiancé eloped with her best friend. Within 24 hours, her Volkswagen Beetle, packed with all of her possessions, was heading west to Bozeman. Lowahna was 21, a clerk-typist who did not like her job at a local industrial works. She didn't want to face the shame and embarrassment she would have felt with her friends. Before dropping out, she had completed one year of college and had earned a certificate from a secretarial school. Her married older sister, Sheila, who had moved to Montana two years earlier, encouraged her to come. She soon found an entry-level secretarial position in a bank, joined a church and moved into her own apartment. In 1984, following a second promotion, she moved into a larger and more luxurious apartment with a lovely garden. By 1990, she was married, five-months pregnant with twins and preparing to move to the Tacoma area with her husband.

While the speed with which she made the decision to leave her hometown was extreme, it was similar to others who spontaneously migrated. She was young, single and had no children. Practically no couples with children or retired couples moved so rapidly. Lowahna had a close personal connection with people already living in the Gallatin Valley, someone she loved and could rely on. She had no strong reasons to stay where she had been. She felt she had been betrayed and rejected. Though her parents and other relatives lived nearby, she wanted to leave. Immediately! She had not begun a career. She had a powerful and painful impetus to leave in spite of her personal history, family and friends in Pennsylvania. She came to Montana for one reason: Her sister lived there and would comfort her in her grief. Lowahna's motives for leaving her place of origin were quite independent of her destination. Her reason for leaving was to escape the horrible disappointment in her life. Essentially any destination would have presented such an escape. She chose to go to where her sister was, which incidentally was Bozeman, Montana. At the moment of her move, she had given minimal consideration to a life plan, job or community.

People who make split-second decisions to move fit into one of two categories. The rarer type, like Lowahna, have experienced some powerful event. These usually involve some devastating episode, such as divorce or the death of a loved one. Heartbroken or heartsick, they want to leave. While extremely rare, the powerful event may be more of a magnetic attraction. One of the few cases of an early middle-aged couple with children spontaneously migrating occurred through a job transfer. Securely settled in a Denver suburb with an upwardly mobile middle-management position in electronics wholesaling, Stan Gonzales received a telephone call one Sunday afternoon from a vice president in the home office in Los Angeles. The branch manager for Montana had to be replaced immediately. Would Stan be willing to take the job? Although a small office, he would be in charge. It would provide some unique managerial experience. Montana was supposed to be beautiful, if cold. There would be a small salary increase and all moving expenses would be paid. Would he let the vice president know by Monday afternoon? The job would be offered to someone else at that time, if Stan didn't want it. Six weeks later, they were living on 10 acres in a subdivision, luxurious by Montana standards, about six miles from town.

"I walked into the living room where my wife and kids were. I was in a state of shock and disbelief as I told them what had happened. My wife and I talked it over and then put it away several times during the rest of the day. Finally, after weighing the advantages the job would offer for future advancement, we decided to take it. Our decision was a combination of being practical, after all the company was asking me to take it, and being cavalier." Their children were three, seven and nine at the time. They were included in the discussion more to reassure them than for their advice. Four years later, Stan and his family were transferred with a hefty promotion to Houston. They were happy to be going back to a major city. The Gallatin Valley had been a pleasant place in which to live, although a bit too cold for their blood.

Most spontaneous migrants did not have an extremely powerful experience that carried them to a new home. Most spontaneous migrants were relatively unattached, drifting or just set adrift. Their backgrounds tended to be unsettled and less committed. As I looked back over their initial interviews, I had often forgotten about them and sometimes could barely recall the interview. Most had moved away before a second interview could be scheduled. Brad Laughton is sufficiently memorable to mention because it took eight failed attempts to contact him before an interview could be completed. He was never at home, a two-room ramshackle house near the railroad tracks with a red late model Turbo coupe parked in front. Finally, we were able to talk.

Brad was a 22-year-old radio announcer. He had adopted his new name when he completed announcer school in Minneapolis just before moving to Montana. His first job was in Miles City, where he lived for a few months before moving to Bozeman. He left Bozeman after a few more months to accept a job in rural Wyoming. Brad had attended two colleges in two years before taking the radio announcer course. He had no close family or friends in the area. He had no outside interests and belonged to no organizations, although he spoke vaguely about maybe doing something sometime. He liked it "a lot" in the Gallatin Valley. The other places had been "okay." He had heard of a job in Bozeman, had called to inquire about it, and had been hired immediately.

Unlike most spontaneous migrants who knew about the area because they or their acquaintances had been drawn to recreation or to hanging out with each other, Brad was solitary. Furthermore, he had a job in hand before moving. More typically, drifting migrants had been told that some kind of work, similar to what their acquaintances were doing, would be available. If it was, they took it for a while before moving on. If it was not, they moved on even more quickly. If they had a stipend, a remittance, then work was less essential, allowing them to recreate or hang out more. A few, very few, remained for more than a few months, although some left, came back, left and came back, drifting in a familiar current.

Another instant migrant was a 51-year-old retired Navy chief who had recently converted to his version of environmentalism, consonant with *Organic Gardening*, which was strewn throughout his mobile home. He had recently completed his third divorce. He despised his new job in the southern California defense industry. So, one day he quit, took his retirement pay and started driving to find the place that he felt best met his ideals of a friendly, supportive and environmentally sustainable life. He settled on Belgrade for two years.

The most extreme version of new migrants who made an instant decision to move to the study area were those who were passing through and decided to stay. A few people, all young, visited friends and took up permanent residence. A few others, who had been tourists, also became permanent residents. Typically, these also were among the newcomers who were first to move away. Millie and Ted Thornleigh, for example, had come to Bozeman to visit friends from their college days three years earlier. Millie and Ted had accepted jobs, out of convenience, where they had attended school. Neither was interested in their work or in spending their lives in Missouri. They were "up for a little adventure" in their lives after so many years in university and being responsible. Two weeks after visiting Bozeman, they drove back to Missouri, resigned, packed their household goods into a U-haul trailer and drove back to Bozeman. Millie immediately began substitute teaching. Ted worked part-time at a photocopy shop. Seven months later, they were heading toward Seattle pulling another U-haul.

The most typical (61%) new residents took less than a year to decide on Bozeman. The rest took between one and two years (18%) or three and five years (7%). People who took more than five years were rare (1%) and usually were waiting for retirement. A typical young childless professional couple described it this way:

We had met in the Peace Corps and completed our education when we returned to the U.S. [his degree was in law, hers was in social work]. We were both working in activist organizations in D.C. and feeling pretty tired and discouraged with the conservative political climate there. We talked for a couple of months about where we would like to go. We wanted to remain active while living in a place where we could see some accomplishments. We also wanted a clean environment where people were concerned with keeping it that way. We considered Boulder and Santa Fe, but finally decided on Bozeman because one of my law school classmates was here.

People who were transferred or who secured employment before moving almost all had taken one to five years to decide to move. One university administrator had attended school at the university and had waited patiently for a slot in his speciality to open up. When it did, he successfully applied. He stayed for nearly 10 years before accepting the same position at a large state university in Oregon for which he had waited equally long and patiently. People who had previously lived in the area tended to take more time than others in moving back. They secured adequate employment or financial security before moving back because they were more aware of how difficult it was to find good jobs.

Newcomers were asked whether they had considered any alternative locations. If they had, they were asked to name those places and to say why they had chosen the Gallatin Valley. It was an exercise in rationality, a chance to explain their choice out of many potential alternatives. The decision to migrate involved two very general sets of choices that ultimately became fused into a single process. The first was the choice to leave a location based upon its relatively low perceived value for satisfying the diverse and idiosyncratic wishes of the migrant. The second was the selection of another location that was also selected to optimize the achieving of the migrants' goals. Some goals could only be achieved at a specific place. If a person really wanted to live near his or her family of origin, then he or she had only one option. Most goals were less personally and situationally specific. One can hunt or work or like the weather in many locations. The relative quality of each may vary with location. If a migrant was solely motivated to pursue one activity, then the choice of locations certainly was reduced, since few places could provide the highest quality of any activity. Realistically, of course, most people had more than one goal and tried to arrive at an optimal choice.

Places can be regarded as having attributes that can potentially give people what they want. As they make their choices, they categorize the attributes they value most and then look to see where they are most likely to find them. For some, there is only one choice. Others don't care to spend much time considering alternatives. Since there are an infinite number of considerations of goals or places, knowing them all is impossible. Not bothering to think or agonize about them saves time and effort, at least at the onset.

Whatever their reason, more than one-third (37%) of our respondents had not considered any alternative to the Gallatin Valley. Respondents were asked what other states and communities they had considered before actually moving. Their first three alternatives to the study area were recorded among those who had alternatives. Another small city in Montana was the most commonly considered alternative. During the 1980s, 39 percent of people with alternatives said their next choice had been somewhere else in Montana. That percentage had dropped to 24 percent by 1990. Three-quarters had considered some other place in the West. Their second and third choices had almost identical distributions. The states most commonly mentioned were, in the following order: California, Colorado, Washington, Idaho, Oregon and New Mexico. Eighteen states were never mentioned as places to where they had thought of moving. Most of these were in the Southeast and Northeast.

Most people who moved to Bozeman wanted to live in the West. Excluding the one-third who considered only Bozeman, another one in six said they had not considered any particular town. Instead, they had been attracted to another state or region before settling on Bozeman, Montana. They were looking almost exclusively for qualities they associated with the area.

Neither of the couples who moved from Hawaii had been to Bozeman before moving there. One had heard the name from a recent acquaintance who had roved about the Rockies looking for the perfect town. Both couples (husband 34, wife 32, childless, husband 42, wife 40, with two teenage children) had liquidated successful businesses before moving. Both had temporarily retired. Both were looking for a beautiful, quiet and restful haven. The older husband said, "I don't care if I don't do anything for the next several years except look out my picture window. I have worked enough to take a long rest. I could have moved anywhere and I chose Bozeman, knowing nothing about it except that it was supposed to be beautiful. Nothing! I don't really care if the people who live here are friendly. I'm not an outdoors man. But, I feel content." Two years later, he had started a new business, which he sold one year later and moved away.

The younger couple had had scarcely any more prior information. She had grown up in Michigan, he in California. They met in Hawaii where both had moved after graduating from college. Having grown tired of a fast-paced life and "feeling isolated because all of our neighbors were retired," they decided to leave during a lull in the island economy. They rented a car in California and started exploring places about which they had heard. They were looking for a place where people "were active and had clean lifestyles. We wanted to enjoy our lives together. We thought we had found it when we drove into Bozeman. The next day, we saw this house and fell in love with it." Both the husband and wife started successful new businesses within two years. They remained in Bozeman and expressed high satisfaction with their choice until their divorce eight years later. He stayed and eventually remarried. She sold her business and moved away. They illustrate that a highly systematic and realistic orientation are not necessary for a satisfactory move. In most instances of instant migration, newcomers moved on much more rapidly.

A young woman (age 22 from Minnesota) described her choice of Bozeman: "My whole family skis. From the time I was in junior high school right up through college, we came to the Rockies almost every spring. I had decided to move to a ski town even before I graduated. I applied for teaching jobs in Jackson, Bozeman and Steamboat, but couldn't find anything. I finally chose Bozeman because it had the college and was more of a normal (nonrecreational) place than the others." She enrolled part-time to work on a masters degree in physical education, found temporary seasonal work and worked as a waitress to support herself. She skied "over a hundred days" each year. She married, gave birth to a daughter who was skiing at age three and moved away six years later.

These examples are fairly typical of people who had had no specific destination in mind. Such people frequently were little different from many people who had thought about towns other than Bozeman or Belgrade. Those who mentioned other places frequently had only heard their names and knew essentially nothing about them.

The importance of a place derives from whether people think it has the qualities that will allow them to meet their goals. A small number of people chose Bozeman because of close personal ties with people who lived there. This was a tangible and already known quality from a reliable source, although quite limited if it had been the sole basis for moving. Considerations people had made regarding work were less tangible. People who moved to Bozeman chose one of the most difficult towns in an economically tenuous region in which to find work. Unless they were independently wealthy or had lined up satisfactory employment before moving, their consideration of economic factors was likely to have been unrealistic.

The primary drawing forces to the area were largely the community and the natural environment. Economic factors were largely the means to that end, rather than an end in themselves. Many had only an imaginary conception of some place in the West, preferably some small town in the Rockies. They were taking a risk, hoping that their illusion, the attributes they thought would be there, would be. The high satisfaction among newcomers would be almost too hard to believe were they not still thinking that their illusions were being upheld.

Moving for most people is no easy chore. Combined with the practical needs of transferring schools, changing addresses, giving up and locating housing, arranging transportation and the myriad other tasks that most households must confront, the physical organization of moving is formidable. Many newcomers grimly joked that they "had better like Montana because they didn't want to ever go through the ordeal of moving again."

The social and psychological responses to moving probably are more profound than the mechanical demands of moving. Deciding on a place with many life expectations tied to that choice requires a powerful commitment for most movers. It implies that where they lived was not good enough. Job transfers, incidentally, are buffered against the negative connotations of this implication. Other reasons, such as moving to avoid health problems or to escape a violent neighborhood, are similarly unquestioned as valid because they share the common norm of responsible migration. But moving to recreational areas such as the Gallatin Valley is unlikely to be for purely responsible reasons.

Moving for hedonistic enjoyment related to community and natural environment demanded some justification among migrants who had taken their move seriously. They had disappointed some friends and family by leaving, while personifying the frontier spirit to others who admired their courage. Many had consciously grappled with the risks and implications of a reduced income or a harsh climate. In the end, they had concluded that the qualities they valued most, and which they expected to find in their new Eden, would compensate for what they were giving up.

Moving is an enormous gamble where the costs and benefits have been considered, the bets placed. Some players take the game more seriously than others, and some seem to play it more skillfully, according to conventional criteria. Unlike a game, though, the judgment of the outcome is based on the kind of payoff the migrant considered important before moving rather than upon a more universally agreed upon criterion like points or cash. When a game is over, it is clear whether a win or a loss occurs, no judgment of the players alters that fact, though extrinsic factors like having enjoyed the game or learning not to play anymore may follow. After moving, the payoff only gradually becomes apparent along with a growing recognition of the accuracy of expectations about the place or one's conception of the world.

People who moved with invalid expectations frequently struggled to preserve them. They were classic cases of cognitive dissonance, having lost their bet without yet realizing or accepting the sad fact. This process applies to migrants who felt impelled to move as much as to optimists who were unrealistic. A middle-aged, empty-nest mother with arthritis maintained her anger and sorrow about having had to move to Bozeman because her husband had been transferred there. After three years, she finally had overcome her dissonance, developed close friends and liked Bozeman.

Cases that overcome unrealistic optimistic feelings were far more common. Initial interviews with optimists frequently seemed to contain words that were out of synchrony with the household setting. One young couple (husband 28, wife 24) with an infant and another child expected described their hopes in a rundown quadruplex on the outskirts of town amidst their unpacked belongings. They had had troubles in the small northern Montana town they had left three months earlier. He had been injured on the job at his family's small logging operation. She had not liked his family who lived nearby. In spite of these problems, they felt torn about leaving. In Bozeman, they were going to create a new life. He would develop a less dangerous occupation than logging, the craft of his family. They would be content doing outdoor family activities in a cosmopolitan town. He was about to go to work as a gas station attendant barely above minimum wage. They expressed certainty that "things would turn out." They were gone within a year, leaving no forwarding address.

COMMITMENT

Residents can derive satisfaction and, conversely, be dissatisfied with any aspect of their lives (Table 7.7). In the Gallatin Valley, people were most likely to mention their satisfaction with the natural environment (81.2%). Cultural and recreational aspects (53%) and constructed aspects of the social environment (51%) were a distant second and third. Satisfaction with the private services (41%), their personal lives (37%), public services (16%) and transportation (6%) completed the list. The positive emphasis was clearly directed toward the natural recreational and constructed environments. Respondents rarely mentioned roads, transportation services or and any other aspects of public services. Residents seemed to take schools, rest homes, welfare, fire and police and other such services for granted rather than criticizing them. The respondents changed somewhat over the years. The 1990s newcomers were significantly more likely to mention public and private services, culture and recreation and transportation than did people during the 1970s. During the interim of two decades, most services had expanded and improved. However, the later arrivals were also more likely to be critical about unsatisfactory aspects of their lives. Their willingness to talk about the sources of satisfaction in their lives, as much as changes in the quality of those sources, seems to be one of the differences between newcomers in the 1990s and earlier cohorts.

Most aspects of the community were appreciated and received few criticisms. Almost no one said anything critical about the natural environment (2%). Very few criticized public services (7%) or local cultural and recreational opportunities (6%). Criticisms of transportation-related services were frequent (28%). Bozeman had essentially no public bus system. There was an airport shuttle and one taxi in 1970. By the early 1990s, the student organization at Montana State University had subsidized a fledgling bus system. Ironically, over half of the residents (53%) criticized the constructed environment in spite of the praise that they also had lavished on it, as a factor that had attracted them to the area. Significantly more criticisms were made by the 1990s new arrivals regarding the cultural, recreational and transportation attributes of the constructed environment.

Having reflected on the satisfactory and unsatisfactory aspects of their lives, new arrivals were then asked whether they were more or less satisfied than they had expected to be. Whatever their demographic characteristics, most (59%) agreed they liked it better than they had expected they would and (74%) better than their previous locations. Most (72%) of their families shared their high evaluations. These high overall evaluations were similar for all demographic categories and for both early and later residents.

Income or, more accurately, the lack of income was consistently regarded as the most important factor that caused people to move away from this Shangri-la in the Rockies. While important, income was not the only reason nor the major factor in a majority of the cases, at least when relative incomes between high- and low-wage earners were considered. How important economic factors were in influencing migration depended on how the information about income was examined. There was considerable difference between the subjective question of whether economic factors were important and the objective question of how much income the household earned. These different economic measures had different effects on out-migration among the respondents. Economic factors also were related to timing, that is, how long they had lived in the area.

People with incomes over $35,000 (1980 dollars) were more likely to remain in Bozeman than they were to move away. Low-income respondents, earning under $15,000, were disproportionately more likely to move away. Nevertheless, one-third of the people who stayed earned less than $15,000 while about one-fourth of the out-migrants were in the highest income group. The effects of low income on moving away were especially evident during the first year. Nearly three-fifths (58.3%) of the movers were in the lowest income category, compared to one-half (49.1%) of the stayers. After the first year, these differences diminished partially because the lowest income residents had already disproportionately moved.

The relative incomes of leavers and stayers, in comparison with each other, seemed to have minimal effect in determining their choices to leave or stay after the first year. Leavers had about the same proportion of low-, medium-, and high-income persons. However, income was also relative to what people might earn elsewhere. Even relatively high-income earners often compared their earnings in Montana with potential earnings elsewhere. In comparison, many of the poorer people who moved away probably would have stayed and been satisfied with the incomes of high-earning out-migrants. In either case, the distribution of jobs and earnings in the Gallatin Valley was a fact which even long-term residents had to face. Relative income within the community did not affect whether people moved or stayed, once they had weathered the first year, which was especially hard on low-income residents. Unlike level of income, the occupational status of residents was scarcely related to whether residents stayed or moved away. Low-status women were almost twice as likely to move away as to stay. But men in every occupational group were more than twice as likely to move away. Men and women for every occupational group were more than twice as likely to have moved away during any 10-year period than they were to stay.

Table 7.7
Community Characteristics Identified by Newcomers during the Early 1980s (N=390) and 1990s (N=47) to Open-Ended Questions about Satisfaction and Dissatisfaction

Percentages of Newcomers Who Mentioned Satisfaction without Prompting			
	1980s	1990s	γ
Public service	14%	34%	.52**
Private service	39%	57%	.35*
Transportation	6%	17%	.53*
Culture/recreation	51%	72%	.43**
Social ties	37%	40%	.07
Constructed environment	52%	38%	-.27
Natural environment	81%	88%	.24
Percentages of Respondents Who Mentioned Dissatisfaction with Prompting			
Public service	6%	13%	.36
Private service	36%	47%	.21
Transportation	25%	47%	.45**
Culture/recreation	5%	13%	.44
Social ties	29%	13%	.44
Constructed environment	49%	81%	.63**
Natural environment	2%	2%	.02
I like it ____ I expected to (male response)			
Worse than	7%	13%	.08
Same as	36%	23%	
Better than	57%	65%	
I like it ____ I expected to (female response)			
Worse than	11%	15%	-.03
Same as	30%	26%	
Better than	59%	59%	

Table 7.7 *continued*

	1980s	1990s	γ
I like it _____ than the last place I lived (male response)			
Worse	7%	10%	-.02
Same	9%	6%	
Better	76%	78%	
Cannot compare	8%	6%	
I like it _____ than the last place I lived (female response)			
Worse	13%	7%	-.03
Same	5%	21%	
Better	72%	62%	
Cannot compare	10%	10%	

*.05 level of significance; ** .01 level of significance

COMMUNITY SATISFACTION

We were concerned with how peoples feelings about Bozeman, their friendships and the place they had left, might change as they gradually experienced their new life. We predicted that they would be more likely to move away if their satisfaction was less than they anticipated and if it declined as they lived there. Among the most surprising findings was that the level of satisfaction people experienced in comparison to what they expected had only a modest effect on whether they left or stayed for several years. The influence that their levels of satisfaction had on their out-migration remained the same from the 1970s through the 1990s. People generally liked Bozeman better than they had expected they would. Men who liked it better were almost as likely to move away as were those who had been disappointed. Thirty-five percent of each type moved away within three years. The men with accurate expectations, those that liked it as much as expected, were a little more likely to stay (73%) than those who didn't like it or liked it even better than they had expected. Women responded more consistently with their feelings. They were more likely to have moved away (44%) if they found it was worse than they expected than if they found it the same as (29%) or better than (31%) they expected. How their expectations had been met mattered more to the women than to the men, at least for the first year or two. A more salient matter that distinguished men and women was how their satisfaction changed over time. Many men who were initially satisfied eventually grew dissatisfied and wanted to move away. Several women who were dissatisfied and stayed eventually grew to like the place and wanted to stay. "I was miserable the first two or three years. Gradually, I made friends. I started to enjoy working at home. Now, I don't want to leave, and he does," lamented Wanda Jolley, a participant who had expressed her misery during the first years after moving to Belgrade.

Another important aspect of community satisfaction was how migrants felt about their new location in comparison to where they had previously lived. Most (77%) liked the Gallatin Valley better than where they had been living. The less that people comparatively liked their new location, the more likely they were to move. Forty-nine percent of the women who liked Bozeman less moved away after three years, in comparison to the 26 percent who liked it more yet moved away. Women who liked Bozeman the same as they had liked their prior home were just as likely to have moved away as were those who disliked it. Men followed the same trends as women, but with less pronounced variations.

Respondents felt about the same levels of satisfaction with Bozeman whether they had children or not. Most (57%) liked it better than they had expected, a few (7%) less. While the presence of children did not influence respondents' expectations, children did influence whether respondents stayed or moved away. Parents who found the area worse than they expected were more likely to move than people without children. Parents who liked it as much or better than they had expected were more likely to stay. In either case, the presence of children magnified the rationale for moving or staying.

Friendship is the emotional bond that ties acquaintances to each other beyond the ties of more formalized responsibilities. We examined how people evaluated the friendliness of the area as an attribute of the place. This dimension is a subjective evaluation of how friendly respondents thought local residents were. We also examined how respondents told us they felt about their own friendships.

We expected that personal friendships would be more important than how the community was perceived. The more friendly and open the community was perceived to be and the more developed friendships were, the more likely people were to have stayed in Bozeman. Most respondents (88%) felt that Bozeman was friendly, although some (27%) felt it was hard to make friends. Most respondents (87%) had made some friends at the time of their last interview. When people thought the community was unfriendly or a hard place to make friends, many (42%) moved away. Those who saw it as a friendly, open place (37%) or an easy place to make friends (26%) were less likely to move.

The personal dimension of friendship followed the same general trend. Most (79%) who had made "discouragingly none" moved away. Only 39 percent of those with some friends and 24 percent with well-developed friendships moved away. The reason newcomers without friends did not have friends was strongly linked to whether or not they moved away. A small number of respondents reported they had deliberately not formed friendships. They had the lowest percentage of out-migrants (17%) of all categories related to friendship. Their preference for the area seemed to be independent of other people, based on a more inner-directed appreciation of their lives.

The Rankins, an early middle-aged (Jeff 43, Sondra 40) couple, explained:

We are not really antisocial. We know we will have friends when we want them. There are a lot of nice, compatible people here. We made this move for ourselves. If anything, we had too many friends in San Antonio and it is kind of relaxing to spend time alone, as a family. The children (Jessica, 11, Tim, 15) are busy with school activities, church and sports. We are plenty busy. We enjoy camping and skiing as a family. I [Jeff] guess we are too busy to have close friends right now.

The Rankins distinguished between friends and acquaintances. Others would consider close friends those people whom the Rankins consider nice people. Lindy Day (29), an energetic woman who varies her seasonal employment between ski instructing and life guarding, defined friends as "people I enjoy doing things with." One of the attractions she found in Bozeman was that "people are so friendly and active. I spend all of my spare time skiing, windsurfing, backpacking or *something* outside. Bozeman is filled with people like me who are up for doing something all the time."

The Rankins and Lindy regarded friends very differently. Yet, both remained in the area longer than most people and reported high satisfaction. Feeling discouraged with a lack of friendships nearly always led to moving away. People who felt discouraged may have followed a path of disappointments that originated with their inability to make friends. People like the Rankins did not need friends, instead finding satisfaction in themselves. They found friends when they were ready. They may be the least likely type of people to move away. Residents who reported they had fully developed friendships also were more likely to still live in the area after three years. Those who gave the more reticent response of having some friends fell in between those who were discouraged and those who were not. Rushing into friendship was not essential for feeling satisfied or for staying. The people who stayed were more likely to make lasting friends than those who left.

Some people seemed to need desperately to be surrounded by acquaintances. Esther Levine, single and 31, spoke of her desperate loneliness when we first interviewed her in 1976. She had thought she wanted to escape from the big city life of the eastern United States. "I miss exactly what I thought I wanted to get away from. I miss being continually surrounded by my family. I miss doing lunch and going to galleries with my friends more than you can imagine." At the encouragement of her mother and her father, she moved on to San Francisco where her sister and brother-in-law lived. Except for the intimacy of living with someone, particularly in marriage, friendship was the most personal form of integration for most people in the area. It may have been the only closely shared relationship for many single people.

Voluntary organizations encorporated many respondents into the community. People sometimes changed their attitudes toward participating in voluntary organizations and found a new source of social support and satisfaction. For example, Kenneth and Mary Davis said they were "not joiners" the first year they arrived. Middle-aged with grown children, Mary was almost a recluse during Kenneth's long sales trips. Three years later, she said she had become active in an evangelical church, where she had made close friends. Her satisfaction soared from "miserable" to "very happy." Joining clubs, belonging to a church and assisting with their operations put people together with others sharing common interests. Affiliation gave them community spirit, contributing to and being accepted by others. Voluntary organizations were important mechanisms for integrating new people into the community. Organizations provided ready-made structures within which people could immediately become members and establish some social foundations in an otherwise unfamiliar place. The longer people lived in their community, the more likely they were to become members. Still, most joiners were likely to seek organizations as soon as they arrived and to become members of several organizations.

Organizational membership was strongly associated with leaving or staying in the Gallatin Valley. Some nonjoiners felt left out. Newcomers who were not members also reported having no friends. People who were socially isolated were also unlikely to seek companionship in voluntary organizations. They usually moved away within a few months. Others did not join because they did not feel committed to community participation, even if they thought they wanted to live there. Over one-half of the respondents who belonged to no organizations had moved away in three years or less. Only 5 percent of those who belonged to four or more organizations moved. The more organizations to which persons belonged, the more likely they were to stay. Essentially the same patterns existed for men and women. People who stayed most typically joined two or three organizations. Only a few (16%) joined more. People who moved away most frequently joined no organizations (35%) or one organization (33%). Only 2 percent of the leavers had joined four or more organizations before moving away.

Laura Killingsworth was the mother of two preschool children when she and her husband, Jeff, moved to Bozeman. Jeff had just resigned his military career as a fighter pilot. At Laura's insistence, he had become a pilot after being awarded an Air Force Reserve Officers' Training Corps scholarship in college. He had intended to become a commercial pilot, but Laura persuaded him to join an insurance firm. She had become a born-again Christian and an antinuclear and antiabortion La Leche League activist during his last Air Force assignment in northern California. She was unemployed, but extremely difficult to make appointments with at times when Jeff could be home. As Jeff put it, "Sometimes I wonder whether I am married! She is gone almost every night." Laura had intensely explained during the first interview that she felt the world had to be saved from evil and that she was dedicated to that goal. She devoted over 30 hours each week to voluntary organizations, not including less formal activities. Jeff belonged to no organizations. He expressed little interest in community or recreational activities. He enjoyed spending evenings at home taking care of their children while Laura was out, in his words, "saving the world."

After four years, his firm encouraged him to relocate to Seattle with a considerable promotion. He agonized, prepared to leave and then decided to stay. Laura had refused to move, remaining steadfast to her community of fellow activists. While atypical, their case illustrates the commitment to organizational memberships that some people make. Organizations anchored Killingworths to the community. For Laura, her precious organizational affiliations were almost synonymous with the community. The more common pattern was for people to have two or three memberships and to distribute their time among a church, a children's team and a service club or professional organization. Most stayers were interested and involved, but clearly not obsessed.

INCOME AND MIGRATION

Income may be regarded as an incentive or as a threshold when migration is considered. An incentive implies that income acts as a continuous gradient. A threshold implies that a minimum or an optimum income is required for determining whether a person stays or leaves. A common myth is that economic decision making acts as an incentive that can be predicted in a linear manner. The more money people earn, the more likely they are to stay. Income as an incentive also implies that the more money they could earn somewhere else, the greater the probability they would move to that place, controlling for the relative costs in moving and living there.

It is hard to imagine that many newcomers to the Gallatin Valley could not have earned more money by living somewhere else. Still, the higher the income, the higher the relative economic satisfaction. For people desperate to live in the community of their dreams, the threshold was very low. Several seasonal workers who relied heavily on State unemployment compensation expressed no intention of moving away, so long as they had enough money to ski, fish and hang out in the fashion to which they had become accustomed. For others who wanted more economic security and material goods, the threshold was much higher. Accustomed to country club membership, new cars and a changing wardrobe, many high-income persons left because they wanted higher earnings than Bozeman could provide. Low-income recreational devotees could have lived luxuriously on incomes too low for out-migrants who had cultivated urban upper-middle-class lifestyles.

How much income respondents felt was acceptable also changed with time and experience. Young devil-may-care migrants who said they needed only $10,000 dollars a year to enjoy life in Montana lost their enthusiasm when a child was born or as a new consciousness of achievement began to challenge their patois of hedonism. Link and Carole Couglan had taken ski vacations to Bozeman several times before moving to Montana. Both had given up steady jobs in the small Upper Peninsula town where they had grown up and married. After high school graduation, he had been a cabinet maker in a local factory. She had been a clerk. Tired of their hometown, their large and dysfunctional extended families and their friends, they were ready for a fun, productive life in Montana.

They had a baby girl two months after arriving in Bozeman in 1980. Link found seasonal construction work during the warm months. The next few months were bleak. They remodeled their mobile home primarily because there was no other work. The following winter, he installed cabinets part-time for a local lumber company. They also had become managers of the mobile home park where they lived. Although financially stable, they had essentially no time for outdoor recreation. A second child was born. Their income was still only $17,000, although they were both working 50 to 60-hour weeks. Previously a hard partier, Link began to hit the bar scene again. Twice arrested for driving while under the influence, he lost his drivers license, his job and, eventually, Carole. Both remained in the area. Their work demanded so much of their time and paid so little that they were never able to pursue the lifestyle that had drawn them to Montana.

Although their experience was more dysfunctional than that of most newcomers, their financial instability and comparative failure were common. The relative loss of income and job instability typically affected college-educated residents even more than blue-collar workers. Attorneys, helping professionals and teachers found the employment opportunities especially tight and incomes unacceptably low. Frequently, people in these professions were wives of men with stable positions, making their family incomes high by the standards of the community. While they could afford to stay, they frequently expressed disappointment, particularly if the woman had resigned a good job in order to move. Former office managers took part-time stenographic work. A former nursing supervisor for a large Portland hospital endured the nightshift at a local nursing home before moving back home.

Not everyone suffered. Comparatively high satisfaction continued for most of the sample who remained. This was particularly true for people who really knew what to expect before moving. People who had moved away earlier, resolving to come back only when they developed more stable and higher income, were almost universally satisfied and stayed longer the second time around.

After arriving, most (75% of men, 69% of women) continued in the same employment throughout the research period, excluding those who retired. People who changed jobs seemed to be as interested in doing something different as they were in maximizing occupational prestige and income. Respondents who frequently changed jobs gave an impression that they were far more likely to move than those who kept their original positions. Fifty-five percent of the women and 71 percent of the men who changed jobs moved away in three years in comparison to 33 percent of all men or women. People often said they were changing jobs because their current job was unsuitable. However, many of the people who changed jobs frequently seemed incapable of remaining committed to either work or place, the reasons they had mentioned when explaining why they had left where they had lived before moving to Montana.

Having determined that people who changed jobs were also likely to move, the next question was whether the relative quality of their new jobs affected moving away after five years. By comparing the occupational prestige of their initial job and the last job they held, a scale of lowest to highest occupational improvements was created. Eighty percent of the men and 65 percent of the women whose job changes were in the lowest category moved away. Nearly one-half of the women in the middle (48%) and high (50%) categories also moved away. Men were even more mobile. Sixty-nine percent of the middle and 70 percent of the high job achievement categories had moved. The relative quality of the new jobs was not nearly as related to their moving away as were their just having changed jobs. Men particularly moved away after they changed jobs no matter how good their new job was.

This finding runs counter to the common notion that job success is the primary reason for remaining in a location. Several of the most successful job changes were moving in order to get a better job elsewhere; this was universally true of men who had been transferred with a promotion. Others who had been most successful in their competition for work left because they had tired of Bozeman for other reasons. For the economically rational, the incentive for earning more money elsewhere provided a rationale for leaving Montana, which was what they wanted to do anyway. The most successful probably had the best prospects because they had already demonstrated their competence and mobility to compete for work.

Employment Factors

During the 1970s, population increase led to new housing construction around Bozeman that spread approximately two miles in each direction through subdivision and small acreage development. Downtown became a fashionable facade, while the commercial sector essentially moved to the malls. Major highway strip developments extended, became denser and took on the appearance of fast-food and car dealer rows. Public and private services and facilities were developed, frequently along the transportation strip. Chain stores, fast-food restaurants and service franchises were complemented by a new library, a law and justice center and a swimming pool, to name only a few municipal developments. Belgrade became the fastest growing town in Montana during the 1980s primarily as a bedroom community for Bozeman.

Having a university and being surrounded by a vast natural recreational area made Bozeman particularly attractive for many potential in-migrants. The economy of the town and adjacent area expanded somewhat independently of the growth. Basic industrial expansion was slight, creating few additional jobs for new residents who otherwise would not have remained in town. Basic industry might have reduced the attractiveness of the area to potential migrants who were looking for a location with minimal industry.

The largest employer in the community, Montana State University (1998), grew from fewer than 2,000 students and 150 faculty in 1950 to almost 10,000 students and 500 faculty in 1988. By 1998, enrollment was approaching 12,000 students taught by 550 faculty (Graduate and Undergraduate Bulletin 1997). This complemented additional employment in small manufacturing firms and recreational and retirement facilities. Additional extractive industry development, traditional primary contributors to the local economy, expanded at a much slower pace.

Actuarial Data

The attractiveness of Bozeman cannot be entirely attributed to the process of economic expansion, where people follow jobs. More commonly, the jobs, poor as they were, followed the people. The area had desirable features for residents and potential residents. It had relatively pollution-free air and water. The recreationally charged industry and natural wilderness made it attractive in addition to having the aura of a small city with a university.

There are inherent strengths and weaknesses in actuarial data. The strengths, which include access to large samples of interval-quality data, permit using sophisticated methods to accurately describe and infer relationships among variables. The weaknesses sometimes seem to be forgotten. A common weakness is generalizing about what is happening to individual cases based on what is known about general processes that affect the general population. This error has been recognized since Robinson (1950) identified the "ecological fallacy." The ecological fallacy pertains to erroneously inferring relationships between properties of actors and their attendant motives. More simply, why a person behaves a certain way is not necessarily a function of the categories with which a person fits. Even when a high proportion of variance is explained across categories of persons and behaviors, the causal inferences that explain the relationships may be in error.

For example, there may be a very high and significant correlation between the levels of literacy and income in several census tracts. This finding means that low income is correlated with illiteracy. The temptation would be to assume that poverty causes illiteracy. This conclusion might be erroneous. It is very unlikely that more than a minority of the population would be illiterate. Consequently, it would be a serious error to conclude that most of the people in the area were illiterate. It would further be unlikely that all illiteracy was among the poor. Therefore, it would be a further error to conclude that most of the poor were illiterate, despite the high correlation. It is even conceivable that a wealthy community, such as an enclave of wealthy expatriates, could exist with high illiteracy. The only way to completely avoid becoming prey the ecological fallacy is to avoid making correlations and causal conclusions across categories. Another way of minimizing the error is to be familiar with and to pay close attention to particular knowledge about the people and their behavior.

OLD-TIMERS VERSUS NEWCOMERS

A considerable body of literature stresses that old-timers and newcomers frequently differ in their sentiments and activities. In rapidly growing communities with high out-migration, differences exist, but become confused. Among already permanent residents in Bozeman, two-thirds moved between 1970 and 1980. That percentage of out-migration persisted into the 1990s. Among newly arrived permanent residents, over four-fifths moved away. Being an old-timer ceases to imply much permanence. During the initial analyses, based on data collected during the 1970s, old-timers were considered to be residents of more than 15 years' duration. By 1980, people who had resided in Bozeman four or fewer years were defined as newcomers. Although four years may seem like a short time for measuring permanence, the residents sampled were relatively more committed to staying than a large number of in-migrants who failed to obtain a permanent address and telephone service.

Table 7.8 shows differences in satisfaction in 1972 between people who had been residents for more than 15 years, real old-timers and less than 15 years, relative newcomers in 1972. The mean (X) scores indicate the average for how respondents rated community qualities on a scale of 1 to 5. The lower the number,

Table 7.8
Satisfaction with Services in 1972 among Relative Newcomers (15 Years or Less of Residence) and Very Old-Timers (15 Years or More of Residence)

Variable	Very Old-Timers (N=39)	Relative Newcomers (N=107)		Difference of Means	Significance
This area has good	X	X			
Restaurants	2.76		3.41	-2.73	.01
Garbage collection	2.59		3.21	-2.03	.05
Road maintenance	3.51		4.23	-4.25	.00
Medical service	2.31		2.79	-2.67	.01
School busing providing access	2.51		3.00	-3.31	.01
Neighbors are more helpful	2.60	11	3.27	-1.92	.04
Schools	2.07	9	2.56	-1.87	.04
Road construction	3.05		3.67	-1.79	.05
Bozeman is a safe place in 1980	2.24		1.78	2.64	.01

1=high; 5=low.

Table 7.9
Changing Evaluations about How the Same Respondents Felt about Downtown, Beginning in 1972 and Later in 1976, 1980 and 1992

Feel Toward Downtown	N	Years: Earlier-Later	Mean: Earlier	Mean: Later	X Test	Sig
Person interviewed	38-60	1972-1976	1.87	1.61	1.61	.12
	58-31	1976-1980	1.62	1.19	3.91	.01
In 2 or 3 panels	48	1972-1980	1.87	1.13	5.72	.00
	42	1980-1992	1.17	1.06	1.27	.28

1=low; 3=high

the more the respondents were satisfied with and approved of the quality. For example, real old-timers on average were neutral (2.76) about local restaurants. Relative newcomers (3.41) were fairly disapproving of them. The scores for differences of means and statistical significance indicate that, in every comparison for 1972, real old-timers were more satisfied than were more recent arrivals. However, newcomers perceived Bozeman to be relatively safer than were old-timers. Some services, especially schools and medical care, were considered to be relatively satisfactory, particularly by old-timers. Others, especially road maintenance, were almost universally criticized.

Differences between old-timers and what we were regarding as newcomers in 1972 were pronounced. The differences changed between the 1970s and 1990s, because life had become worse in many cities and because the Bozeman area had so many more amenities by the 1990s. During the first years of the study, newcomers were much more critical of restaurants, garbage collection, schools, busing and road maintenance. Newcomers less frequently saw neighbors as more helpful than in other places. By 1980, newcomers for the first time reported that Bozeman was a safer place to live more frequently than did old-timers.

The differences between newcomers and old-timers convey only one important aspect of the complex differences in relative satisfaction among various categories of residents. Old-timers were not entirely satisfied with what was happening in Bozeman, although they typically were more satisfied than were newcomers during the 1970s and 1980s (Table 7.9). As time passed, old-timers were becoming more dissatisfied with the appearance and commercial quality of the downtown area. Table 7.9 shows how the same respondents measured between 1972, 1976, 1980 and 1992 liked the downtown. They became increasingly dissatisfied throughout the period. In 1972, the average evaluation (1.87) of downtown by old-timers was slightly positive. Old-timers consistently evaluated downtown lower with each passing interview. The dissatisfaction with downtown among old-timers had become so profound (1.17) by 1980 that their responses could scarcely be lower (1.06) by 1990. Ironically, the facade of downtown had been one of the most attractive characteristics mentioned by newcomers. The facade may symbolize broader differences between newcomers and old-timers.

Chapter 8

Conflict Between Newcomers and Old-Timers: Confusion about Being Local or Cosmopolitan

Community structure cannot be entirely described by secondary data. Too many idiosyncratic characteristics affect variation from one place or one time to the next to be validly understood solely on the basis of data collected for some other purpose. The collection of census data on April 1 makes those data especially inappropriate to use for explaining behavior in seasonal tourist areas. The tourist season between Memorial Day and Labor Day attracts large numbers of seasonal employees. Seasonal tourist areas frequently depend upon college-age employees to do much of the labor. Young seasonal workers also are commonly associated with many varieties of criminal behavior. Consequently, such communities are likely to experience more crime because they have so many young transients (Jobes, 1999), which is disproportionately high because the April 1 population figures understate the actual town size during the economically active months. These idiosyncracies of tourist towns could lead to invalid analyses. If data for tourist towns then were compared to agricultural towns, the analyses would have to be interpreted cautiously to avoid biases. Since the populations of agricultural towns have more old people and swell less during some seasons, they are less likely to have as much chance of deviance occurring there,

IDENTITY

No problem related to growth in Bozeman and in other towns in scenic recreational locations is more evident than is the rancor between newcomers and old-timers. These two categories are highly subjective, even mythical. From the perspective of recent arrivals, people who have lived there a few years longer than themselves are old-timers. Before the 1980s, the caricature was of newcomers buying a pair of Tony Lamas and a Resistol within a few months after arriving. Their new plumage made them essentially indistinguishable from people who had been born there. They were almost old-timers except for a few subtle cues. Fashion-conscious newcomers even learned those cues after awhile. I felt relieved of the burden of being a newcomer when Montana license plates were attached to my pickup truck and an in-state fishing permit was in my wallet. Two years later, when I bought my first pair of cowboy boots and Sorels, I felt legitimate and authentic. After all, I was fencing, haying, raising sheep, heating with firewood, gardening and engaging in a long list of other activities that made me a Montanan.

The distinction between newcomers and old-timers is not reserved for western towns. Lewis Ploch (1989) discussed the distinction between old-timers and newcomers in rural Maine. Ploch also studied a town that was experiencing problems, as exurbanites sought solitude, safety and community. The town meeting became severely tried as hosts of newcomers strained the traditional political system beyond endurance. Traditional communities from biblical times through the Middle Ages frequently preserved themselves from outsiders by fleeing or fighting. Walls and moats protected inhabitants from invading armies and undesirables wanting refuge or property. The Yugoslav republics are attempting to establish spatial boundaries around social identity between newcomers and old-timers.

Robert K. Merton (1949, pp. 441-474) made an influential and enduring sociological distinction between a dimension that is often crucial between recent and long-term residents. Merton contrasted what he termed "locals" with "cosmopolitans." He focused upon styles of leadership. Locals were "inside operators," almost exclusively dedicated to and knowledgeable about local community matters. They were motivated to engage in activities out of a desire for personal gain, albeit justified from their perspective as for the good of the town. Their success hinged upon a network of locals like themselves. Through extensive membership in many organizations, they knew who to call, what to say and how to say it. Their orientation was toward the real local social and natural environment.

Cosmopolitans were more likely to be experts, informed about and concerned with broad issues that extended beyond the local community. They were motivated primarily from intellectual interests and principles. When they joined local organizations, they sought to satisfy their more ecumenical appetite. Locals looked upon cosmopolitans as interesting-idea people whose feet were not entirely on the ground. Cosmopolitans thought locals lacked a worldview that could be utilized for the benefit of the town and surrounding area.

Merton made clear that the difference between locals and cosmopolitans was not merely one of newcomers and old-timers. Locals in Rovere, the town he studied, tended to be locally born and raised, leaving town solely to go to the service or to college. However, some cosmopolitans also had local origins. Their differences were a matter of perspective, how and why they engaged in activities.

In rapidly changing towns with heavy migration like Bozeman, newcomers are seen as a constant source of problems as well as vitality. In Bozeman, the problems were simplistically seen as the ways of the city being imposed on those of the town. Those ways included the direct effects of in-migration, such as population growth, subdivision, traffic, increased taxes, crowded schools and welfare transients. In southwest Montana, many problems were stereotyped around wealthy, professional, city people who were believed to be imposing their aggressive yet stylish city style of life on the its hapless local residents. Newcomers were identified as the carriers of new and frequently objectionable solutions — initiators of new modes of education and religion, new ideas for Main Street, new designs for housing and recreation, new protections for the countryside. They were the initiators of the new, sometimes exploitive and exclusionist plans. In short, the cosmopolitans were seen as newcomers. If the cosmopolitans were criticized, locals were hardly lionized. Their frequently self-serving and short-sighted intransigence built around development seemed to balance the equally insensitive orientations of more aloof new residents and their attendant impacts.

There are essentially no old-timers in a residential sense in towns like Bozeman. A small proportion, ranging from zero to 20 percent, have roots of more than two generations. "Local" is a symbolic concept. Merton was absolutely correct that local and cosmopolitan are dimensions based on how people were oriented to issues and how they got things done. He did not anticipate a town that has few or no long-term residents. The few long-term residents are indeed likely to be in businesses based directly on development, such as real estate, hardware, fuels, lumber and construction, businesses that prosper due to staying power. Long-term businesses are the residuals of successful establishments that have not left. They remain ever poised to capitalize on any upturn in the local economy.

Many businesses are owned by newcomers. In the Gallatin Valley, as elsewhere, banks, real estate agencies and much of the commercial establishment are branches of regional or national corporations. Their managers frequently had been transferred from other locations. Their strategies were often largely based on externally driven decisions. Their financing came from outside investors or from entrepreneurs who had recently moved there. Their development and planning strategies were sophisticated methods and philosophies used in other places.

Nick O'Tool, a real estate developer, participated in the study from the early 1980s. The author was able to talk with him on several occasions in addition to five interviews. Nick was a central figure in planned developments in the area during the 1980s and 1990s. Admired by some and vilified by many residents, he was locally oriented. He drew upon his skills and connections in real estate honed in California and Oregon. He sometimes consulted with environmentally sensitive architects and designers to establish a veneer of environmental sensitivity. He developed land for a profit. He used whatever advice and design that was necessary to achieve that goal. He appreciated long-term environmentally sensitive plans and maximized his short-term investment. Soft-spoken, athletic and sophisticated, Nick was concerned with healthy lifestyles and with the prosperity of the local economy.

One participant from the 1970s sample, Bella Thomas, had amassed a considerable fortune with her husband. Their wealth also was largely from real estate. She was a member of several influential and effective local boards. Among other activities, she was credited with organizing a cadre of politically influential and financially dominant local families to build a large sophisticated regional natural science and art museum. Except for their hope of profiting within the local market, Nick O'Toole and Bella Thomas seemed to be pretty cosmopolitan.

Who, then, were the cosmopolitans in the study area? They exemplified some aspects of what Merton said cosmopolitans should be. They were selectively active, motivated by principled conviction. They were oriented toward the outside issues and solutions. They were not local joiners for the sake of joining, although some were active in organizations devoted to their interests. Through their activities in local organizations, they also developed a network of like-minded acquaintances.

University faculty were particularly represented among the cosmopolitans. Ron Smith, a social science professor in the Business School, contributed several hours each week to environmental and planning organizations. His involvement reflected his love of hiking, fishing and cross-country skiing, his professional skills in environmental management and his dedication to creating a beautiful and sustainable environment. He had been a gratis member of the planning board, the pathway committee and several environmental boards. Johan and Sweda Ernst joined the art department faculty during the mid-1970s. After Sweda achieved international recognition for her rustic sculpture, the Ernsts left the classroom, devoting themselves to art and horses. They remained instrumental in the local art community by hosting gatherings and visiting artists.

PSEUDODISTINCTIONS

The difficulty in distinguishing local from cosmopolitan is evident from these examples. Nick and Bella would recoil at the insinuation that they were less cosmopolitan than Ron Smith and the Ernsts. Nick and Bella maintained that their effective tactics were legitimate and sound procedures for local business or public service. They also believed their developments contributed to the growth and development of the town and area.

In Rovere, Merton found that locals were concerned with local matters. They associated and worked with a network of others like themselves to accomplish their goals. In highly mobile recreational and scenic towns, "local" has two common meanings. The first is the symbolic, and mythological, old-timer, a multigenerational resident whose knowledge and orientation are essentially limited to the local area and community. This is an ideal type, the local end of the local-cosmopolitan continuum. In towns like Jackson and Aspen, authentic old-timers are essentially nonexistent. In Livingston and Cody, there are a few. Whether there are genuine locals, then, is largely determined by how long and how fast a town has been growing. New recreational developments, like Vail and Big Sky, have none. Sleepy agricultural towns way off the beaten path have many.

The second meaning of "local" is what pejoratively is referred to as the Chamber of Commerce mentality. These locals are identified with local business, finance and real estate. They have been criticized since Sinclair Lewis wrote *Main Street* for being profit-oriented and self-serving to the destruction of the higher interests of the community. They are labeled as locals by self-designated cosmopolitans who regard themselves as operating on a higher ethical plane. They see themselves as holding a broader environmental and aesthetic view for developing and preserving its natural qualities. The cosmopolitans prefer to think of themselves as the protagonists, the locals as the antagonists.

While this pseudodistinction between local and cosmopolitan is conceptually very different from Merton's terms, it more accurately expresses what happens in rapidly growing recreational areas. Fast-buck developers and business people scarcely give lip service to aesthetics or to historical and environmental preservation. Their philosophy, if present, is founded on power and profit: the Invisible Hand will miraculously clean up the destruction they wreak. A few of the purest environmentalists and preservationists comprise the cosmopolitan extreme.

Most residents fell toward the center of the continuum and were critical of the extremes. Most residents, pseudolocals and cosmopolitans wanted to protect the natural beauty, the relaxed pace and the sense of community, although their understanding of these qualities may have been superficial. Most business people and developers did not object to working with the local planning office. Some wanted to create a good place to live. Others simply complied. Whatever their motive, they knew their activities were more protected by having worked through the planning structure. Increasingly, historic preservation and environmental planning were recognized as good business. A beautiful town which has tastefully preserved and incorporated its natural and historic assets into development is a sounder place for continuing growth, investment and profit.

As aesthetically pure as pseudocosmopolitans in the Gallatin Valley may have been, they also contributed to the very problems they claimed to want to resolve. They were part of the collective flow of people into and out of the area. The collective effects of their needs for housing, roads, shopping areas and recreation sites inescapably were development, growth and change. Many pseudo-cosmopolitans had a deep appreciation for nature and wanted to live in nature. They were ready clients for outlying, large-lot subdivisions that were among the most destructive and exclusionary uses of land. Such people, ironically, have been found to consume more electricity, gas and other natural resources than people who live in town. Despite their environmental rhetoric and benign orientation toward development, they were significant contributors to the problems they blamed on locals (Fuguitt, Heberlein, and Rathburn, 1991).

Lacking genuine locals and cosmopolitans, a more accurate distinction may be between pseudolocals and pseudocosmopolitans. The struggles between pseudolocals and pseudocosmopolitans usually focus on environmental and development issues. Their relative contributions to the community as a social system are rarely considered. Each represents a destructive process to the sustained personal, dependable, predictable informal social structure that comprises community. Community is undermined by the lack of permanence and commitment which earmarks both pseudolocals and pseudocosmopolitans. Their struggle may involve an objective, rational discussion of the physical and even social properties of the place. Yet, they personify a lack of the essential integration into the rich human stew of community.

Some styles and motivations among community members are more effectively described by substantive issues in the local-versus-cosmopolitan distinction. Religious zealots were among the most unusual and extreme examples of newcomers who selected the area for noneconomic yet substantive reasons.

Belgrade had a regional reputation as a conservative Christian community. The reputation was partially due to a local radio station that broadcasts a traditional Christian religious message. The surrounding farming area had been settled at the turn of the century by a traditional ethnic Protestant sect. Farmers on one side of Belgrade continued to actively support and affiliate with the sect. Two energetic born-again ministers with churches in or near Belgrade were well-known in the region. The Christian Right was well-organized, active in campaigns opposing abortion, supporting home schooling, opposing sex education in public schools and other causes that frequently engage conservative Christians. Belgrade had the additional attraction of remaining a working-class small town in an agricultural area, personifying the virtues of the traditional rural mystique. Never mind that Belgrade was becoming largely a bedroom community for Bozeman. Never mind that it was among the fastest growing towns in the region, quickly becoming a suburb for a small city. It still was small and rural by the standards of most modern Americans, and it symbolically represented a traditional Christian perspective.

Any confusion the reader might feel about local and cosmopolitan is to be expected. There were very few multigenerational old-timers in the study area. The high turnover of residents made nearly everyone experienced and knowledgeable about the world beyond Bozeman. The high turnover also created a fluid social system, easy to fit into and to move out of. The style of the business people and other pragmatic residents had an air of personal folksiness, but most were too cosmopolitan to be accurately labeled as locals. Authentic locals can only exist in a community that has a sufficiently large and persistent permanent population to establish a network comprised of people whose experience is limited to their surroundings. The struggles between planning and development advocates and opposers is between two cosmopolitan groups, neither of which contains many members who will remain long enough to be authentically local. The difference between local and cosmopolitan, then, is largely symbolic in recreational towns. Both claim legitimacy or virtue regarding the highest interests of the community. The pseudolocals claim authenticity that only locals can have.

CHANGING PERCEPTIONS OF THE COMMUNITY: NEWCOMERS AND OLD-TIMERS

Old-timers have already been shown to have generally higher satisfaction about living in the Gallatin Valley than newcomers. However, how the relative satisfaction of newcomers and old-timers has changed over time has not been discussed. Considering their evaluations from different perspectives in time allows comparing how newcomers and old-timers liked the community both in comparison to each other and in comparison to other newcomers and old-timers. It may be that the smaller size and slower pace of the early 1970s were more appreciated by both groups. These comparisons provide some insight into the nature of community qualities that residents liked or disliked. The answers also provide foundations for conjecturing about dynamic factors that will continue to influence future growth and satisfaction in the area.

Tables 8.1-8.3 summarize how respondents answered exactly the same questions beginning in the early 1970s and ending in the early 1990s. Respondents were asked questions that measure global satisfaction, more specific measures of satisfaction with public and private services and measures related to future population growth and job opportunities. Table 8.1 summarizes whether respondents believed Bozeman and the surrounding area had everything necessary for a happy life, a general subjective measure of how respondents felt about the area. If everyone strongly agreed with the statement, the mean score would be 1. If every one strongly disagreed, the score would be 5. Respondents in the original 1972 panel and also interviewed in 1976 and in 1980 are compared with respondents in 1992. The responses by old-timers and newcomers for each of the time periods also are shown.

The responses of old-timers reflect a historical perspective of what how they were reacting to the place at different periods. First, as time passed, panel participants more strongly agreed that the area had everything that was necessary for a happy life. As they became older, they were more globally satisfied with the community. The 1992 respondents did not evaluate the area as highly as members of the panel study. Second, old-timers, those respondents who had lived in the area more than 15 years at the time of the interview, incrementally liked the area better from 1972 ($\bar{x}$ = 2.26) until 1980 ($\bar{x}$ = 1.82). Their responses in 1992 ($\bar{x}$ = 1.97) reversed what had been a trend of liking the area better. It is possible that the negative effects of development were causing the otherwise satisfied old-timers to become more critical by the early 1990s. Third, newcomers gradually evaluated the area more positively throughout the study period. Unlike old-timers, newcomers continued to like the area even into the 1990s. Fourth, old-timers liked the area better than newcomers at every time period. Even in 1992, more old-timers ($\bar{x}$ = 1.97) believed that the area had everything necessary for a happy life than did newcomers ($\bar{x}$ = 2.22), despite the growing dissatisfaction among old-timers during the previous decade.

POPULATION GROWTH

Both old-timers and newcomers were becoming were aware that population growth presented problems for the area. Between 1972 and 1992, there was a steadily growing awareness of the problematic nature of population growth by the panel and by old-timers. Newcomers reversed that trend until the 1990s. Lacking any local perspective of growth, newcomers during the 1980s typically did not see any problem. A recent in-migrant from Chicago in 1980 ridiculed letters to the editor that complained about traffic problems in Bozeman: "For the past ten years, I spent an hour each way commuting between my house and my office. Here (a subdivision seven miles from town), I drive almost as far as I did then, and it only takes fifteen minutes. Hell, it can't take more than ten minutes to drive all the way across town at five o'clock on a Friday afternoon." In 1972, population growth was seen as relatively unimportant ($\bar{x}$ = ca. 2.5) by all categories. The recognition that population growth carried negative implications for the area indicates a

Table 8.1
Mean General Satisfaction and Attitudes about Population Growth among Newcomers and Old-Timers to Bozeman Between 1972 and 1982*

	Number of Responses	Bozeman has Everything for a Happy Life	Population Growth Presents No Problems
1972	146	2.35	2.51
1976	60	2.02	2.75
1980	17	1.76	2.51
1992	149	2.02	2.76
Old-timers 1972	107	2.26	2.58
Old-timers 1976	96	2.04	2.73
Old-timers 1980	71	1.82	2.77
Old-timers 1992	104	1.97	2.75
Newcomers 1972	39	2.59	2.56
Newcomers 1976	11	2.64	2.41
Newcomers 1980	9	2.33	2.37
Newcomers 1992	45	2.22	2.83

*1= strongly agree; 5= strongly disagree.

growing sensitivity to the consequences of growth for the local area. Despite the growing sensitivity, population growth was still being evaluated somewhat neutrally ($\bar{x} = 2.76$) into the 1990s.

Public Service

Public services contribute to the quality of community. Satisfaction with public services is one indicator of how effectively the community is providing for a happy life. Table 8.2 summarizes how residents evaluated local schools, road maintenance and garbage collection. Comparison of these services illustrates how widespread the evaluation of different aspects of community infrastructure can be. Schools consistently received relatively more positive appraisals than road maintenance. Garbage collection fell somewhere in between. In addition to these varying levels of approval among services, several differences are evident in these data. With few exceptions, old-timers evaluated local services higher than did newcomers. There is a tendency for all categories of respondents to systematically rate the services better from 1972 until 1980. In 1992, there is an abrupt reversal of that positive trend, with a few exceptions. The panel had reversed its more positive evaluation of schools by 1980. Newcomers continued to positively evaluate local road maintenance even through 1992. For other evaluations some significant and negative changes seemed to have occurred by 1992. This growing negativity reflects dissatisfaction. Newcomers were most likely evaluating services from the perspective of their previous home. They gave garbage collection an average grade of good ($\bar{x}$ = 2.00) in 1980, the highest evaluation of any service by any group, only to significantly reduce that evaluation ($\bar{x}$ = 2.78) by 1992.

Shopping and Employment Opportunities

Public services are only one important aspect of a satisfactory community. Table 8.3 summarizes how respondents between 1972 and 1992 evaluated shopping facilities in Bozeman. Their evaluations are remarkably similar to how they had evaluated public facilities. Once again, the responses became more positive between 1972 and 1980, only to reverse that trend by the 1990s. Newcomers were especially likely to report that shopping had improved through 1980. They increased their evaluation of shopping by an entire measurement unit from 1976 (3.09) to 1980 (2.00), only to become more negative (2.98) by 1992. The responses among panel members and old-timers followed similar variations.

Difficulties in finding employment plagued many new residents in the Bozeman area. There is a paradox associated with adequate employment in scenic recreation areas with high in-migration. Adequate employment from the perspective of the majority of marginally employed newcomers might imply both a rapid increase in jobs and an escalating population. Yet, there is widespread recognition that population growth would destroy much of the scenic and recreational qualities, as well as undermine the already fragile foundations of social life in the community. As a result of this paradox, residents hold mixed opinions about more job opportunities being desirable in the area. Among people whose incomes were derived independent of the area, there is relatively little support for more economic development or population growth. Such residents are a minority. More typical are those newcomers hoping to become comfortably established. They are complemented by people who have become established and who are trying to avoid being replaced by newcomers looking for solid employment.

Attitudes about the adequacy of employment opportunities among respondents between 1972 and 1992 are summarized in Table 8.3. Most people believed that the local area offered poor job opportunities and that more and better jobs were needed in the study area. Between 1972 and 1980, slightly more newcomers and old-timers believed that employment opportunities were improving. Newcomers continued to agree with this orientation into the 1990s. Old-timers abruptly changed their minds in 1992. One interpretation for their change in attitude is that even established old-timers were finding it difficult to earn what they considered a decent living, especially in comparison to the new cohort of in-migrants. It also is possible that old-timers had accepted some broader notion that more jobs means a better community, a notion not shared by the newcomers. In any case, by 1992, old-timers seemed to have become more critical of employment opportunities than they had been in years past, just as they had become more critical about other aspects of the community.

Table 8.2
Average Evaluations (Means) of Public Services Between 1972 and 1992 by Residents in Bozeman*

	Schools	Road Maintenance	Garbage Collection
1972	2.44	3.71	2.75
1976	2.08	3.43	2.22
1980	2.48	3.13	2.03
1992	2.36	3.50	2.49
Old-timers 1972	2.11	3.41	2.46
Old-timers 1976	2.06	3.40	2.26
Old-timers 1980	2.07	3.10	2.06
Old-timers 1992	2.33	3.48	2.42
Newcomers 1972	2.79	4.23	2.89
Newcomers 1976	2.18	3.72	2.27
Newcomers 1980	2.55	3.66	2.00
Newcomers 1992	2.48	3.57	2.78

*1=excellent; 5=very poor.

HOPES FOR IMPROVEMENTS, LIBERATION AND SALVATION

Newcomers contributed in numerous ways to the community, in spite of their propensity to soon move on. Many aesthetic and practical achievements in the area were initiated by new arrivals who had long departed when their ideas reached fruition. The bike paths in Bozeman had been a cause of Sonya Lowell, the wife of a university professor. San Francisco born and raised, she left soon after their divorce, several years before the paths became established. The local planning ordinance in Bozeman was doggedly advocated by a professional planner who had recently migrated to the study area from Florida. He volunteered his time and professional skills, aggressively carrying the plan through a gauntlet of opposition. His was the last of a series of attempts to establish a plan by newcomers spanning two decades. The summer festival was largely conceived and developed by relatively recent arrivals. The Museum of the Rockies, the gem of local cultural constructions, was facilitated by a director who came, did an incredible job at fundraising and coordinating ideas and activities and then left. These accomplishments also are noteworthy because each involved both locals, pseudolocals and cosmopolitans working together to achieve their notion of community.

Table 8.3
Mean Evaluations of the Quality of Private Goods and Services and Job Opportunities among Panel Members, Old-Timers and Newcomers in the Bozeman Area Between 1972 and 1992

	Shopping Facilities*	Local Area Has Poor Job Opportunities**
1972	2.83	1.90
1976	2.54	2.25
1980	2.19	2.19
1992	2.49	1.92
Old-timers 1972	2.62	1.91
Old-timers 1976	2.57	2.33
Old-timers 1980	2.12	2.14
Old-timers 1992	2.39	1.85
Newcomers 1972	2.90	1.77
Newcomers 1976	3.09	1.91
Newcomers 1980	2.00	2.13
Newcomers 1992	2.96	2.26

*1=excellent; 2=very poor.
**1=strongly agree; 5= strongly disagree.

The most common resolution to commitment lies somewhere between the extremes of moving tomorrow or staying for life, of moving for no reason in particular or moving with a passionate motive. Most newcomers had moved with the hope and intent of staying forever. The qualifications and conditions of staying forever usually were not clear and, consequently, could not be articulated very well. There was an unstated exit clause: If . . . I don't like it enough, . . . I can change my mind. For a fortunate few, there was no need to refer to this clause. The lackadaisical few had the clause written into their commitment to transience. Their expectations might have been perfectly satisfied and they still might have wanted to see what living in another town felt like. One couple in their 20s, who were perceiving life as an adventure, moved to Bozeman after a stint in Africa with the Peace Corps. They took off to Kathmandu after two years. They retained undeveloped rural property outside of Bozeman and left saying, "We really like it here. I am sure we'll come back someday."

Howard Becker (1960) has described commitment as placing side bets. Moving is related to a gargantuan number of bets on one's own tastes and on the ability of a place to satisfy them. Commitment comes from not wanting to break the ensuing friendships, job opportunities, time invested in house and organization, local economic investments and so forth rather than from the idea of commitment as life-long permanence in the community. To break those real, tangible side bet commitments would involve their loss. On the other hand, one might give up those investments, cut ones's losses and leave. Self-knowledge is probably as filled with error as is knowledge about a place. As one's tastes change or become clearer and the inability to satisfy them becomes apparent, the precise wording in the exit clause appears. Forever indicates a state of being as responsible as one can feel, even to the exclusion of other fairly likely outcomes that were not considered when the commitment was made.

Permanence was important for most migrants in our research. Otherwise, they would not have stressed their responsible intentions. Permanence was especially important to many migrants who were moving for reasons of a preferred lifestyle. They were attached to a belief that there was a better way for them to live. Their motives were different from those people who imagined they moved for economic reasons. The extreme rationality of seeking income and property led only a few people to articulate the importance of economic factors in comparison to all other influences. Whether people actually believed their own rhetoric seemed unlikely even as they spoke. Their decisions to leave or to stay were influenced by family and friendships, and by natural and constructed environmental characteristics, although they might not have been aware of the influences.

Quality-of-life migrants placed their bets on an optimal community or natural environment that held the key to their future happiness. Their formula contrasted with the conventional maximum income and consumption formula which receives so much credibility in industrial society. They held their values as perhaps purer and more timeless, as the idea of living forever in a nearly perfect place requires. Having developed some sensitivity about what was needed for their happiness and having found a place to meet those needs, quality-of-life migrants took the meaning of forever more seriously, as considering perfection deserves. In time some of the economic rhetoricians introduced more concerns about the good life into their single-minded interpretation, just as quality-of-life migrants introduced more economic rationality into their decision making.

Migrants are searching for something better in their lives. Among primitive societies, migration was most likely to hospitable conditions, food and a sheltering environment that would allow perpetuation of the way of life they knew. Since any alternatives were largely unknown, they could scarcely be considered superior or inferior. Migration among relatively rich and educated people in an industrial society is likely to be based on the desire to satisfy a different hunger, a sense of diffuse personal anxiety and alienation. Ironically, they became aliens through the very process of moving. Theirs was a search for something which, once gained, would bring happiness. The conventionally recognized goal was income and property. They felt that their lives would be better if they could have more job security or another $20,000 a year. Taken to extremes, economic motives are intrinsically alienating because they are endless. There are always more dollars to earn or objects to buy. More frustrating is the fact that others like oneself want those same dollars and objects. Gaining more of either is both difficult and inevitably defeating for most who are in the competition. The fortunate eventually reach a station in life when they say "this is enough." The unfortunate reach no such place and settle for a truce or even defeat. Meanwhile, the threshold of what is acceptable within the collective desire is continually rising. Possessions coveted for a comfortable middle-class standard of living in 1950 are taken for granted by people living near poverty in the late 1990s.

Many migrants in modern societies try to alleviate their alienation by feeding hungers other than economic consumption. Some Gallatin Valley migrants were hostile to the idea that economic success was associated with personal happiness. They were convinced that their way was best for them and probably for others, if only the others could realize it. These people felt that there were qualities which transcended the crass value of money, economic security and possessions, although a little more wouldn't necessarily hurt. For some, a close-knit supportive community of caring souls was the solution to alienation. In one four-day period in 1981, three newcomers confided that they had moved to Belgrade because of the nurturing Christian community there. Others, responsible hedonists, thought that their hunger could be satisfied by the right amount and kind of play. They were enthusiastic about skiing, fishing, hunting, motorcycle riding and several other outdoor activities. Whereas migrants to a metropolitan center might feel their hunger could be fed by museums, galleries, restaurants and singles bars, high natural-amenity areas offer scenery outdoor recreation and cowboy bars to make them feel at home at last.

Our research provides insight into the geographic restlessness of modern America, a search to fill the void for self with place. Alienation ends when home is found. Home is likely to be "found" followed by the discovery that the restlessness within has simply been lying dormant for awhile. Once reawakened, the process of searching for home began anew. People who consciously divided their motives into categories and then pursued one goal to the exclusion of others had the shortest respite to their search. People who moved for recreational reasons without much realistic consideration of relationships or of economics were especially likely to change. They either broadened their interests or left. Just as several respondents had come to Bozeman from Boise, Aspen and Jackson, a few moved on to Alaska, the San Juans and even the Alps and the Himalayas.

LOSS AND ALIENATION

There is little reason to expect that integration into community will occur completely or frequently in modern society. As long as society divides the worlds of fulfillment into categories and offers a smorgasbord of choices to each, knowing where home is will remain difficult. Stating one preference, whether friendship ties, income or recreation, to the exclusion of others leads most people to search eventually for what they are missing. As long as people are certain that they have found home, perhaps that is as near as most can come to escaping being an alien. It is a tenuous process searching for a permanent home in places filled with aliens, like oneself, searching to satisfy their temporary notion of community.

Alienation is the feeling of being an alien, of being foreign. The search to quell the sense of being foreign is to find home or the qualities to make one feel at home. John Denver's plaintive wail for a country road to take him home expressed a more universal message than having breakfast in West Virginia. If migration takes the migrant back home, then it is ironic that so many move again so soon. The move to reduce alienation probably will increase it rather than reduce it. As a process, it may act as a catalyst to help reduce it in the future. Places like the Gallatin Valley are terminal locations, homes for migrants who satisfactorily come to rest there. They provide a reality for satisfying the illusion-proven-accurate of the migrant. They are reality testers, temporary pacifiers if not satisfiers, for those migrants who conclude that they belong somewhere else. Through them, people may reach the realization that another place is the right place for home.

Terry Amersen (age 30), an architect, and his designer wife, LuAnn (age 37), moved from Denver to Bozeman to escape the dangers and disorganization of urban society. They believed that urban society was deteriorating and meaningless. They were certain that they had escaped these pitfalls of modernization when they first arrived in Bozeman. Both became active in community service projects in addition to starting a design and planning firm. Tellingly, they never developed close friends in spite of their zealous participation. They seemed certain that their three children would flourish in the smaller, socially supportive school system.

Although their design firm became successful by local financial standards, Terry regarded it as a failure. Their household income declined to about one-half of what it had been in Denver. One son became seriously delinquent. After four years, they began to call it quits, floundering between moving to still another high natural-amenity town on the Washington coast or returning to Denver. In the end, Denver was their choice. Shortly after moving there, LuAnn died after a brief battle with cancer.

During a return visit to Bozeman the following year, Terry told me about the return to Denver.

When I left Bozeman, I felt terribly bitter. The people here just didn't care about quality. They didn't want to protect its (the natural and constructed environment) intimacy or beauty. And they didn't care about tastefully developing it either. I grew to feel so angry I just hated the place. I was especially angry at the people at the university, because they should have realized what a precious place Bozeman is. I have found I have everything in Denver that I wanted to find in Bozeman and with over twice as much income. All I had to do was open my eyes. I am grateful to Bozeman. If I had never lived here, I might have gone on thinking that life would be better in a small, sophisticated university town. It gave me the realization that the kind of place doesn't make people dependable or sensitive to where they live. Living here made it possible for me to feel at home in Denver.

Chapter 9

Losses and Gains, Alienation and Transformation: Aesop Meets Durkheim, Simmel, Parsons and Thomas

The loss of a dream and the conversion of a social structure are sad. They also are uplifting. Neither the dream nor the community change turned out the way that migrants thought they might. Despite the discrepant paths, there were wonderful experiences both among the residents and for the community.

Nearly everyone learned something. Many did not like what they learned, because often they disagreed with the lesson. Many have moved on wiser and happier for having been able to test their dream. The few who stayed, for the most part, appreciated being able to stay. The Northern Rockies, the region, the towns are wonderful places. The few established old-timers often prospered, at least by local standards, as they stayed.

Their prosperity was largely in exchange for reductions in the natural beauty and solitude of the physical environment. Given that inescapable fact of growth and development, the towns in the study area were still comfortable, liveable and enjoyable. Their scale remained human. They had fewer of the artificial and inauthentic contrivances that define attractive urban places after 30 years of unremitting growth. The beauty in Montana still is largely natural rather than constructed.

The institutions became relatively well-developed during the period of research. Hospitals, schools, libraries, roads, police and fire protection and churches have kept pace with services in other comparable towns. The natural environment, while not as pristine, uncrowded and accessible as it once was, still is a virtual paradise for almost any activity a devotee might seek in mountains or plains. There has remained much to be enjoyed at levels unthinkable in most places.

The subjective interpretation of change for the newcomer, of course, may seem to be exactly the opposite. For professionals accustomed to the pressure-cooker intensity of the city, a small town in the Rockies, a nearby stream, even a quiet house on an acre may seem utterly liberating. For recent college graduates or young workers who grew up in an Eastern suburb, skiing or kayaking within a few minutes' drive seems close to heaven. These types of newcomers are unlikely to be deeply aware of the relative loss that they have, in effect, caused. The professional enjoys looking at the small creek adjacent to his house. But that creek is no longer accessible to local kids on bicycles as it had been a few years earlier. The kayakers filled with enthusiasm are defensive or even oblivious to their incursion into the privacy of a stream once remote to masses of people. Only people who have lived in the area long enough, who have used the area sufficiently to recognize particular changes and who care passionately about the undeveloped state of the environment are able to recognize the magnitude of the losses that have occurred in exchange for the newcomers' gains.

PLANNING

Given the stakes that people have invested in their choice to live in scenic recreation areas, it seems imperative once again to consider the issue of planning. It would seem that people would want to preserve the qualities that had attracted them to southwest Montana. Table 9.1 summarizes responses to questions about planning asked between 1972 and 1992.

The distinction between more centralized planning, that is state and federal planning, and local planning is important. For some people, centralized planning carries the specter of Big Brother, socialism and loss of individual control. Local planning has a more personal connotation, local people familiar with the facts of the surrounding environment and sensitive to social idiosyncrasies deciding how to develop or preserve their area. Local planning implies grass-roots participation, as residents in the area make wise choices to preserve what is valuable. They decide whether and how it will be changed. Central planning implies top-down decision making imposed on the area and its residents.

The above comparisons between suppositions that people often make about central and local planning are grossly simplified and largely inaccurate. State and federal planning procedures rely on information provided by local residents. What passes as local planning often involves minimal local democratic representation. Local planning often is based on preferences of a small number of influential interests who are not even local. They may be people and organizations from distant locations who have economic resources and professional support that exceed any that locals can assemble. Most rural areas and towns are not equipped to plan in situations that involve large-scale development and population growth. Fortunately, a considerable safety net of state and federal laws protects local areas to some extent from this vulnerability. What passes as local planning in small towns is largely the implementation and execution of state and federal laws. Furthermore, local planning is essentially limited to statutory powers. Local ordinances have neither the breadth nor strength of legislation. Local and state planning have both, although they may have some aspects that do not really fit needs of the local area.

Support of centralized planning, as opposed to local planning, is largely a philosophical orientation rather than an empirical one. The most doctrinaire position against planning is to oppose both local and central planning. The intermediate position is to oppose state and federal planning and to support local planning. About one-quarter of respondents favored both types of planning. Practically no one opposed local planning while favoring central planning. The responses to the questions on planning ranged from 1, that is, strongly support, to 5, strongly oppose. In 1972, respondents were relatively opposed to state and federal planning. The average in 1972 was 3.35. More people of every category in the samples supported local planning than state and federal planning at every time period (Table 9.1). During the 1970s, there was increasing support for both types of planning by newcomers, old-timers and the panel, in general. A pivotal shift in attitude occurred over the span of the research. By 1992, that support had reversed for all groups. Newcomers and old-timers were again moderately opposed to state and federal planning, and moderately in favor of local planning. Old-timers were consistently more favorable toward both types of planning throughout all time periods than were newcomers.

Most residents in the Gallatin Valley seem to place their hopes for protecting what they like about the area on local planning. There also remains a large contingent of residents who oppose any planning, including local planning.

Table 9.1
Opinions about Planning among Bozeman Residents, 1972-1992

	State and Federal Planning*	Local Planning Only*
Panel 1972	3.35	2.60
1976	3.24	2.30
1980	2.75	2.06
1992	3.24	2.34
Old-timer 72	3.24	2.60
Old-timer 76	3.07	2.29
Old-timer 80	2.73	2.01
Old-timer 92	3.22	2.29
Newcomer 72	3.79	2.95
Newcomer 76	3.42	2.32
Newcomer 80	2.80	2.08
Newcomer 92	3.35	2.57

*1= strongly support; 5= strongly oppose planning.

Newcomers were even more likely to oppose planning, whether central or local. Newcomers did not like most aspects of the area as well as did the old-timers. Old-timers, perhaps hoping to preserve what they liked, were very slightly more supportive of both types of planning. There is a dynamic implication from these findings. The constant onslaught of newcomers, who are simultaneously less enamored with the community and more opposed to planning, ensures that the area and its towns will find only moderate appreciation for their qualities and little support for preserving them.

THE PROBLEMS OF MISPERCEPTION OF COMMUNITY: SOCIAL AND ENVIRONMENTAL ISSUES

When people move for reasons based upon what is discussed here as reality, they inevitably encounter some problems. When their moves are founded on illusion, they frequently encounter more problems than they had dreamed of. These shared misconceptions may lead to a problem in itself. The most frequent problems were associated with economic failure and disillusionment with interpersonal qualities of the community. The disillusionment with interpersonal qualities of the community is especially interesting because it lacks the more tangible rhetoric associated with economic failure or with environmental characteristics. If employment is hard to find and pays little, then newcomers can conclude that opportunities are more obtainable somewhere else. Similarly tangible, when the temperature hovers below 30°F, no one can argue that the weather is not cold. Disillusionment around community is much more elusive.

Community dreamers who had moved under the illusion that they would find friendly, cooperative residents were shocked by what they found. After a year or two, recent migrants frequently became more analytic about the community than they had been during their first euphoric interview. Married couples living in outer suburbs frequently said something like "We have lived here for two years now and we still have not been invited into any of our neighbor's homes. What is it with Montanans?" or "I thought they were friendly, but they aren't nearly as friendly as where we came from." Tim and Sue Brown continued, "In Minnesota, we were constantly with our friends. We played softball in the summer and bowled in the winter. We rode snow machines together at night and on the weekends. We had a potluck or went out with this group of friends we had at least twice a month. We had both been born and had grown up in Elm Falls and knew everyone there."

Kevin and Shari Ogilvey gave a more urbane description of what people had done in Redondo Beach, California, to experience community:

We lived in a condominium. Every Saturday, sometimes two or three times a week, someone in our complex would buy a keg of beer. Everyone who lived in the complex was welcome. We played volleyball, drank beer and talked. As soon as you moved in, you were part of the group. That sort of thing seems to occur only around the bars in Bozeman. Maybe it is just the neighborhood we've moved into or that we are getting older, but people here don't seem to really care about each other. We have talked about this a lot with the people we have met and they say the same thing is true for them.

Each couple expected to find as much or more community as they had had where they came from and instead found less. The kinds of community each had experienced and the meanings of what was important that they brought with them were very different. A small agricultural hometown in Minnesota probably is a close proxy for traditional community, with the same people sharing the same activities generation after generation. A southern California condo is another extreme — a social system which functions to batch-process highly migratory people with maximum pleasure. By paying rent and taxes, residents are assured that a complex infrastructure of roads, schools, police protection and myriad other services will be provided without further consideration. An "instant" community capable of temporarily satisfying the sociation wishes of temporary people emerges as a superficial ideal.

High-amenity recreational towns are composed of people who assume that what they took for granted in their prior communities are natural and will also be in their new community. Newcomers imagine that they will find the qualities they left. Instead, they find a hodgepodge of new residents with different competing notions of what good community is and become discouraged with this discovery. Such towns lack the long-term personal attention of traditional communities or the mechanical efficiency and superficial ease of the high-tech submetropolis. Places like the Gallatin Valley have the disadvantages of small-town inefficiency while simultaneously offering little permanent or even dependable temporary support networks.

Realizing how fragile acquaintance with newcomers is, people who became permanent residents insulated themselves from contact with the new arrivals. Some adopted a wait-and-see attitude to allow enough time to find out whether new people really were going to stay. They knew better than to believe that people would remain committed to staying merely because they love everything about the place. The less-calloused old-timers remained aloof and insensitive to the process of migration turnover. The community, as a distinct unit, also suffered from this process of rapid in- and out-migration. The ideal cherished by people who believed in traditional community became impossible because of the temporary commitment and residence of newcomers. They moved on almost as fast as the residents who lacked an interest in traditional community and those who believed that an "instant" community was possible.

Rapid migration posed special difficulties to established institutions like churches and political parties. Sustained political activities, particularly those related to community planning or advocacy, are difficult when the constituency constantly changes. I was frequently invited by local political parties, professional associations and churches to speak about the impacts of local migration. All such groups talked about how hard it was to sustain participation, even to keep their membership or client rolls up to date. Most constituencies had little institutional memory. New people did not know what issues were locally important or had been recently discussed. Leaders frequently used the cliché of newcomers wanting to reinvent the wheel, in reference to capturing the energy and participation of recent arrivals. Old pros in the local political parties talked about how difficult it was to get party members to run for election. They also said that there was little consistency among voters with regard to issues or candidates. Lack of participation and widespread ignorance about local issues among newcomers consolidated the power and influence among the small number of longer term participants. These leaders realized that they were speaking for and acting as representatives of an elusive and shadowy constituency. Meanwhile, established political leaders and leaders of other formal institutions must endure the incessant and grating demands of newcomers who want to make the place a little more or less like the place they came from or the place where they aspire to live. And the newcomers must tolerate the establishment, who, having heard the new ideas many times before, resist or ignore them.

A few of the more cognitive urban people consciously established support groups which they referred to as "my community" or "our neighborhood community." These were micropolitical activities that transcended the larger and less personal political arena. They personified what has come to be referred to as communitarian activity, an attempt to establish community in the context of modern society. The author knows of no such local groups that persisted for more than a few years. Such attempts were praised by their members. They provided temporary support for the disconsolate among them who were experiencing difficulties in their fragmented world. The author was aware of two groups that some respondents referred to as "my community." Both were composed of a few scattered neighbors and close acquaintances of these neighbors. Both organized weekly potlucks, neighborhood play days and clean-up-fix-up days. Members consciously assisted each other, caring for them during illness and emotional upsets or helping them pack and move away. The members of one group were primarily married couples with children who lived on a cul-de-sac just outside of Bozeman. The adults were full-time, middle-class employees. The central figure was a nurse whose husband was a sociologist. She extended her philosophy of nurturing care into her group. The other group was self-acknowledged New Age. The central figure was a witch. Full moons, equinoxes and solstices were special days for celebration. The members were a polyglot of marginally employed single mothers, unmarried couples and lesbian couples. The life span of both of these groups was about the same, four or five years.

The people change and the values of people who stay also change in high-migration communities, increasing the grounds for political conflicts while reducing opportunities for thoughtful, long-term resolutions. Each new proposed division or suggested modification of a forest-use plan in the study area erupted as a unique and unanticipated surprise. Local residents operated as a public rather than as a community. They were unable to accept uniform guidelines for land use, economic development or other crucial considerations. People opposed to growth arriving from Boulder, Missoula, Salt Lake or Jackson railed about the need to preserve Bozeman from the fates that they witnessed befall their communities, only to grow discouraged and move away or to decide that trying to prevent the problem involved just too much effort. Some joined the development by subdividing their properties into 20-acre lots. Meanwhile, people encouraging of, cynical about or oblivious to growth were moving in at the same time, effectively nullifying most opposition to development.

Newcomers into the Gallatin Valley sometimes perceived their new environment very differently from each other, which led to serious disagreements. Suburbs frequently become battlegrounds because of conflicting visions about country life. An airline pilot and his wife developed a small hatchery for endangered species of ducks and geese on their property just outside the Bozeman city limits. At sunset, dozens of wild birds sought refuge on the small pond at their hatchery. Neighbors immediately objected that the fowl operation violated the tenets of the subdivision. For the pilot's family, their new move was to bring them closer to nature as participants in the cycle of life. The other families saw theirs as a move to a well-manicured and prestigious estate. They did not wish to be associated with bird-raisers operating a quasiagricultural operation no matter what its contribution might be to wildlife preservation or to the aesthetics of its caretakers.

SUBSTANCE VERSUS FORM IN COMMUNITY

Migrants who are dissatisfied are prone to confuse content with form, as George Simmel (1950) conceived them, or substance with form as the distinction is more popularly described. Deborah Winger, in *Urban Cowboy*, asks John Travolta, "Are you a real cowboy?" which, of course, he was (Bridges and Lathan, 1980). She couldn't tell by appearance since most of the men in Gilley's Bar looked the same. She was searching for form, not substance, knowing that the real value of western man comes from a structure deeper than the fit of his jeans and the roll of his hat.

Distinguishing content and form is no simple matter. Deep underlying and often invisible structure separates form from content. Content is visible and mitigable. Content is frequently misunderstood, taken as the presence of the qualities of structure that are really being sought. For lack of other information, people assume that what they are looking for in a place is likely to be there because of the image it presents. This erroneous assumption is especially likely when conceptions are based largely on illusions about the underlying structure. Content is visible, on the surface. In slow-changing, traditional social environments, the surface authentically reflects the deeper form. In changing environments, content and form become disassociated. Content takes on symbolic meaning. As symbols, they are assumed to refer to what is real in an authentic setting. But the authenticity of the setting, hence of the symbols, does not exist. The symbols are taken as real, as if they are authentic, when they may be dissociated from the form that once exited. Stockbrokers and bus drivers look like cowboys in Gilley's, and John Travolta is not a real cowboy.

Many people who moved to the Gallatin Valley assumed that it would be structurally superior for their goals because of its appearance. The people composing its relatively small population were assumed to be knowable, personal and familiar. They were assumed to be members of a community where intimacy and concern were part of the form of social structure. This common theme among

American intellectuals assumes that cities are intrinsically alienating and inhospitable to the formation of community (Mumford, 1946). That community can occur in urban settings, especially among working-class ethnic populations, need not concern us here. What is crucial is the assumption that small towns are where community exists. There may be a higher probability of community in rural places than in urban. Rural areas also may be scarcely more than symbolic social environments, lacking the form, the underlying structure essential for community and populated by residents who don't know the difference between symbol and reality.

Driving into Bozeman, traditional images of the manageable small town are likely to be evoked. The postfrontier Main Street filled with shops is still there. Many streets are still lined with old ash trees. It is small in comparison to most towns, especially since it is not part of a metropolitan area. It is relatively free of industrial air pollution. Its buildings are well-maintained and its homes are in good condition. Walking around, this image is complemented by the cordial informality with which people treat each other. Clerks talk and smile at customers. People dress casually. The poverty and insanity visible in large cities are not apparent. It looks like a small town should look. And it is assumed to have the qualities of community that small towns should have. The image of Main Street has remained relatively unchanged during the past three decades, however, the elements composing it have changed. Few locations contain the same businesses they did 10 years ago. Malls and franchises have decimated local hometown businesses. New businesses downtown are largely affluent specialty shops where people of means browse and find leisure rather than make essential purchases. The image of the traditional healthy downtown is illusory. Similarly, the houses are well-maintained. Trees have been removed from some streets, but the appearance of most continue to be improved. But the inhabitants change. Homeowners in Bozeman move with the same regularity as urban residents in the rest of the United States. The image of a stable, committed population is illusory. The place looks much the same, the buildings have the same facades, even the people look the same, but, upon closer examination, they have different faces.

Back on the streets or in the bars or at community activities, the interaction has remained cordial and informal. But, again, the faces have changed. What one is likely to see are mirror images of oneself, relatively recently arrived people, maintaining the style in which they want to live and which they feel is appropriate for the face with which they live. With few exceptions, they are not long-term residents committed to sharing activities to make the community work. They adopt the style, the content, but rarely become part of the permanent structure. Again, the imagined characteristics of community structure based on the visible image are largely illusory.

Social structural characteristics of uncommitted impermanence in settings that capture a visual essence of tradition are not unusual. They are typical of gentrified urban neighborhoods or suburbs. They are not intrinsically problematic or undesirable, but they are different from what newcomers expect to find in small towns in the Rockies. That Bozeman or Belgrade do not have the qualities they were presumed to have gradually occurs to newcomers carrying the illusion. More analytic residents interpreted the differences between form and content once they discovered them. Most who were surprised by the facade plainly didn't like what they were observing, without consciously distinguishing between inauthentic symbols and structure.

Several migrants to Belgrade mentioned they were drawn to it because of its conservative and traditional religious reputation. Nevertheless, its conservative qualities were sometimes romanticized to a point of making realistic judgments in error. One recently married couple of born-again Christians described their decision to move from a Wyoming boomtown to Belgrade. The first interview occurred in a tiny and tidy rental house just off Main Street, where the middle-aged couple and nine children lived. The interview the second year was in a run-down mobile home.

The Lord spoke to us to move here. I had spent time here as a girl and knew He was right. We trusted in the Lord that a true Christian community would take care of its own. Gillette was no place to raise these kids [there were nine]. Everybody down there hangs around the bars and there are lots of problems. The kids can't help themselves. Both Joe and I know. We was both married twice before we found each other and the Lord. Things have worked out just like we thought. Joe is working as a hand [on a nearby ranch] and the kids are more settled in school than they ever have been.

Joe was working on a different ranch the following year. The couple was worried that he might lose that job, too. The third year, the couple had disappeared, leaving no forwarding address. The assumptions that they made about community content and form did not seem to gel.

When respondents realized that what they had assumed to be the real form of Bozeman was primarily a substantive style, they often became irate, as if the town had deceived them. A few approached their discovery like a practical joke had been played on them because of their own gullibility. One woman cynically remarked, "Store owners must hire their clerks for their smiles. After a while, I realized they were smiling because they were getting my money, not because they were happy to see me." Another laughed, "The twinkling in their (store clerks) eyes was from the light shining through their ears."

A young single man (age 29), who had raved about how friendly the town was during the first interview, had this to say the second time we talked to him:

I used to think Bozeman was the friendliest place I had ever been. As soon as I sat down in the bars, people would start talking. People smiled and said "hello" on the streets. Everybody was really friendly and mellow. Then, one night last spring, I was sitting in a bar and started looking around. Except for two old hard-core alcoholic barflies, I was the oldest regular in there. People were still just like they had been, but none, except for a couple of helpless old drunks, of the guys who were there when I moved here [eight months earlier] were still around. We had done a lot of things together, but they weren't around anymore. I started thinking, these people are not friends. You can depend on friends, but not these guys. They just act friendly. I got really depressed. I haven't been going to the bars much since then.

He moved to Seattle with his small design consulting firm a few weeks after his second interview.

There are undoubtedly small towns that more closely conform to the idealizations people have about their image and their structure, places where people stay and share the joy and grief of sustaining a community. Slow, stable, unchanging agricultural towns are unlikely to be attractive places to many outsiders though. The more desirable a place is in terms of environmental criteria, like weather or scenery, the more likely people will be attracted to it. If the place sustains the level of in-migration that California has, then gemeinschaft explodes into gesellschaft. If, like Bozeman, the migration cannot be sustained, then the rate of turnover in the population destroys the opportunity to maintain long-term informal interaction essential to gemeinschaft, except for the small minority who stay. If community is the primary goal of potential migrants, they would be well advised to move to a small, stable town where few Americans would consider living because such places are perceived to have low environmental quality and offer few economic opportunities. There, in a small town in central Oklahoma or North Dakota, they might find the structure of community they imagine they want.

Romantic migrants will continue to be attracted by the appearance of places like the Gallatin Valley. The more they are, the more such places will lose whatever stable characteristics they have. Their erroneous illusion will become apparent all the quicker, and the quicker they will search anew for a dream place. Many will surmise that they can find no better place to satisfy their wish for a desirable environment, a decent job and acceptable friends. Through this realization, they become realists and may join others to forge an imperfect community for themselves and for others. As this lengthy process unfolds, form and content subtly merge. The merging, though, occurs quite incidentally to what is visible to outsiders.

Migrants move for substantive reasons, whether they consider only themselves or others in so doing. Talcott Parsons (1949) referred to this distinction as being oriented toward self as opposed to a collective, that is, other people (Table 9.2). Their substantive reasons for moving fall across a continuum of conventional social responsibilities. People may move to try to get experiences that are idiosyncratic and of limited value to the society as a whole. Some outdoor devotees move to remote natural areas to fish and hunt, while culture lovers might choose a city of museums, galleries and theaters. However desirable either of these types of activities may be, they are independent of conventional social responsibilities in their purest form. Migration is socially responsible when the substance sought has social approval, and when the form contributes to others. The norms of migration are expectations that people should optimize employment and community participation.

ORIENTATION OF SELF OR COLLECTIVE

When an individual takes only himself or herself into consideration for idiosyncratic reasons, that person is an *unrestricted hedonist* or grasshopper (Aesop, 1985). If a selfish migrant moves in order to maximize earnings and community recognition, he or she is a *conventional egoist* or Friedman (Friedman, 1962). If a person moves to gain a singular dream that he or she wishes to share with (or impose upon) family or others, that person is an *unconventional altruist* or protestant (Weber, 1930). Finally, if motives and substance are based only on social responsibility, then the migrant is a *responsible conformist* or ant (Aesop, 1985) or saint or martyr, depending on the personal justifications of the person. Although this paradigm was developed independently, it is similar to the four wishes of W. I. Thomas (1923): desires for new experience, recognition, response and security. The basic idea is that inevitable tension exists between wanting to be an individual and a group member, between being free to follow one's own desires versus the desire for social recognition and accomplishment.

Inherent strains are involved in moving from one category to another. While no terminal state exists, grasshoppers and ants are hypothesized as being more stable than the other categories. Conventional egoists and unconventional altruists both face social disapproval. Conventional egoists, by failing to share their experiences, are recognized as selfish because they are engaged with conventional others. Although a continuing thrust to be egotistically conventional is rewarded in the United States, such people are nevertheless felt to be missing an essential element of life and frequently are feared by group-oriented types. A successful, socially responsible bachelor or spinster is free and happy to move to display the level of personal commitment expected by either the protestants or the ants. The hedonistic grasshoppers expect social responsibilities to be cast aside because they interfere with the purity of new experience. The responsible ants disapprove of the selfishness that motivates individuals to pursue a life free from the restricting bonds of the colony. Unrestricted hedonists do not have to care about such group-oriented disapproval, although loneliness and deviant status may eventually lead them to climb onto the social treadmill. Unconventional altruists face broader social disapproval. They enjoy the support of each other. However, even that group support may be lost if their imposition to achieve their idiosyncratic goals drives members out. Some back-to-nature communards and New-Age zealots have remained committed to their groups and their ideals, but most have moved on. The

Table 9.2
Motivations for Migrants

	Substance To Be Gained by Moving		
		Personal and Idiosyncratic Rewards	Collective and Approved Rewards
Who Will Benefit from the Migration?	Self	Unrestricted hedonist — grasshopper (new experience)	Conventional egoist — Friedman (recognition)
	Group	Unconventional altruist protestant (response)	Responsible conformist ant (security)

most common category, responsible conformists, meanwhile, gains approval from their friends and family as well as the society-at-large. They wrestle with their inner self, wondering what life would be like if they were independent or if they tried something new and daring. Current divorce and migration figures indicate that people are increasingly bolting to find a different star. Attempts to resolve the dilemma of selfishness and altruism express the underlying norm that says that a person is collectively expected to be independent.

There is a strain involved in moving from any cell to adjacent cells because of the eternal struggle between individual wishes and social responsibility and between wanting to share with others or to live without the inevitable restrictions that accompany sharing. The primary tendency will be movement from being a grasshopper to being an ant, that is, toward social support. Migration allows individuals to express their idiosyncratic preferences for a particular place in conjunction with the diverse opportunities all other places have to offer. Although legally free of external regulation, their choices are based upon individual opportunities for what may be optimally achieved in particular locations. Their preferences are based upon interpretations of how the needs imposed by the positions they occupy may be met. People who occupy few positions of responsibility generally feel fewer constraints. They have relatively less for which they are expected to be accountable. Having fewer of Becker's side bets to wage, they are relatively freer to move. Most others feel restrained by responsibilities of employment, consumption patterns and family care.

SOCIAL ORDER AND MIGRATION

Migration expresses constraints of social order. Economic opportunity with its close linkage to social responsibilities is a major determinant of opportunities to provide for responsibilities. Norms guide behavior toward conventional definitions of social responsibility. Behaviors that potentially place demands on the society which are hard to ignore — unemployment, child care and low community participation — are undesirable, deviant, from a collective perspective. Migration almost always has the potential for being disruptive. The tendency has been to socialize people to internalize norms for taking on social roles with their attendant responsibilities. That socialization has encouraged most people to stay put and to remain part of the group, if possible, and to be productive and adaptive, if they must move (Cumming, 1968, p. 7). Some alienation, being caught between exclusive orientations of self or collective, is inevitable.

Migration reflects this strain. It is played out as people move. The consequences of their choices create a new stage. Migration has great disruptive potential when people avoid socially responsible roles. It is an expression of individual notions of responsibility to oneself and to others. People are monitored by norms governing work, family and community participation. They are controlled by the availability of opportunities in the form of jobs, housing, services and other amenities. Deviant migration occurs when people decide to move to places that fail to meet socially approved expectations.

Migration, as a deviant act, is distinct from migration by people who engage in behaviors that are conventionally considered deviant. Social scientists since Durkheim (1933) have recognized that migration is closely linked to social problems. Social Disorganization theorists identified profound negative influences of migration on urban areas, immigrants and especially, the children of immigrants (Shaw and McKay, 1969). In my own research of crime and high-school dropouts in Montana, I also found that migrants and their children were at much greater risk of committing crime or leaving school (Jobes 1999). The socially disorganizing influences of migration are by no means universal. Many migrants and their children present few problems. Despite such problems, it also is important to keep in mind that migration is simultaneously economically beneficial for host communities and immigrants. Nevertheless, migrants are disproportionately likely to be deviants (Sanua, 1970).

Many respondents in our research would be considered as sufficiently selfish and irresponsible to lead most reasonable and responsible people to conclude that they were deviant. We observed (and did not report) obvious violations such as growing marijuana and driving while intoxicated. Many respondents also became deviants in conjunction with their migration. We were told about many cases of spouse and child neglect and abuse. We learned about difficulties that respondents and their families were experiencing with local schools. We were aware of charges against participants in this study. Most were common such as driving under the influence of alcohol, misdemeanor drug violations, simple assaults and vandalism. As far as we know, only three participants in our research were sentenced to prison during the research period from 1972 until 1994.

The study of deviance is devoted to behaviors that lie beyond the boundaries of social acceptability and approval (Rubington and Weinberg, 1995). Crime, mental illness, drug addiction and disabilities are typical subjects because society defines them as deviating from the norm. The general social response is to acknowledge deviant behavior and then to try to control it. During the past 30 or so years, there has been an effort to redefine many types of behavior as "special" rather than deviant. Many formerly deviant behaviors, for example, homosexuality, divorce and physical and mental handicaps, have received widespread redefinition. Divorce merits a brief discussion because it was so frequently mentioned during interviews with respondents. Difficulties between spouses seemed to be a central factor for initiating many moves. Divorce also was often discussed with considerable anger and anguish as a problem and as a solution.

Migration is related to divorce in two general ways. First, migrants themselves have long been recognized to be more likely to exhibit certain types of deviance, for example, mental illness or crime, than are long-term residents (Park, 1952). Second, migration itself may be deviant, which is socially unacceptable beyond some normative standard. The free migration in America and most Western societies is not the norm in many societies. For some groups, individual migration without the support and approval of the family may even lead to exclusion and murder. In some Islamic nations, such responses to individualism are fairly common and acceptable.

No specific questions were asked about deviance. As a result of the way in which the questions were asked, respondents were free to choose whether to discuss matters that might be considered deviant. Other classic types of deviance were mentioned less frequently than divorce. The possible exception was alcohol abuse, which was also frequently mentioned. Sexual preferences or activities were almost never mentioned. One openly gay couple who had moved from Houston said that they thought the gay scene in Bozeman was "refreshing, less jaundiced and stylized" than in the big cities. A couple of women, one 34, the other 28, spoke indirectly of difficulties that they had experienced with placating the parents of the younger partner. The couple publicly and actively acknowledged that they were lesbians. They never specifically mentioned their sexual preference during the interviews. In this respect, they were no different than the hundreds of other respondents, whatever their sexual preference might have been.

Social order is fundamental to society. Role commitment and acceptance of social norms are essential for social order (Wood, 1974). Migration implies changes in both roles and norms, increasing the likelihood of deviant behavior. Migration has historically been regarded as a potentially disruptive behavior and has been regulated as such. Enforcement, and more recently, legislation tightly control migration for the preservation of society. In fact, free migration, the willingness of the host location to receive people and the willingness of the sender location to let them move away, is a relatively new phenomenon. Both formal (e.g., laws and bureaucracies) and informal (e.g., family and community) rules have historically been involved. The rules have specified whether or not migration would be permitted, for whom and under what circumstances. These rules have differed across time between sender and host locations. Primitive societies forced their criminals into exile and forced slaves into servitude. They used forced-migration as a way of life. Their response to migrants was the same to deviants: outsiders would be killed. Britain forbade the out-migration of textile workers. Modern communities and societies prefer stable, educated, monied in-migrants and have enacted laws preventing or discouraging others.

Michael Sobel (1981, p. 28) has defined lifestyle as "a recognizable mode of living." Although conceptually independent, lifestyle is actually interrelated to attitudes, values and behavioral orientations held by individuals and groups. It is related to historical position as well as to social and economic status. Sobel maintains that lifestyle expresses *consumption* preference more than any other attribute, even work or leisure. Migration can also be a lifestyle. Migrants are consumers of a new environment. Being free to migrate in order to satisfy lifestyle preferences, migrants are given license to flirt with behaviors that historically have been deviant. Respondents frequently broached subjects and experiences that articulated the difficulties they were having in establishing boundaries between what was socially acceptable or unacceptable, conforming or deviant.

Large numbers of people are imperfectly socialized, particularly when they are being conditioned for a future in another place. They fail to take on conventional roles and choose alternative paths. Many potential migrants are free to move by default because of overpopulation or recession. Others are free due to the gradual emergence of a lifestyle which has favored unrestricted individual experience over conventional responsibilities. A new premise of individual satisfaction has been evolving for decades, evident through avoidance or periodic rejection of conventional traditional roles by remaining single, childless and marginally employed. Most continue to struggle to optimize individual preferences and satisfaction around their social obligations. Much of the malaise of being confused, uncommitted and anomic undoubtedly derives from the constricting and contracting nature of the social structure. There are fewer job opportunities. Family, schools and churches seem ineffective and irrelevant to many young people. But some of the malaise may reside in confusion and lack of faith in the broader structure itself than in the rejection of particular institutions.

HEDONISM, SOCIAL RESPONSIBILITY AND MIGRATION

There is inherent strain in moving from the responsible hedonism of the egoist to unrestricted hedonism or to conventional responsibilities. There is an inherent strain to move from any cell to adjacent cells over time, between being alone and wanting linkages. The tendency will be to move toward the middle, to seek both support and control for the person and for the society. But the logical consistency is consonant with the extreme, being an unrestricted hedonist or a responsible conformist. Alienation, being caught between two exclusive orientations, is inevitable once a person recognizes the notion of autonomy.

Migration becomes deviant when it fails to prevent people from conducting themselves in socially irresponsible ways, that is, from avoiding conventional roles. The potential deviance is controlled as individuals act on internalized notions of social responsibility operating in conjunction with the opportunities to perform roles responsibly in any particular location. Conformists, nondeviants, are monitored by their sense of social responsibility, of accepting work, family and community participation. They also are monitored by the availability of opportunities in the form of jobs, places to live and suitability for dependents. Deviant migration also can occur when people decide to move to places that meet social expectations.

At one conceptual level, modern humans are no freer than were earlier generations. The very idea of being free to choose, free to move, is itself a model, a template for behavior. Modern humans may be as trapped by their conforming to that model as were hunters and gatherers.

As I have pursued my research, I have modified my interpretation of community. What I understood to be community in 1970 and what most persons treat as community now is in error. My fascination with why people move to high natural-amenity areas began nearly 40 years ago when I lived near Sante Fe. I watched and listened while avant-garde urbanities described why they had left Philadelphia or Dallas for this bohemian promised land. During the interim, I lived in Boulder, Colorado, near Las Vegas, Nevada and small towns outside Seattle, hearing variations on a similar theme.

Development is an expression of the same structural antecedents as the industrial and urban revolution. It poses a threat to both values and behaviors of conservative institutions. Ironically, modern-day conservatives are among the most adamant defenders of laissez-faire economics, which acts as a radical force by encouraging personal choice and movement and which gradually erodes commitments to family and community. Free migrants choose to move primarily for personal reasons based on considerations for themselves as individuals or for the sake of the group of which they are a part. This choice expresses the continuum between selfishness and altruism or, as Parsons has defined them, an orientation toward oneself as opposed to an orientation to a broader social collective. The difference between other and self is not causally distinct. Individual ideas originate in the group. American idealizations of individualism are acquired within the culture. People are expected to accept and conform to collective norms.

I am subject to biases. The analytic approach, which compares what people want with what they find, illusion with reality, can be easily confused to mean how their experience differs from my ideal of a community. My intention is to convey how immigrants and residents felt. The values they sought to satisfy and their experiences in satisfying them are theirs, not mine. I prefer small towns. I love gemeinschaft, community, yet regret that it can occur so imperfectly in most places. I also am intimately familiar with the infringements that community makes on its members. Most contemporary Americans would feel enraged and violated by behavior that is considered normal in Romania and Pakistan. The lack of community in modern society might bother me less if people were more realistic about it. However, fantasy is an integral aspect of the human condition. William Saroyan (1943) called it "the human comedy." Zorba called it "the Great Catastrophe" (Kazantzakis, 1952). I have no expectations that the quality of community in America will become more integrated and cohesive in the foreseeable future. I hope that people may at least understand some of the processes that work against gemeinschaft in the contemporary world, even in small, somewhat isolated towns.

Chapter 10

The Future of Rapidly Growing Small Towns in High Natural-Amenity Areas

In this chapter, the discussion focuses on what I imagine will happen as migrants and communities in scenic recreational areas move into the 21st century. Change is universal, inescapable and, when it occurs, is especially evident in small remote places. A prediction that such places will continue to grow and to lose much of their social structure built around personal relationships seems fairly safe. Prediction can range from mysterious suppositions for eternity obtained through a crystal ball to the simple extrapolation of measured events into a very immediate future. Our predictions are loose extrapolations mixed with a few tea leaves. This chapter is about how the processes of migration will be played out into the next few decades by individuals and will leave an imprint on local communities located in beautiful places.

Two extremes of migration and community change have been occurring in small towns in the Rocky Mountains since the 1950s. The more persistent extreme has been the dogged survival of agricultural towns and communities. Most have gradually lost population and have attracted few newcomers. At the other extreme are scenic and recreational communities that have high in- and out-migration and, in many cases, rapid growth. These extremes encapsulate geographic character-istics, economic foundations and social structures.

AGRICULTURAL TOWNS

Agricultural towns and their surrounding areas that have lost population are generally in relatively flat farming areas or are far removed from transportation routes. There is no clear dividing line between the farming areas and the broken topography more typical of logging and ranching areas. Forests and tablelands are more beautiful than flatlands to most outsiders. Scenic locations are more likely to have attracted newcomers since the 1960s in spite of failing local natural resource economies. Despite their small size and slow growth, the social structures of agricultural areas are more retentive. Their populations are largely composed of people who have stayed while others have moved away. Most adult residents are permanent, frequently from multigenerational local families. Mobile residents who would like to become permanent are usually discouraged to do so unless they have independent sources of income. Retirees with pensions and frequently with local roots are welcomed back. Poorer transients are given marginal jobs similar to the work done by the small residual population of nonrespectable residents. In research we conducted in 10 small towns in Montana, we found that stable, salaried employment was rare. It was scrupulously given to dependable long-term residents. Established local women were given job preferences. When no competent local residents were available for permanent positions, such as for professional positions, nonlocals were hired (Jobes, 1997).

The primary concerns within isolated agricultural towns are survival within the broader society. They encourage and support established institutions: families, schools, churches, government and businesses. For all institutions, existence is threatened because of efforts to cut costs and increase efficiency. The communities struggle to survive and to accommodate by creating a modest and measured community administration. It can afford no more. Buildings, equipment and people must be selected carefully to do the job for a long time. The appearance of agricultural towns reflects the struggle to survive. Many are sentinels of the past with boarded windows, wind-swept elevators and railway tracks overgrown with weeds. Their decimation usually occurs gradually and painfully. Local businesses close as the farmers become fewer. Schools consolidate, towns share ministers and athletic teams and the post office closes. A bar and a church seem to be the last establishments to close. The fortunate survivors have plain worn buildings. The state of the local economy is reflected in the buildings. Dependably prosperous farm areas have solidly constructed and well-maintained structures. Those near developed petroleum and mineral reserves usually have more modern buildings and civic improvements, although poorly maintained if they are experiencing a bust cycle.

Willis Goudy (1990) and Willits and her colleagues (1982, 1990) have repeatedly demonstrated that residents in agricultural towns know what they have. Their facilities are rarely cutting edge. The competence is rarely state-of-the-art, though easily accessible and personally administered. There are no lines and few formalities. The schools still turn out successful scholars and victorious teams. Their residents know what exists in the cities. Their children and their siblings live in them. They may have lived there for awhile. Most prefer the slower, more personal, predictably conventional way of life. The prediction for these places is that more of the same will occur. In the next decade or two or three, many probably will continue to lose population. I optimistically predict that gradual growth will occur as these bypassed and vacated places slowly attract and retain spillover from the broader national growth and dispersion.

SCENIC TOWNS

Scenic towns are consistently in close proximity to outdoor recreation. The more developed the recreational resource, the more the community attracts people and development, which differentiate it from agricultural communities. Downhill ski areas have become magnets for development. Famous areas such as Jackson and Sun Valley are complemented by dozens of less well-known ski areas. National parks create a similar magnet for development. Some of these Rocky Mountain areas are among the fastest growing in America. Scenic recreational locations undoubtedly will continue to grow. At the same time, their populations will become less permanent. The continual growth and influx of newcomers in scenic recreational towns creates diverse and efficient services compared to most rural areas. Some services, particularly restaurants, airports and financial services, resemble posh suburbs more than agricultural towns. Recreational towns actually have more services than suburbs of the same size because rural towns provide a range of goods and services to large geographic areas. Suburban towns usually rely on the broader metropolitan areas for their needs. The continual influx of newcomers is a constant source of new ideas for every type of institution. Tourists and the local residents, themselves largely recent exurbanites, have high expectations about quality and efficiency.

Recreational towns are organized around fairly reliable and established institutions that cater to a largely uncommitted and transient population. A small core of committed residents keeps the place operating for the rest of the residents and tourists. This small core is established in local administration, industries and relatively stable businesses such as construction, transportation and real estate. The core is not socially homogeneous. It includes laborers, white-collar employees and an established local elite. There is a filtering effect that rewards people who stay. People in the core who have lived there for several decades may have incomes and social status that are disproportionately above average. The more growth and development a town has had, the smaller the relative size of the core. At some point, when and if population growth and transience slow, a sizeable, stable core may evolve. That is unlikely to occur for several decades in the most rapidly growing localities.

GROWTH

The demise of small towns has many faces. Environmental destruction and the loss of community are two types of demise. A more tragic loss has occurred in thousands of rural communities that atrophied or disappeared since early in this century. They are a tangible backdrop for interpreting the current conversion throughout the beautiful regions. Scenic recreational towns endure a loss of community. Many agricultural towns have lost their very existence. The scenic recreational towns are filled with some life, prosperity and hope. They inspire many people to live in community rather than society. They hold promise, if indeed community is to reemerge, for society, during the centuries to come.

If the concern in agricultural communities is with survival and accommodation to the broader society, the concern in recreational towns is with growth and symbols of life quality. Their residents are ambivalent about growth. The greediest favor it without mitigation and the most reclusive oppose it all. Those in between generally dislike the disruption and depersonalization that follow development and transience while enjoying the more diverse goods and services, and the support it provides for their livelihood. Growth and its consequences often are a local obsession. Residents are concerned about its goodness and badness and about what to do about it. They talk about the loss of community, something which many of the critics themselves have never experienced. They are irritated by the brashness and impatience of new city people.

The concern and communication about growth does not stop it or even slow it down. The discussion molds the growth and directs attention to tangible symbols. Ironically, the attention given to antigrowth sentiments and the cultivation of development to make the growth more attractive and humane probably increase the growth and population instability. Since progressive and foresightful people are attracted to the promise of progress, they head straight for such places, accelerating the process of development.

Tangible symbols are activities, conditions and objects that are established to protect or maintain valuable natural or social characteristics of the community. Their value may be imagined, romanticized and have little substantive foundation for the symbols being advocated. Numerous tangible symbols become successfully established as practical accommodations to growth. In areas where clearcutting and other aesthetically ugly forestry practices are common, view sheds have been developed around the visual perimeter of towns. The unsightly forest is removed from sight and, to some extent, mind. Green Belts ostensibly create outer boundaries for growth development. While development usually hop scotches around protected areas, Green Belts do preserve park lands for the future which otherwise could be lost. They also provide space for nearby low-impact recreation and for pathways. A few wise communities protect small streams and other natural settings for public pathways. Small streams are gems for effective landscaping that often are lost to public use because of local administrative short-sightedness.

SYMBOLS OF COMMUNITY

Cultural qualities also are drawn upon to establish tangible symbols that the community is energetic and vital. High cultural examples include the establishing or expanding institutions such as museums and arts complexes. Institutions and events tangibly symbolize that the town is viable, culture with or without haute. The Aspen Institute and the Sundance Film Festival are replicated throughout the region. Farmers' markets and fairs frequently are established, or symbolically reestablished, as linkages to the land. Local crafts glorify products hewn from nature through skills developed in the past.

For decades, I have wanted to tell this story about goat ladies. Goats are beautiful, graceful and affectionate animals that provide milk and delicious meat. Some of my friends claim that the word barbecue is derived from the Latin word for goat. The classic Mexican barbecue is *cabrito*. Some goats provide valuable wool. All provide decent manure. They are ideally suited for small, self-sustaining acreage. They also have a few less-attractive traits. Billy goats smell like a concentration of rancid butter and urine. They can climb almost anywhere, though they particularly prefer neighbors' porches. They can eat almost anything and have special appreciation for gardens and fruit trees. They must be milked twice each day while they are wet. And, because they have multiple offspring, half of which are billies, their numbers quickly proliferate if the billies are not butchered and the nannies sold.

I have observed six women who call themselves goat ladies. There were no goat gentlemen. There were patient husbands and partners who assisted with fencing, feeding, milking and care of the animals. They also often paid for what was otherwise an expensive hobby for their wives. All but one had moved from urban areas and wanted to live a quasiagricultural life. All loved their goats greatly. Two of the six gradually ran very efficient, well-fenced operations that specialized in breeding registered animals for sale. They carefully measured growth, birthing, conformation and milk production. They constantly communicated and traveled in the national goat network. After 26 years, one is still settled in her task on 15 acres north of Bozeman. The other, after 11 years, switched from goats to sheep. Neither of these women were bohemian. They were no-nonsense, practical, hardworking and organized small-animal zealots.

The other four women were former or continuing vestiges of the 1960s, gently loving life and nature. They fell in love with their goats. One, the only single woman, instantly took to goats in a small commune. The others quickly acquired them through the rural bohemian network. All four even looked much like the others, with long naturally hanging hair and no makeup. All dressed exclusively in ankle-length skirts or jeans. The three married women got rid of their goats and husbands within three years, although none claimed any causal order. Most goat ladies are an extreme form of rural illusion, so sure at first and so different later. Hearing a young bohemian woman recently moved from the city lovingly talking about her goats and the wonderful country life was an instant signal that there would soon be a disillusioned urban pilgrim, a divorce and another out-migrant. Goat ladies personified sustainable agricultural activity for practical reasons. Their pseudogemeinschaft character masked the lack of presence or representativeness of the events and their participants. What seems to make sense in a small, beautiful way is out of context for the people and their lives. Schumacher (1973) had part of the right idea. Although small can be beautiful, that does not mean that it is. Goat ladies symbolize social characteristics of community that many people fervently want to believe will last. Such people and their practices are likely to quickly pass on. Not incidentally, I have only met goat ladies in scenic recreational areas.

SYMBOLIC CONSTRUCTED ENVIRONMENTS

Recreational communities encounter many more dynamic impacts on their physical and social environments than do their agricultural counterparts. Tangible symbols are responses to environmental and cultural changes that are spreading concentrically away from the social epicenter. One by one, the small towns surrounding the glamor towns adapt to and replicate the pattern of the town that dominates the locale.

Cultivating symbols helps to create physical appearances in both the natural and the constructed environments. The natural and social gradually become mixed together. Distinguishing where one begins and the other ends becomes difficult. Among the most universal, evident and definitive physical characteristics of recreational areas is their sprawl. Even carefully planned unit developments, like Vail and Big Sky, quickly lose control of population dispersion into surrounding valleys and hills. Since these areas were aesthetically beautiful before development, many of the environmental qualities are soon modified or destroyed. The little gems (springs, creeks and sledding hills) are broken up, sold and closed off. Air quality, so vulnerable in high mountain valleys, changes from clear and pure to smoggy and polluted, requiring protective ordinances against behaviors that had been part of the authentic rural lifestyle, like fireplaces and open trash burning.

The rapidly expanding constructed environment also changes. With the exception of totally new planned unit developments, most of these communities have grown around a small downtown that was first constructed between about 1880 and 1920. During their early heyday, the Main Streets were wide enough for four teams of horses to pass side by side. They were robust local agriculture and transportation centers, well-maintained, spacious and open. Even now, they have solid ornate facades typical of their era. Except for the few with a high proportion of brick buildings, made possible by a continual reliable influx of capital, most rural towns have not been well-maintained. The fortunate few, like Livingston, Montana, a railway center, Red Lodge, Montana, a gateway town with a ski area, and Sheridan, Wyoming, with a federal hospital, had capital. The postfrontier facade of these vestiges of the late frontier era made them especially attractive for development. Some historical buildings and districts have been preserved. Neighborhoods with Victorian houses have become cherished reflections of the social life and craftsmanship of an earlier era. They also became choice real estate. The well-preserved older buildings became local landmarks, symbolic loci for parks, shopping areas and subdivisions.

Many of the historic preservation efforts in scenic recreational towns have been led by planners and architects who especially appreciate beautiful classic structures, their relationship to their settings and their integration into the developing community. Architects also are central to the new construction which so visibly distinguishes recreational towns. Some new buildings are wonderfully imaginative and creative. Their designs and materials are beautifully and practically integrated into lovely spaces. They frequently are inspired by symbolic visual and social themes of the formative era. Located on acreage at the continually expanding perimeter of town, many of these are architectural jewels that complement the natural setting.

CONSTRUCTED ISOLATION

The best new construction sometimes is evident in architectonic rural residences and represents the conversion of the past into a symbolic reference for the present and future. Even in their beauty, they often stand as citadels that represent the processes of transformation and illusion in scenic areas, apparitions, beautiful isolated edifices, visible only from a distant road. Some are remote, invisible to anyone but their residents and visitors. Physically atomized, separated from the town, they communicate the separation from community that their owners imagine they want. Their isolation often is at the loss of being part of the community. Two families of participants who did not know of each other built grand custom-designed neo-Tudor houses on subdivision acreage several miles from downtown. One was the home of an agricultural engineer, recently remarried with young children. Jim Schultz had just sold an agribusiness in the Midwest and planned to become semiretired on his profits of several million dollars. He was 48 and Elizabeth, his wife, 10 years younger. They spoke lovingly and patiently of staying there and building a family life around their children. Within four years, he had organized a new firm in animal husbandry. The following year, they moved to a prestigeous Denver suburb to be nearer to their new business and because they thought that their children, now adolescents, would benefit from the cultural opportunities of the city. Though they attended a local church, they never formed close friendships in the Bozeman area.

The other couple, Theodore and Elke Bondon, were artists and illustrators. Originally from Europe, they had extensive professional experience and success. They had heard of Bozeman while living in New York. They moved to Bozeman shortly after their first visit. Their success as illustrators was not diminished by their move, which was unusual for professionals who depended upon outside contracts. They said that the isolation of their house perched alone on a hill had increased their productivity because they were no longer interrupted by the urban art world. They found inspiration in the beauty and solitude. They moved back to the city, essentially cosmopolitan nomads, after eight years. In their last few years, they had become more and more critical about local growth, mediocre development, local aesthetics and social justice.

Like Elizabeth and Jim Schultz, the Bondon's had no close friends nor were they active participants in local community organizations. Both couples built beautiful homes on the distant outskirts of town. However beautiful their homes and their surroundings, however secure their financial well-being, most people who were geographically isolated moved away. Some symbolically used their place as a seasonal or holiday retreat, a geographic reference point in their lives. Their land was usually taken out of production and tightly posted out of public use. These people come and go and, in a sense, speak of Michelangelo. The symbols implied something valuable, the ability to appreciate the authentic that was being lost.

Some few residents in scenic recreational areas became active in cultural planning. Such people usually lived in the beautifully restored historic houses or in the newer architectural gems outside of town. People of modest means lived in less elegant older homes or mass-produced subdivisions. The social system itself is complex and many-faceted in rapidly growing towns like Bozeman and Livingston. Essentially no one is fully integrated into the community. Recreational community structures, like the residents themselves, are fragmented and specialized. Yet, those people who are active are often passionate and convinced that theirs is a good community, a progressive community and a good way of life. They participate, compete, contribute as part of the community whatever their diverse motivations for becoming locally engaged. They are satisfied, rewarded, thrilled and frustrated, discouraged, bored and sometimes angry. The people who are involved rarely succumb to the attraction and fascination with living isolated, independent and alone. That distinguishes them from the majority of people who pass through, residents by legal, but rarely social definition.

AUTHENTICITY

Recreational and agricultural towns and their respective residents have all been formed by different molds. Our descriptions are probably representative for most. Once established, recreational scenic towns eventually dominate the surrounding area. Towns beyond the periphery of the recreational center gradually become more like the recreational center. Land use incrementally changes from commercial agriculture to hobby farms, acreage and subdivisions. Land values increase, adjusting to their more privileged owners. The gradual domination of the entire Roaring Fork Valley and surrounding vicinity by the development of Aspen is a process that has occurred on a smaller scale throughout the Rocky Mountains. The farther away an agricultural town is from scenic recreational development, the more its residents struggle to retain people, jobs and local services. Their way of life is taken for granted as good. The other edge of the sword cuts in scenic recreational towns. They struggle symbolically to retain that way of life, which, for the most part, has been destroyed by the processes of developments as their populations, jobs and services multiply. Between these extremes of isolated farm town and trendy pseudorural lifestyle enclave is a broad range of towns and people.

"Authenticity" has crept into the modern lexicon. One meaning of "authenticity" is genuine, as opposed to being false. In this sense, an antique, an art piece, a gem stone and a community is the real McCoy rather than an imitation. The second meaning is natural, as opposed to being manufactured. "Natural" means something has been formed by natural forces, as opposed to making it with hands, the literal translation of "manufacture." The conceptual problem with distinguishing natural from manufactured is what to do with humans as makers? Are we part of the natural order or are we distinct from it, acting upon it? If humans are part of nature, then their creations, whether a remote aboriginal village or Las Vegas at night, are equally natural. If humans are distinct from nature, manufacturers, then at some time in our genetic archives, somewhere between beast and human, the transition was made to conceptualize human nature. That unrecorded moment may be considered as the absolute event that abruptly and forever set humans apart from nature. A more gradual way of considering the distinction between human and nature hinges on the extent of domination humans have over nature or their immediate surroundings.

People may have no final control over nature. When the Big Bang comes, there is precious little that humans will able to do to prevent it. Even less extreme natural catastrophes are humbling reminders of our limited control over nature, although, certainly, wiser planning for such events is possible. From a relativistic perspective, indigenous cultures that have evolved to sustainable adaptation survive in their natural settings are more natural than a manufactured construction lacking sustained adaptation on a natural setting. From this perspective, Las Vegas and Aspen or Jackson are less natural, less authentic than the isolated aboriginal community or modern agricultural communities. The level of authenticity of small towns is all the more apparent if their residents act out a pseudostyle that was not part of the local repertoire before newcomers came. When people take on new and imitative ways of talking and being with each other like they don a pair of boots and a cowboy hat, they are inauthentic.

Forty years ago, Mexico border radio stations advertised "genuine simulated diamond rings." The most manufactured of the recreational towns, Telluride, Sisters or Big Sky, are close approximations of genuine simulated western towns (or Bavarian villages). Their symbolic appearances and activities replicate what is imagined to be real. Their lack of historically continuous support from the surrounding natural area make then inauthentic. They are manufactured imitations of some designers' imaginings of real and natural. They are not the quaint, personal, modern frontier facades that they symbolically pretend to be. But they are 100 percent pure of the kinds of community they are. And many people just love them, for a while.

The question of authenticity may have little relevance. People have a right to be themselves and to talk, act and dress as they want. They have the right to make claims, to imitate what they imagine authenticity to be. If there is any danger to making the claim, it probably lies in not being able to distinguish the real from the false, and the consequences of that ignorance. The natural areas and towns were true gems. Do they change from diamonds in the rough to polished and cut stones with many facets? Or are they exchanged for bogus, glittering artifacts? Is the ability to tell the difference in the eye of some discerning observer? Or is what is discerned merely a pretentious opinion?

FATE OF MINING TOWNS

Along the continuum between purely agricultural towns and purely recreational towns are some types of communities that deserve special consideration. Each of these has had historical precedents and each promises to be noteworthy into the future.

An entire set of communities also depends upon nonrenewable natural resources, where resource plays out, the primary source of jobs and incomes is eliminated and the towns shrink, disintegrate and often collapse. It is hardly a matter of coincidence that hard-rock mining towns are the origins for many modern recreational theme towns like Aspen, Carson City, Park City and Telluride. The ore played out, residents looked desperately to another resource to mine. Hard-rock mining towns have a boomer mentality, rarely concerned with environmental preservation. They also have ready-made images to be substituted, fabled names of characters and mines. They have many scenic residues of mines, headers and shafts that provide symbols to further authenticate the local theme. Perhaps most importantly, hard-rock deposits are often in rugged, beautiful mountains with mother lodes of snow.

The centuries-old phenomenon of boom and bust has been a recurrent theme for the entire discipline of social impact analysis and is beyond the scope of this book (Albrecht, Amey, and Amir, 1996; Murdcch et al., 1986). Perhaps the most important lesson to be learned by considering mining communities that have become scenic and recreational towns is to avoid mining the resource in a nonsustainable manner. Protect nature because it is the sustainable resource upon which the community is physically and socially constructed. Destroy the scenic and natural resources and the quality of the location is forever changed.

The great faith and hope invested in theory, particularly the use of theory to implement planning, is that once a good plan is agreed upon and incorporated, the undesirable alternatives will be eliminated, once and for all. True believers hope and believe that a good plan will take care of the problems. Such faith neglects the complexities of both the environmental and the social systems. A timeless countertheory will eventually resurface in the idiosyncratic conditions of Everytown, just as crucial flaws are part of Everyman. This resurfacing will occur partially because not everyone was convinced that the plan was a good one. Newcomers arrive who were not part of the planning process. Even supporters become disillusioned with the plan they advocated. Objections to a plan which has been agreed upon and set into motion involves more than personal resistance. The individual responses against a plan reflect the inevitable inadequacies of the plan and the theory upon which it was conceived. There are systemic reasons for the objection to any plan, beyond the obvious and petty selfishness of individuals. Even resistance for the most selfish personal reasons implies the failure of theory to accommodate errant nonbelievers who do not want or act according to theory.

One might be tempted to abandon trying to develop plans based on theory, given the inevitable resistance to them. Social systems demand and require constant, vigilant attention, especially when they are experiencing change. A structure does not take care of itself once it is designed. How long it will last is partially a matter of how effectively and realistically a plan was designed and constructed to work in a particular social and natural environment. That success will largely be determined by how people in that system continue to nuture it. A good garden has a plan and is never without a good gardener. Some garden plans are easier to maintain than others. Human systems are not nature. They are more similar to gardens, planned, designed and constructed apart from nature in order to achieve what is conceived as socially desirable.

SMALL, ISOLATED ENCLAVES, ANARCHISTS, RUGGED INDIVIDUALISTS

Rural areas also attract enclaves based on experimental or countercultural lifestyles, groups who wish to establish their own isolated social world. Monasteries have been constructed in remote areas for millennia in order to find peace, solitude and safety (Coser, 1974). Rural areas provide enclaves with essential food, energy and construction materials to sustain themselves. The honest and simple toil brings the members back to the Earth: digging, planting, harvesting, preserving and eating; growing, cutting, splitting, stacking and burning; tapping, hauling, pouring and drinking. Natural cycles of birth and death, of seasons, of day and night and the work devoted to those cycles connect the members back to nature, community and, frequently, to God.

Rural areas promise freedom, anarchy, to some groups. My knowledge about escapist, religious and paramilitary groups comes only slightly from the interviews. However, during the late 1980s, I conducted one research project on a religious organization which had relocated to Montana. It is not possible to know how many members of such groups were in our samples. We only know those members who voluntarily identified themselves.

One long-term sample member, Stuart Barnes, was a local political gadfly. He opened a motorcycle and snowmobile business shortly after coming from Chicago in 1980. He gave up the motorcycle shop in order to devote more time to editing and publishing a small libertarian newsletter. He confronted the local school system regarding pedagogy in the education of his children. His wife, a university professor, dissociated herself from him following their divorce. Barry Lynch was another well-known local conservative political activist. He regularly and unsuccessfully ran for public office under the Libertarian Party, when he was in town. He left the Gallatin Valley four times between 1976 and 1994. These and other group members openly discussed their philosophies and orientations with enormous glee during interviews. They believed and enjoyed what they were doing.

I also lived in close proximity with several rugged individualists and a few politically conscious anarchists. The Rockies is probably the best-known haven in America for such people. Most people who are attracted to isolation and independence from society's control are not members of organizations. Scenic recreational areas have the essential features to satisfy the myths that sustain many isolated rural romantic anarchists. The mountains and streams are the places where a real man can be a real man, independent and dominating nature. The streams are full of fish, and the hills abound with game for the skilled outdoorsman. Modern rural anarchists can wander contentedly without the constraining noise of society and its whistles of justice. The bars on the boundaries of national parks and wilderness areas are filled with such characters. More elk are shot and fish caught in any bar in West Yellowstone and Gardiner than in all of the surrounding meadows and streams.

Most independent anarchists are extremely transient. They stay for a few weeks, a year or two. Although many are social isolates, they constitute a subcommunity within the scenic recreational communities. They are colorful, energetic and frequently more than a little outside the law. Even the outlaws often believe their violations are acceptable within their code. Taking game out of season, beyond legal possession limits and on property closed to hunting are common violations that follow a historic tradition of poachers challenging authority. Drug paraphernalia and marijuana plants were sometimes visible during interviews in the more remote households. Hard drinking and drug use are common to these areas, fueling minor assaults and other nonprofessional legal violations that are acceptable in the code of rural anarchists.

Their violations clearly cross the boundary of unacceptability. A begrudging tolerance usually is afforded even to some of those who are clearly criminals if their crimes are justified by some political principle. The Unibomber probably falls at the extreme end of a continuum of survivalists. The most extreme of the outlaws include guides who offer clandestine trophy hunting in the national parks and drug dealers. Their deviant subcommunities throughout the region are analogous to deviant subcultural enclaves in marginal areas of the cities. They are disapproved of yet left alone, as a concession to a shared appreciation for individual freedom. Their presence adds credibility to myths that vestiges of a postfrontier world are still alive.

SECTS, CULTS AND RADICAL POLITICS

The most recognized and in a few cases, notorious newcomers often are members of unconventional organizations. Scenic recreational areas continue to attract religious sects and cults and political radicals who have deliberately located in rural areas for the same reasons of sustenance, security and aesthetics that have attracted such groups to rural areas for thousands of years. The number of members is small, although the proportion may be high in particular pockets, such as the Idaho Panhandle. Their zealousness is feared by others who sometimes organize opposition within the immediately surrounding area.

CONFLICT AND VIOLENCE

Zealots are especially feared if they are religious and advocate militant self-defense. There is credibility for some of the fear that local people and the public-at-large feel toward such groups. Leaders at Rajneespuram sprinkled *Salmonella species* bacteria at the salad bars in restaurants in surrounding towns as part of a political plot (Carter, 1990). The business manager of the Church Universal Triumphant (CUT) was convicted of providing false information during the purchase of weapons more suitable for hunting armored vehicles than big-game animals. There have been several armed clashes between militia-survivalist group members and law enforcement authorities in the region. On the other hand, the presence of religious zealots and political radicals is an illustrious extension of the American civil tradition into the West. The Great Basin was settled by the Latter Day Saints who had religious beliefs and social lifestyles at odds with convention. They also had an effective militia. Dozens of religious and lifestyle communes have been established between the West Coast and the Rockies. Archaic branches of the Mormons continue to practice polygamy here. Although they may be rural isolates as they become recognized as zealots, the origins of most are from somewhere else, most likely the city. The Unibomber, like most rural zealots, was a troubled urban character gone feral.

Conditions which stimulated the formation of rural communes in the past will persist and perhaps increase into the future. The strains will be particularly evident in scenic recreational areas because they are simultaneously attractive to cosmopolitan exurbanites, religious zealots and escapist militant groups. The distinction among these is arbitrary. It is possible to fall into any or all of these categories. As the availability of such places declines and polarization around violence increases, conflicts probably will become more common. Responses to them quite likely will remain as they have been — fear, distrust and, occasionally, violent reactions. They will be feared more than the independent anarchists because they have a collective identity which distinguishes them as critical of conventional society.

Small, isolated religious, political and lifestyle enclaves are not particularly dangerous as social movements. Zealots attracted beyond the fringe of conventional society are not likely to attract many followers, certainly not a critical mass for significant social change. If anything, they personify the foolishness, even the craziness of American society, fortunately tucked away in remote areas. Their uniforms, the orange and red of the Rajneeshees, the crystals, purple and white of CUT, the camouflage clothing of survivalists, are locally ridiculed as symbols of beliefs and activities that are seen as silly, foolish or dangerous. At the same time, the causal forces that generate such groups and then drive them to remote areas of the countryside probably are multiplying.

The greater dangers from such groups are that they invite militant responses and that they have a few unmanageable dissidents. When these factors are combined, they almost inevitably will lead to confrontation. The loose cannon, the constantly enraged, probably insane, independently violent member, is more likely to act if a provocation has occurred. Convinced of the urgency and legitimacy of their beliefs, the most zealous create havens for the uncontrollable and violent who ultimately may force a confirmation of their beliefs. Confrontations further solidify the group, the opposition and a continued escalation of their struggle against each other. The struggle of the groups are believed to be based on high ideals: religious, economic, political and lifestyle freedoms. The greatest dangers to local communities and society occur when radical zealots or militant social control agents act in manners that are unacceptable even for most of their respective groups. When that unacceptable and violent act has occurred, their members are in the unenviable position of justifying and defending evil.

Becoming engaged in the emotional turmoil of an armed confrontation with the state confers great power to anarchists and other groups of zealots. It is important to keep in perspective that they generally present little more threat than being a nuisance. Judiciously avoiding confrontations may keep them from attaining credibility by being regarded as "folk devils" (Cohen, 1985). There are more murders on any given night in many cities in the United States than in confrontations in rural areas that receive television coverage for weeks.

Unconventional communities will persist into the future in the Northern Rockies. How the broader, more conventional communities, municipalities and states should respond is not amenable to formula. A moderate course following constitutional guarantees for the rights of individuals, the well-being of communities and the society is sensible. Zealots in rural areas may be thought of as exhibiting the essence of what attracted many more moderate residents to scenic and recreational places. The dream of the zealots is more clearly stated and identified than for most residents. It is more specifically organized, often a caricature with simplistic beliefs, activities and appearances that its members passionately believe are appropriate and right for the place. It is an immoderate illusion, a modern version of the old romance for freedom, a magnified version of the same dream that attracts so many people to the region.

CONVENTIONAL IN-MIGRANTS

Although religious groups and survivalist zealots receive inordinate attention among rural newcomers, the great masses of more conventional in-migrants pose a much greater risk to the local communities and natural environment. The large and unrelenting flow of in-migrants who are demanding change makes disruption to social life and impacts upon the environment inevitable. Nature is the primary attraction of the study area.

Some of the future of the Northern Rockies and its communities has been set in place by development that has already occurred. Existing development probably has established a pattern that is likely to be followed into the future. Table 10.1 summarizes a few facts about development that identify some of the pressures that are being exerted on the natural environment and communities in the region. Each has implications for development in other scenic recreation areas. Problems associated with development in scenic recreation areas seem to be multiples of problems found in their broader region.

Table 10.1 indicates how development and population growth have exerted pressure on land resources in Gallatin County in recent years. These pressures were considerably more intense there than in Montana as a whole. These measures are notable because they were collected during the relatively slow period between the mid-1980s and 1990. Housing increased by nearly one-quarter (24.3%). New housing in rural areas typically requires new land. More than 5 percent (5.5%) of agricultural lands in Gallatin County were lost to development. The reasons for

Table 10.1
Indicators of Pressures Imposed on Land Resources by Recent Development in the Gallatin Valley: Comparisons with the State of Montana

Indicators of Development	Montana	Gallatin County
Increases in housing 1982-87	10.0%	24.3%
Loss of agricultural land 1982-87	-.06%	-5.5%
Rental vacancy rates 1990	9.6%	4.5%
Median housing values 1990	$56,100	$70,300
Rural housing without public sewer connections 1990		8,089 (74%)

Source: County and City Data Base: 1994, U.S. Bureau of Census, U.S. Government Printing Office, Washington, DC.

new housing are made obvious by the rental vacancy rates and median housing values. Proportionally, only half as many rentals were available in Gallatin County as in the State. The demand for housing also drove up the value of housing. With the median priced house in Gallatin County selling for $70,300 in 1990, the value of housing was much higher than the State average, over $5,000 higher than the next most expensive county. These figures understate many impacts because they are restricted to Gallatin County boundaries. For example, the new housing in Gallatin County (24.3%) was second only to Madison County with an astronomical 42 percent increase. Most of that growth was almost directly related to Gallatin County and Bozeman. Most of the growth in Madison County was due to construction at Big Sky, a destination ski and golf resort. Big Sky, though largely located in Madison County, is in a cul de sac accessible only through roads in Gallatin County. The destruction of the natural environment and access to the natural environment because of the development have been enormous.

CHANGING ORIENTATIONS ABOUT WILDERNESS

Wilderness has many meanings. One meaning is based upon legally defined protection for relatively undeveloped areas. This legal definition has become increasingly recognized during the past 30 years. Corporations and environmentalists spend millions arguing the legal meaning of wilderness. The more general and historically conventional meaning, stripped of legal language, is a relatively natural environment. It is important to designate these meanings when discussing the following tables. We began to ask participants in the research about whether they favored more wilderness in the local area in 1972. It is likely that what they considered to be the meaning of that question may have changed by 1992. As Tables 10.2 and 10.3 indicate, their responses changed markedly between 1972 and 1992.

In 1972, the initial cohort ($\bar{x} = 2.15$) generally wanted more wilderness in the area (Table 10.2). By 1976, the new subsample was neutral ($\bar{x} = 2.70$) toward developing more wilderness. By 1980, the new subsample was negative about the idea. These shifts indicate that, during the 1970s, people had become more opposed to developing more wilderness. The reasons for their growing opposition are unclear. One factor may have been increased involvement in federal designation of wilderness lands. The federal Roadless Area Review and Evaluation (RARE) proposals of the 1970s may have satisfied some people that, in conjunction with legal definitions, sufficient local wilderness had been set aside (Wellman, 1987). It also is likely that people who opposed state and federal planning were reacting to central government intervention. Discussions about wilderness beginning in the 1970s became increasingly polarized. Opponents to wilderness became more organized. They claimed that the establishment of wilderness denied individuals the rights to develop and use lands in manners that were acceptable in a free market political economy. Special interest groups, like snowmobile riders and four-wheel drivers, became bitterly estranged from the legal notion of wilderness. Commercial interests, especially realtors and extractive industries, opposed the closure of potentially developable land resources. By 1992,

Table 10.2
"I Favor More Wilderness in the Surrounding Area": Responses by Cohorts Interviewed Between 1972 and 1992

	Changes Between Total Samples							
	1972	N (%)	1976	N (%)	1980	N (%)	1992	N (%)
Strongly agree	38	25	13	12	8	10	24	16
Agree	65	45	39	36	17	21	37	25
Neutral	26	18	25	23	22	18	41	27
Disagree	17	12	27	25	22	28	37	25
Strongly disagree	0	0	3	3	10	13	10	7
Total	146	100	107	100	79	100	149	100
	$\bar{x} = 2.151$		$\bar{x} = 2.701$		$\bar{x} = 3.075$		$\bar{x} = 2.16$	

Table 10.3
Favor More Wilderness: Responses in 1992

	Year Respondents Were First Interviewed					
	1970s	N (%)	1980s	N (%)	1990s	N (%)
Strongly agree	1	3	14	19	12	26
Agree	7	24	16	21	16	35
Neutral	4	15	24	32	14	30
Disagree	12	41	17	23	3	9
Strongly disagree	5	17	4	5	0	0
Total	29	100	75	100	45	100
Mean	$\bar{x} = 2.90$		$\bar{x} = 2.73$		$\bar{x} = 2.18$	

the cohort was much more supportive of increasing wilderness. More longer term residents were opposed to increasing the amount of wilderness in the area. Simultaneously, newcomers were not only more supportive of increasing local wilderness, each successive cohort, particularly of newcomers, was more supportive.

Table 10.3 summarizes how people in 1992 felt about developing more wilderness, distinguishing responses among people who had initially been interviewed in the 1970s, 1980s and 1990s. Their responses are to the same question about wilderness that they had been answering for at least one and, in some instances, two decades. The most obvious difference is that the earliest cohort to be interviewed was the least sympathetic toward developing more wilderness. Respondents first interviewed during the 1990s were the most sympathetic. The reasons why the earlier cohort and successively the 1980 cohort were less supportive about wilderness are not entirely clear. The people interviewed for the first time in the 1990s were all newcomers. Newcomers may have been more supportive to wilderness. In 1992, newcomers were also younger than old-timers who already had lived 10 or 20 years in the study area. Newcomers had more recently lived in the city. An expanding body of literature indicates that people worldwide are becoming more supportive of preserving and protecting the natural environment (Inglehart, 1997). Residents in First World nations are more supportive of environmental issues than are people of the Third World. In addition, there is more support for environmental issues now than there was 30 years ago.

There also is evidence that the differences between how the 1970s', 1980s'and 1990s'respondents felt about wilderness in the 1990s may have been due to changes among the old-timers themselves. Most (70%) of the 1972 respondents agreed or strongly agreed that they favored more wilderness. The average in 1972 ($\bar{x} = 2.15$) was significantly more supportive than in 1992($\bar{x}=2.9$). Barely a quarter (27%) of the remaining 29 people from that initial subsample felt the same way in 1992. It is conceivable that the wilderness supporters had been more likely to have moved away in the interim years. However, newcomers who left and those who stayed did not differ about their attitudes regarding the natural environment. It seems unlikely that the people who were still in the sample 20 years later were initially more opposed to wilderness than early respondents who had moved away or died. The more telling evidence is apparent by looking at the responses about disagreeing or strongly disagreeing among the respondents from the 1970s. In 1972, not a single person strongly opposed more wilderness. Only 17 (12%) disagreed. Only 13 respondents from all of the subsamples of the 1970s had strongly disagreed. Yet, a majority (58%) of them disagreed or strongly disagreed by 1992. Many people changed from supporting more local wilderness during the 1970s to opposing it by the 1990s. Meanwhile, respondents from the 1980s, largely remaining newcomers, had become slightly more supportive by 1992 ($\bar{x} = 2.73$) than they had been in the early 1980s ($\bar{x} = 3.07$). The countervailing influences of becoming more supportive, as part of a national trend, and becoming more opposed, because of increasing age and provinciality, were operating.

FUTURE OF COMMUNITY

The future has inevitably been grander than and different from any predictions. One obligation of science is to predict. Predicting where a line will intersect another or under what load a structure will collapse is a relatively easy matter in physical science. Predicting long-term social events is infinitely more difficult and tangential. There are many more variables, all indeterminate and interactive. Estimating how many years of school people will attend or how many babies will be born to a known population next year is feasible and relatively accurate. Predicting what the nature of community and society will be 50 or 100 years from now borders on science fiction.

Community is a factual phenomenon that can only exist with certain conditions. It requires a small stable population residing in the same place over a long period, preferably generation after generation. Given these conditions, routine rules and behaviors emerge based around familiar, informal, face-to-face interaction within the cohesive population. These conditions are likely to occur less and less often, unless some devastating catastrophe markedly reduces migration and other forces that destroy social cohesion. Conditions of stability have not been typical in the industrializing world for 200 or more years. Backwater pockets in developed nations have experienced them in relatively pure form, but most of modern society has not. There has been a mixed presence and absence of some of the conditions. Even postfrontier towns in agricultural areas often were migratory, although frequently sharing a legacy of norms and behaviors that facilitated cohesion. Similarly, ethnic enclaves in inner cities have sometimes shared conditions of community (Suttles, 1968; Tamney, 1975).

The future seems likely to be an extension of the present for rapidly growing beautiful places and the people who inhabit them. The complexity of the meanings of such places and their residents should be evident. Places which are smaller and more personal and populated by people sharing a common orientation will be more community-like than larger, less personal populations that lack common identities, places, behaviors and beliefs. Small newly formed towns will strive to claim and to convey gemeinschaft, though their newly arrived residents lack the essential fellowship, kinship and neighborliness.

The problems of development that confront these beautiful places will persist. The issues and the ways the problems are articulated will also be murky. That most of the critics of development and growth are the same people who generate the processes that they despise will remain ironic. What once seemed to be easy dichotomies of newcomers and old-timers, and of support for development and opposition against it, will become even murkier. Length of residence will become a red herring. Residents who oppose or support development will be found among both newcomers and old-timers. The distinction between newcomers and old-timers will become increasingly indistinct. The condition for lifetime residence as a condition for claiming to be an old-timer will give way to whether a person has lived there for 20 years, or 10, or five, or for more than one winter.

Community is a need within humans, whether or not the integrating structure exists. It is a lingering desire for affiliation, to be part of a group and a place, to be recognized and to recognize. This longing is increasingly denied a place and a people of which to be part. It is there, not as a vestigial organ like the appendix with an almost forgotten function. It is there, gnawing for satisfaction, needing to be in a community structure. Simultaneously, there is a need for independence and freedom, struggling against affiliations, a social analog to eros and thanatos, thesis and antithesis, community and independence. We, people, will continue to resolve the tension with our struggle to be together and to be apart.

Believing in community, holding some elements of a common orientation, is only one small aspect of community. Community can scarcely be held together as a social construction. Yet, that element which is superficially called sense of community will command most attention as the meaning for community. A recognition of community is not sufficient to create community. When sense of community is evoked, superficial symbolic planning will attempt to perpetuate the planners' notion of community. Populations brought together with a common hope and expectation will be disillusioned over and over again unless the structural elements — stability, dependence on the local social and physical environment and an interlocking set of rules and beliefs — also are present.

While not foreseeable in the immediate future, true community may become inevitable in some future and less mobile age. In the interlude, if in fact such a slower and more sustainable world eventuates, there is much that will have to be done: to work, learn and give thanks; to protect the environment, to cherish loved ones, friends and neighbors. These simple acts may become increasingly difficult as competition becomes more intense as a result of declining resources and growing, more-centralized populations. Continuing to dedicate oneself to family, friends, neighbors and community activities may become especially exhausting as the more solid bedrock of stable, personal support disintegrates. The reasons for disintegration must be appreciated and honored. Whatever their supportive character, communities also are likely to be composed of inbred and unjust people incapable of adapting to rapid and intense changes which have been shaking the social world for so long. The resolution and synthesis will incorporate the structural and inner needs of individuals and of groups with the environments where they live.

Bibliography

Aesop
    1985   *Aesop's Fables*, selected by Michael Hague, London: Methuen.
Albrecht, Stan L., Robert G. Amey, and Sarit Amir
    1996   "The Siting of Radioactive Waste Facilities: What Are the Effects on Communities?" *Rural Sociology* 61(4)649-673.
Argyris, Chris, Donald Putnam, and Diana McLain
    1985   *Action Science: Concepts, Methods, and Skills for Research and Intervention*, San Francisco: Jossey-Bass.
Arrington, Leonard J.
    1966   *The Great Basin Kingdom*, Lincoln: University of Nebraska Press.
Augustine, Saint
    1972   *The City of God Against the Pagans*, translated by William M. Green, London: Heinemann.
Barsby, L. and R. Cox
    1975   *Interstate Migration of the Elderly*, Lexington. MA: Lexington Books.
Beale, Calvin L.
    1975   *The Revival of Population Growth in Nonmètropolitan America*, Washington, DC: U.S.D.A., E.S.C.S., E.R.S.
Becker, Gary S.
    1962   *Human Capital*, Chicago: University of Chicago Press.
Becker, Howard S.
    1960   "Notes on the Concept of Commitment." *American Journal of Sociology* 66(3)32-40.
Biggar, J. C.
    1982   "Who Moved Among the Elderly, 1965-1970: Comparison of Types of Older Movers." *Research on Aging* 2(2)73-91.
Blackwood, Larry G. and Edward H. Carpenter
    1978   "The Importance of Anti-urbanism in Determining Residential Preferences and Migration Patterns." *Rural Sociology* 43(1)31-47.

Blau, Peter M.
    1960   "Patterns of Deviation in Work Groups." *Sociometry* 23(3)245-261.
Bridges, James and Aaron Lathan
    1980   *Urban Cowboy*, produced by Robert Evans and Irving Azoff, executive
            producer, C. O. Erickson, for Paramount Pictures. Screenplay by James
            Bridges and Aaron Lathan, based on a story by Aaron Lathan.
Brown, David L. and John M. Wardwell (eds.)
    1980   *New Directions in Urban-Rural Migration,* New York: Academic Press.
Buttel, Frederick H., Olaf Larson, and Gilbert W. Gillespie, Jr.
    1990   *The Sociology of Agriculture,* New York: Greenwood Press.
Calvert, Jerry W. and Patrick C. Jobes
    1990   "The Economic Value of Wilderness: A Critical Assessment." In *Outdoor
            Recreation Policy,* pp. 59-74, edited by John D. Hutcheson, Jr., Francis P.
            Noe, and Robert E. Snow, New York: Greenwood.
Campbell, Angus, Philip E. Converse, and Willard L. Rogers
    1976   *The Quality of American Life,* New York: Russell Sage.
Carter, Lewis F.
    1990   *Charisma and Control in Rajneeshpuram,* Cambridge: Cambridge
            University.
Cebula, Richard J.
    1979   *Determinants of Human Migration*, Lexington, MA: Lexington Books.
Cohen, Stanley
    1985   *Visions of Social Control*, Cambridge: Polity Press.
Coser, Lewis A.
    1974   *Greedy Institutions*, New York: Free Press.
Costner, Herbert L.
    1965   "Criteria for Measures of Association." *American Sociological Review*
            30(3)341-353.
Crutchfield, Robert, Michael Geerken, and Walter Gove
    1982   "Crime Rates and Social Integration: The Impact of Metropolitan Mobility."
            Criminology 20(3)467-478.
Cumming, Elaine
    1968   *Systems of Social Regulation,* New York: Atherton Press.
DeJong, Gordon and J. Fawcett
    1981   "Motivations for Migration: An Assessment and a Value Expectancy
            Research Model." In *Migration Decision Making*, edited by Gordon DeJong
            and Robert Gardner, New York: Pergamon.
DeVall, Bill
    1984   *Deep Ecology,* Salt Lake City, UT: G. M. Smith.
de Vaus, D. A.
    1995   *Surveys in Social Research*, fourth edition, Sydney: Allen and Unwin.
Durkheim, Emile
    1933   *On the Division of Labor in Society,* translated by George Simpson, New
            York: Macmillan.
Ferguson, Adam
    1973   *Principles of Moral and Political Science*, New York: AMS Press.
Fichten, Janet S.
    1991   *Endangered Spaces, Enduring Places: Change, Identity and Survival in
            Rural America*, Boulder, CO: Westview.

Finkelman, Paul
    1986   *The Law of Freedom and Bondage,* New York: Oceana.
Flynn, Cynthia
    1982   "General versus Aged Migration 1967-1970." *Research on Aging* 2(1)165-176.
Freudenburg, William R. and Robert Emmett Jones
    1991   "Criminal Behavior and Rapid Community Growth: Examining the Evidence." *Rural Sociology* 56(4)619-645.
Friedman, Milton
    1962   *Capitalism and Freedom,* Chicago: University of Chicago Press.
Fuguitt, Glenn V. and Calvin L. Beale
    1996   "Recent Trends in Nonmetropolitan Migration: Toward a New Turnaround." *Growth and Change* 27(1)156-174.
Fuguitt, Glenn V., David L. Brown, and Calvin L. Beale
    1989   *The Population of Rural and Small Town America,* New York: Russell Sage.
Fuguitt, Glenn V., Thomas A. Heberlein, and Pamela R. Rathburn
    1991   "Migration Consequences for Household Energy Consumption in a Nonmetropolitan Recreation-Retirement Area." *Rural Sociology* 56(1)56-59.
Gibbs, Jack
    1989   *Control: Sociology's Central Notion,* Urbana: University of Illinois.
Glaser, Barney G. and Anselm Strauss
    1967   *The Discovery of Grounded Theory,* Chicago: Aldine.
Glasgow, Nina
    1980   "The Older Metropolitan Migrant as a Factory in Rural Population Growth." In *Rebirth of Rural America: Rural Migration in the Midwest,* pp. 153-170, edited by Andrew J. Sofranko and James A. Williams, Ames, IA: North Central Center for Rural Development.
Gober, Patricia and Leo E. Zonn
    1983   "Kin and Elderly Amenity Migration." *The Gerontologist* 23(2)288-294.
Goffman, Erving
    1974   *Frame Analysis: An Essay on the Organization of Experience,* New York: Harper Colophon.
    1959   *The Presentation of Self in Everyday Life,* New York: Macmillan.
Goldscheider, Calvin
    1971   *Population, Modernization and Social Structure,* Boston: Little Brown.
Gorham, Lucy
    1993   "The Slowdown in Nonmetropolitan Development." In *Population Change and the Future of Rural America,* edited by Linda L. Swanson and David L. Brown, Economic Research Service, Washington, DC: USDA Staff Report AGES 9324.
Gottfredson, Michael and Travis Hirschi
    1990   *A General Theory of Crime,* Stanford, CA: Stanford University Press.
Gottlieb, Martin
    1993   "One Who Would Like to See Most Architects Hit the Road." *The New York Times,* March 28, 142 #4, p. E7, col. 1.
Goudy, Willis
    1990   "Community Attachment in a Rural Region." *Rural Sociology* 55(2)178-198.
Gouldner, Alvin W.
    1970   *The Coming Crisis of Western Sociology,* New York: Avon.

Hawley, Amos H.
    1986   *Human Ecology: A Theoretical Essay*, Chicago: University of Chicago.
Hirschi, Travis
    1969   *The Causes of Delinquency*, Berkeley: University of California Press.
Hobbes, Thomas
    1991   *Leviathan*, edited by Richard Tuck, Cambridge: Cambridge University Press.
Horowitz, Irving Lewis
    1975   *The Use and Abuse of Social Science*, New Brunswick, NJ: Transaction
            Books.
Howell, Frank, M. and Wolfgang Frese
    1983   "Size of Place, Residential Preferences and the Life Cycle: How People
            Come to Like Where They Are." *American Sociological Review* 48(4)569-
            580.
Humphrey, Craig R. and Frederick R. Buttel
    1982   *Environment, Energy and Society*, Belmont, CA: Wadsworth.
Inglehart, Ronald
    1997   *Modernization and Postmodernization*, Princeton, NJ: Princeton University
            Press.
Jacobs, Jeffrey C. and Merlin B. Brinkerhoff
    1986   "Alternative Technology and Part-Time Semi-Subsistence Agriculture: A
            Survey from the Back-to-the-Land Movement." *Rural Sociology* 51(1)43-59.
Jobes, Patrick C.
    1999   "Migration and Social Problems in Small Towns: An Empirical Analysis of
            Awareness Among Public Administrator." In *Research in Community
            Sociology*, pp. 201-220, edited by Dan Chekki, Stanford, CT: JAI Press.
    1997   "Gender Competition and the Preservation of Community: The Allocation
            of Administrative Positions in Small Rural Towns in Montana." *Rural
            Sociology* 62(3)315-334.
    1991   "The Greater Yellowstone Social System." *Conservation Biology* 5(3)387-
            394.
    1987   "The Disintegration of Gemeinschaft Social Structure from Energy
            Development: Observations from Ranch Communities in the Western United
            States." *Rural Studies* 3(3)219-229.
    1986   "A Small Rural Community Responds to Coal Development." *Sociology and
            Social Research* 70(2)174-177.
Jobes, Patrick C., William F. Stinner, and John M. Wardwell
    1991   *Community, Society and Migration*, Lanham, MD: University Press of
            America.
Johnson, Kenneth N.
    1989   "Recent Population Redistribution Trends in Nonmetropolitan America."
            Rural Sociology 54(3)301-306.
Kant, Immanuel
    1934   *Critique of Pure Reason*, translated by J. M. D. Meikle John, London: J. M.
            Dent.
Kanter, Rosabeth Moss
    1972   *Commitment and Community*, Cambridge, MA: Harvard University Press.
Kazantzakis, Nikos
    1952   *Zorba the Greek*, translated by Carl Wildman, New York: Simon and
            Schuster.

Kemmis, Daniel
    1990   *Community and the Politics of Place*, Norman: University of Oklahoma Press.
Knop, Edward and Patrick C. Jobes
    1997   "The Myth of Rural Stability: Population Turnover in Colorado and Montana." In *Population Change in the Rural West 1975-1990*, pp. 113-138, edited by John M. Wardwell and James H, Copp, Lanham, MD: University Press of America.
Lichter, Daniel T., Glenn V. Fuguitt, Tim B. Heaton, and William B. Clifford
    1981   "Components of Change in the Residential Concentration of the Elderly Population." *Journal of Gerontology* 36(3)480-489.
Lundberg, George
    1961   *Can Science Save Us?* Second edition, New York: David McKay.
Lynd, Robert S.
    1939   *Knowledge for What?* Princeton, NJ: Princeton University Press.
Machiavelli, Niccolo
    1944   *Il Principe*, edited by Hardin Craig, Chapel Hill: University of North Carolina Press.
Mannheim, Karl
    1936   *Ideology and Utopia,* translated by Louis Wirth and Edward Shils, New York: Harcourt, Brace and World.
Marriott, Alice
    1948   *Maria the Potter*, Norman: University of Oklahoma Press.
Marx, Karl
    1970   *Capital*, Volume 1, London: Lawrence and Wishert. First published in 1864.
McHugh, Kevin
    1984   "Explaining Migration Intentions and Destination Selection." *Professional Geographer* 36(3)315-325.
McPheat, David
    1996   "Technology and Life Quality." *Social Indicators Research* 37(2)281-301.
Mead, George Herbert
    1934   *Mind, Self and Society,* edited by Charles H. Morris, Chicago: University of Chicago Press.
Merton, Robert K.
    1949   "Manifest and Latent Functions." In *Social Structure and Anomie*, pp. 73-138 and 215-248, New York: Free Press.
Michelson, William N.
    1977   *Environmental Choice, Human Behavior and Residential Satisfaction*, New York: Oxford University Press.
Mills, C. Wright
    1959   *The Sociological Imagination,* New York: Oxford University Press.
Montana State University
    1997   *Graduate and Undergraduate Bulletin*, Bozeman: Montana State University.
Mumford, Lewis
    1946   *Values for Survival*, New York: Harcourt Brace.
Murdoch, Steve H., Sean-Song Hwong, Rita R. Hamm, and F. Larry Leistritz
    1986   "Project Related Migration: Empirical Evidence from Western USA and Some Policy Implications." *Project Appraisal* 1(3)191-203.
Nearing, Scott and Helen Nearing
    1970   *Living the Good Life,* New York: Schocken.

Nietzche, Frederich
　　1955　　*Beyond Good and Evil*, translated by Marianne Cowan, Chicago: Gateway Editions.
Pareto, Vilfredo
　　1976　　*Sociological Writings*, edited by S. E. Finer, translated by Derick Mirfin, Oxford: Basil Blackwell.
Park, Robert Ezra
　　1952　　*The City and Human Ecology*, Glencoe, IL: Free Press.
Parsons, Talcott
　　1949　　*Essays in Sociological Theory,* New York: Free Press.
Peterson, William
　　1961　　*Population*, New York: Macmillan.
Ploch, Lewis A.
　　1989　　*Landoff-Then and Now*, Orono: University of Maine, Maine Agricultural Experiment Station, Bulletin 828.
Price, Daniel O. and Miriam M. Sikes
　　1975　　*Rural-Urban Migration Research in the United States*, Bethesda MD: National Institute of Child Health and Human Development Center for Population Research.
Radcliffe-Brown, A. R.
　　1952　　*Structure and Function in Primitive Society,* Glencoe, IL: The Free Press.
　　1935　　"On the Concept of Function in Social Science." *American Anthropologist* 37(2)394-402.
Rapaport, Amos
　　1990　　*History and Precedent in Environmental Design*, New York: Plenum.
Ravenstein, E. G.
1885, 1889　　*Max Weber on the Methodology of the Social Sciences,* translated and edited by Edward A. Shils and H. A. Finch, Glencoe, IL: The Free Press.
Riesmann, David
　　1953　　*The Lonely Crowd*, New Haven, CT: Yale University Press.
Ritchey, P. Neil
　　1976　　"Explanations of Migration." *Annual Review of Sociology* 2:363-404.
Robinson, William S.
　　1950　　"Ecological Correlations and the Behavior of Individuals." *American Sociological Review* 15(3)351-357.
Roseman, Curtis C.
　　1984　　"Labor Force Migration, Non-Labor Force Migration and Non-Employment Reasons for Migration." *Socio Economic Planning Science* 19(1)114-123.
　　1983　　"A Framework for the Study of Migration Destination Selection." *Population and Environment* 6(3)151-165.
Rosenbaum, James E.
　　1983　　*Careers in a Corporation: The Internal Stratification of an Organization*, New York: Academic Press.
Rousseau, Jean-Jacques
　　1911　　*Emile,* translated by Barbara Foxley, London: Dent.
Rubbington, Earl and Martin S. Weinberg
　　1995　　*The Study of Social Problems: Seven Perspectives*, New York: Oxford University Press.
Russell, James S.
　　1992　　"Defending Communities." *Architectural Record* 180(8)1-3.

Sanua, Victor D.
1970   "Immigration, Migration and Mental Illness: A Review of the Literature with Special Emphasis on Schizophrenia." In *Behavior in New Environments*, pp. 28-35, edited by Eugene B. Brady, Beverly Hills, CA: Sage.
Saroyan, William
1943   *The Human Comedy,* New York: Harcourt and Brace.
Schumacher, E. F.
1973   *Small Is Beautiful: A Study of Economics as if People Mattered*, London: Bland and Briggs.
Seamon, David, (ed.)
1993   *Dwelling, Seeing, and Designing: Toward a Phenomenological Ecology*, Albany: State University of New York Press.
Sell, Ralph R.
1983   "Analyzing Migration Decision: The First Step Whose Decision?" *Demography* 20(3)299-311.
Shaw, Clifford and Henry D. McKay
1969   *Juvenile Delinquency and Urban Areas,* revised edition, Chicago: University of Chicago Press.
Simmel, Georg
1950   *The Sociology of Georg Simmel*, edited by Kurt Wolff, Glencoe, IL: Free Press.
Small, Albion E.
1916   "Fifty Years of Sociology (1865-1915)." *American Journal of Sociology*, index to volumes 1-52.
Smith, Adam
1992   *An Inquiry into the Nature and Causes of the Wealth of Nations*, edited by Fred R. Glahe, Savage, MD: Rowman and Littlefield.
Smith, David
1994   *Geography and Social Justice*, Oxford: Blackwell.
Sobel, Michael
1981   *Lifestyle and Social Structure*, New York: Academic Press.
Speare, Alden, Jr., Frances Kobrin, and Ward Kingkade
1982   "The Influence of Socioeconomic Bonds and Satisfaction on Interstate Migration." *Social Forces* 61(4)551-574.
Sumner, William Graham
1940   *Folkways,* New York: New American Library, Mentor edition.
Suttles, Gerald D.
1968   *The Social Order of the Slum: Ethnicity and Territory in the Inner City*, Chicago: University of Chicago.
Tamney, Joseph
1975   *Solidarity in a Slum*, Cambridge MA: Schenkman.
Thomas, William I.
1923   *The Unadjusted Girl*, Chicago: University of Chicago Press.
Turner, Jonathan L.
1991   *The Structure of Sociological Theory*, Belmont, CA: Wadsworth.
Tsonis, Anastasia
1992   *Chaos,* New York: Plenum Press.
U.S. Bureau of Census
1994   *Census of Retail Trade Montana*, Washington, DC: Department of Commerce, U.S. Government Printing Office.

1994   *County and City Data Book*, Washington, DC: Department of Commerce, U.S. Government Printing Office.

1950, 1960, 1970, 1980, 1990 Census of the Population: Montana, DC: Department of Commerce, U.S. Government Printing Office.

Vale, Lawrence J.
1992   *Architecture, Power, and National Identity*, New Haven, CT: Yale University Press.

Veblin, Thorstein
1899   *The Theory of the Leisure Class,* New York: Macmillan.

Walkerstein, Imanuel
1989   *The Modern World System III*, New York: Academic Press.

Ward, Carol
1995   "American Indian High School Completion in Rural Southeastern Montana." *Rural Sociology* 60(3)416-434.

Ward, Lester Frank
1906   *Applied Sociology*, Boston: Ginn and Co.

Wardwell, John M.
1977   "Equilibrium and Change in Nonmetropolitan Growth." *Rural Sociology* 42(1)89-104.

Weber, Max
1946   *From Max Weber: Essays in Sociology,* translated and edited by Hans H. Gerth and C. Wright Mills, New York: Oxford University Press.

1930   *The Protestant Ethic and the Spirit of Capitalism*, translated by Talcott Parsons, London: Unwin.

1885, 1889 *Max Weber on the Methodology of the Social Sciences*, Translated and edited by Edward A. Shils and H. A. Finch, Glencoe, IL: Free Press.

Wellman, J. Douglas
1987   *Wildlife Recreation Policy,* New York: John Wiley.

Willits, Fern K., Robert C. Bealer, and Donald M. Crider
1982   "Persistence of Rural/Urban Differences." In *Rural Society in the U.S.: Issues for the 1980s*, edited by Don A. Dillman and Daryll J. Hobbs, Boulder, CO: Westview.

Willits, Fern K., Robert C. Bealer, and Vincent L. Timbers
1990   "Popular Images of 'Rurality' Data from a Pennsylvania Survey." *Rural Sociology* 55(4)559-578.

Wood, Arthur Lewis
1974   *Deviant Behavior and Control Strategies,* Lexington, MA: Lexington Books.

Wrong, Dennis H.
1961   "The Over-Socialized Conception of Man in Modern Sociology." *American Sociological Review* 26(3)186-193.

Index

About the Author

PATRICK C. JOBES is Senior Lecturer in the School of Social Science at the University of New England in Australia. He was a founding member of the Environmental Sociology Section of the American Sociological Association, chaired the Natural Resources Research Group, and has held numerous regional and national appointments related to research and professional service.

Lightning Source UK Ltd.
Milton Keynes UK
UKHW012031110123
415190UK00002B/16

9 780275 966898